Toward Freedom Land

TOWARD FREEDOM LAND

The Long Struggle
for Racial Equality
in America

HARVARD SITKOFF

THE UNIVERSITY PRESS OF KENTUCKY

Scholarly publisher for the Commonwealth,
serving Bellarmine University, Berea College, Centre College of Kentucky,
Eastern Kentucky University, The Filson Historical Society, Georgetown
College, Kentucky Historical Society, Kentucky State University, Morehead
State University, Murray State University, Northern Kentucky University,
Transylvania University, University of Kentucky, University of Louisville,
and Western Kentucky University.

Editorial and Sales Offices: The University Press of Kentucky
663 South Limestone Street, Lexington, Kentucky 40508-4008
www.kentuckypress.com

14 13 12 11 10   5 4 3 2 1

Library of Congress Cataloging-in-Publication Data

Sitkoff, Harvard.
    Toward freedom land : the long struggle for racial equality in America /
Harvard Sitkoff.
        p. cm.
    Includes bibliographical references and index.
    ISBN 978-0-8131-2583-1 (hardcover : alk. paper)
    1. United States—Race relations—History—20th century. 2. Civil
rights movements—United States—History—20th century. 3. African
Americans—Civil rights—History—20th century. 4. African Americans—
Social conditions—20th century. 5. Race discrimination—United States—
History—20th century. 6. United States—Social conditions—20th century.
I. Title.
    E184.A1S614 2010
    305.800973—dc22   2010001912

This book is printed on acid-free recycled paper meeting the requirements of
the American National Standard for Permanence in Paper for Printed Library
Materials.

Manufactured in the United States of America.

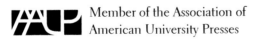

Member of the Association of
American University Presses

Contents

Acknowledgments   vii

Introduction   1

The Preconditions for Racial Change   11

The New Deal and Race Relations   21

The Detroit Race Riot of 1943   43

Racial Militancy and Interracial Violence
in the Second World War   65

African American Militancy in the World War II South:
Another Perspective   93

Willkie as Liberal: Civil Liberties and Civil Rights   129

African Americans, American Jews, and the Holocaust   147

Harry Truman and the Election of 1948:
The Coming of Age of Civil Rights in American Politics   175

Martin Luther King Jr.: Seeing Lazarus, 1967–1968   197

The Second Reconstruction   215

Index   225

Acknowledgments

Many have made this volume possible. Over four decades, my intellectual debts have mushroomed far beyond my ability to list or remember. I only hope my friends and colleagues are aware of how deep my gratitude is for their candid counsel and critiques, for their nurturing of me, and for the genuine and generous inspiration they have provided me. In particular, I thank my fellow scholars of the civil rights movement, whose perceptiveness and encouragement for so many years have kept me writing and thinking anew. I thank, as well, the initial editors and publishers of these essays, both for improving my original drafts and for granting permission for the articles to be reprinted in this volume.

A special debt of gratitude is owed to my publisher Steve Wrinn. A gentleman and scholar, Steve initially suggested I create this book and then shepherded it through every stage of preparation and publication. As always, I cannot fully express my appreciation for all that my mentor—I'm tempted to say coauthor of these essays—William Leuchtenburg, has taught me about the historian's craft. I am indebted to him for whatever extent these essays exhibit dogged research, judicious analysis, and vivid prose. Finally, and not open for argument, I thank my playmate and wife, Gloria Singer, for what I treasure most—her love.

Introduction

In the pages that follow I have assembled a selection of my essays on the "long" black freedom struggle. Written over the course of five decades, they exemplify my sustained interest in a cluster of themes associated with the struggle for racial justice and equality.

In rereading these essays for inclusion in this book, I was sorely tempted to tidy up some of the prose, temper or amplify a few arguments, revise an outdated perspective, and generally make use of the wonderful scholarship on race done in the recent past. In part, because too many books of essays with the usual disclaimer of being just lightly retouched leave me wondering how much has been changed, and in part, to be fair to those who initially commented upon or criticized them in print, these writings, however vulnerable, are presented here as they originally appeared.

They all deal broadly with the struggle for black equality, but writ ten between 1969 and 2008, for different venues and purposes, they do not present a single coherent interpretation. Moreover, arranged chronologically by subject rather than by publication date, so as to provide a linear sense of that topic's history, they sometimes counter and at other times echo one another. Indeed, I occasionally repeat myself in pieces written years apart and for different audiences. So did Mozart, but alas, the analogy ends there. The overlapping and interlocking, however, do mirror one historian's effort to grapple with changing times and changing historical scholarship.

They are, I believe, still of value as historical scholarship. It is my hope that in gathering together in a single volume works written for many journals or scholarly collections, some no longer in print, they will be more accessible to future generations of scholars. This volume also reveals (hopefully) the evolution of a mind. It can be read as an account of a historian's growth or, at least, his changing views. It is evidence of how one historian confronted and articulated some of the attitudes and issues central to civil rights history during the past five decades.

Like most others making their way in the profession, I always felt too busy, too eager for the next project, to indulge in introspection about past works. Reflecting upon oneself—one's background, one's experiences, one's values—is not what historians generally are taught. We're too self-conscious to bare ourselves before the gaze of outsiders. The chasm between recollections and truth, moreover, leaves me wary of distant hindsight. Still, assembling this volume left me no out.

At the very least, however dimly apparent to me at the time, my general disposition to challenge dominant points of view and, in particular, my inclination to assert interpretations at variance with others writing civil rights history appear clear in retrospect. This contrariness may well be in my DNA, or in the New York City air. Then again, it might be the way I was brought up. Much as we can never fully free ourselves from the influence of the past, we can never fully free our view of the past from all that influences us.

Extended, extensive verbal bouts are what I most remember of family life in my world as a child. Every Sunday, my immigrant father and my mother, who was the first in her family born in the United States, would gather with their many siblings. All lived on the Lower East Side of Manhattan or had recently migrated to other Jewish neighborhoods in the Bronx or Brooklyn. All worked in the needle trades. Drinking tea out of glasses, they lovingly (for the most part) sparred with one another about the week's events. Some were communists in Ben Gold's furriers' union. Others, in David Dubinsky's ladies garment workers' union, claimed to be socialists. A few considered themselves Roosevelt liberals, and one, I think, a syndicalist. Whatever their politics, they all could talk, and talk. And did so. Some shouted. Some even screamed. None felt inhibited to dispute this or denounce that. And after the bickering came the inevitable good-bye hugs and kisses. I understood little of it other than the joy of the joust, the delight they shared in the tussle.

A similar feeling of pleasure attended my immediate family's squabbles. The tradition in which I was gratefully raised honored disputation. Although my father could neither read nor write, he carefully looked and listened and never shied from expressing his mind.

He talked fast and combatively and, however humble his beginnings, instilled in my sister, brother, and me a similar craving to speak up and speak out. At no time was this more the case than when my family returned from the synagogue on Saturdays. Since we could not watch TV or go out and play ball until the Sabbath ended, we had hours to question everything in the rabbi's sermon and much in Judaism as well. And we surely did. Likewise, the dinner table bristled with opinions; someone or other was always challenging another's contention. One would assert a notion, and others would immediately rib and rag. Raised on the dialectic, we found disagreeing fun. Because my father adored the Brooklyn Dodgers, my older brother became a Giants fan, and I had little choice but to root for the New York Yankees. Within a loving family context, I absorbed the facility to express myself forthrightly and to be accepting of someone else's jest or blunt riposte.

To the extent I can remember, my education in New York City's public schools did little to curb my candor. Bickering did not help me do well in arithmetic, but I was a whiz in Problems of Democracy. Fantasizing about being William Lloyd Garrison, I starred in Brotherhood Week. Yankee fan or not, I followed my father in his adoration of Jackie Robinson and of Paul Robeson as well. In high school I became an avid reader of the *New York Post* and thrilled to the desegregation of Little Rock High School and the Montgomery bus boycott. I saw racial issues through the liberal lenses of Murray Kempton and James Wechsler and dreamed of being Lincoln Steffens or Clarence Darrow.

Next came Queens College, then a campus mainly of World War II Quonset huts, and my discovery of press-pot French roast coffee and, especially, philosophy. Whether the Socratic method or Marx's dialectic, I could not get enough of parrying with my friends at all-night stand-up pizza joints. My newest idol, Martin Buber, grounded my ethics in a Judaism of dialogue, and Albert Camus reaffirmed my Quixote-like opposition to unfairness. Like the mythical Sisyphus of his philosophical essay, I imagined myself pushing on and on for justice. Far less dramatically than eternal labor at the rock, I started a student chapter of the NAACP, wrote articles on school desegregation in the South for the campus newspaper, and led groups of students to rallies and pilgrimages for civil rights in Washington, D.C. In my senior year, as student body president, I met the initial cadres of black college students in the sit-in movement at conclaves arranged by the National Student Association in 1960. I was smitten, swept away. If I could only do what they were doing. . . .

But as a child of the Depression, I worried about having a job and earning a living. I knew I wanted no part of the business world. My father, whose failures in fur enterprises had ruined his health, often paraphrased what Jacob says to his grandson in Clifford Odets' *Awake and Sing*: "Make your life something good. . . . Go out and fight so life shouldn't be printed on dollar bills." To go as far as one could get from being a furrier, I would—what else?—teach. I began graduate work at Columbia University in European intellectual history, which seemed the closest thing to my undergraduate love of philosophy.

But I disliked Columbia's curriculum in the history of ideas and hated the university. I never felt comfortable, never thought I fit in. Having spent all my years of public schooling among students and teachers like myself, from working families like my own and with as little education as my own, I suddenly envisioned myself as different, an outsider. A lower-middle-class son of a Jewish immigrant from a *shtetl* in eastern Europe, I feared rejection by the prep school–to–Ivy League graduates. None of my fellow students and teachers had names like mine or backgrounds remotely close to mine. Or so it seemed to a hypersensitive outlier. A furrier's son, I felt like the runt I had been at age six. Marginalized and restless, I quit.

I headed south to join my heroes in the civil rights movement. I wish I could write that I fought on for years or that I did something significant. Not me. I joined in several marches. I sat-in. I picketed. But I never conquered the fears of a too-bookish New Yorker facing the scorn of enraged southern whites. My brief, episodic experiences in the movement frightened me out of my wits. I did not have the courage to be an activist on the front line. I lacked the guts to keep doing what those I most admired were doing. Guilt-ridden for failing to help others in the way that I thought mattered most, I retreated to New York. There I began to understand, only very slowly, that I could help the movement in other ways. I could, for example, do my part by teaching and writing history that would aid the struggle for racial justice. My battleground would be the classroom, my bullets would be the words I wrote.

When I finally decided to conquer my awe and envy and return to

Columbia, both the university and the history profession were in the throes of rapid change. I now easily discovered others who felt "different"—Jews, women, even some ethnic minorities—and others who did not fit in or did not want to fit in. Many graduate students, of every background, were joining the battle for a new paradigm of American history called the "new history" or "New Left history." That now motivated me more than my class-based self-consciousness.

The civil rights movement, the war in Vietnam, and all the campus and national upheavals of the 1960s affected the new history as much as the Cold War struggle against communism had influenced the "consensus school" of history. The latter's consoling version of American history as a success story posited our inevitable progress toward ever-more freedom, equality, and justice. While obscuring the price paid by ordinary people laboring to change their society, it emphasized the fundamental agreement of most Americans on basic ideas about politics and society and the broad continuities in American life over time. Written mostly by white men comfortable with the nation as it was, it downplayed race and class tensions and depicted the absence of conflict as a sign of American greatness.

The "new" historians, contrariwise, saw divisions over race, class, and gender as the essence of the American past. They brought to the historical fore the groups ignored by "consensus" historians, particularly African Americans, Native Americans, immigrants, the poor, and women, generally depicting them as victims of the dominant elites. Rather than a Fourth of July version of America's past, they harped on all the failed promises of justice and equality. Every major theme of the consensus school was turned on its head. For the new historians, eager to take aim at their elders, to stand in judgment of the historians who had come before them as well as the historical actors of the past, parricide became a form of scholarship.

The young scholars I associated with, moreover, sought to make the past speak to the present, to make a new past that suited current ideas and needs. This politicization of history was nothing new. It had been going on since our forefathers first looked backward. Our turn had now come. Unhappy with what the United States had become, we replaced celebration with critique; multiculturalism and diversity supplanted unity and uniformity. The once hidden underside of American history now became the preeminent subject of our scholarship.

How lucky I was to be in the forefront of an effort to revolutionize the study of American history, especially as it related to what groups of people to study and what issues to study. Nothing pleased me more than being a cog in an academic machine contesting the consensus viewpoint of our teachers. As usual, I eagerly spoke up. I posed questions relevant to the dissident politics of the 1960s and interpreted the past through the prism of my values. I longed to add my voice and pen to those making a difference in the world, making a better world. Wanting my teaching and writing to count, I set out to be a scholar-activist like my latest role models, John Hope Franklin and C. Vann Woodward.

I never did for racial equality and social justice what they did. But I took up what was then called "Negro history," writing it to emphasize the shortcomings of liberalism and to serve the cause of the New Left. Thus my earliest publications decried the Roosevelt administration's racial policies during the Second World War, took President Harry Truman to task for his limited and very mixed record on civil rights, and emphasized that the social injustice of whites—not black rabble—caused the race riots of 1943 (and, by implication, those of the 1960s).

Over time, my scholarship changed. I could cite Freud's view that there is nothing in behavior that does not have a cause. But I've barely begun to understand my reasons. Conceivably I learned a lot more history and even a lot more about doing good history. Then again, stepping away from New York's scholarly correct environment for the less radically charged atmosphere of a Midwest hub might have played a part. Perhaps it reflected my growing pessimism that I would soon see a radical restructuring of American society, or the hurt I felt when some demanded that only African Americans write or teach black history. Maybe it's just what they say about getting older. Or perhaps, as others in the profession increasingly shared viewpoints similar to mine, I simply (stubbornly) needed to be oppositional. Whether just being a wiseass or still compensating for my physical cowardice, I relished going out on a scholarly limb.

Whatever the cause(s), as I worked on those changes in the 1930s that would help lead to the emergence of civil rights as a national issue, I began to have second thoughts about stomping New Deal liberalism. Doing my research in the era of President Richard Nixon, I no longer scoffed at such goals as full employment, better wages for workers, more assistance for the unemployed and underemployed, and quality education, decent housing, and medical care for all. Most of all, I now better understood how spunky Franklin Roosevelt's even minimal interventions on behalf of African Americans had been at the time. The extreme denunciations of his most racist detractors, the scorn heaped upon him by virulent white supremacists, now made sense. The differences between liberalism and conservatism on civil rights, mocked by New Leftists, stared me in the face in the 1970s.

Increasingly I thought it worthwhile to emphasize what brought blacks and whites together, what made a liberal alliance possible and successful. Thus my *A New Deal for Blacks*, and essays based on it, highlighted the diverse fighters for racial justice in the 1930s—the artists and athletes, the trade unionists and communists, the Southern Tenant Farmers' Union and Association of Southern Women Against Lynching, the lawyers and judges, and even the New Dealers—who helped plant the seeds for the civil rights movement that flowered in the postwar years.

Other essays of mine, focusing on the 1940s, furthered the notion of a "long" civil rights movement. They dealt with individuals such as Wendell Willkie, who played significant roles in vanquishing Jim Crow, and they reconsidered alliances such as that of Jewish and African American organizations, which dented the walls of racial discrimination and segregation. Without minimizing black agency or traditions of black resistance, I also sought to deepen our understanding of successful social movements by highlighting those external and impersonal factors that created the context conducive to advances in civil rights. Less concerned with exposing or indicting others, I grew more interested in those structural socioeconomic changes, Karl Marx's "circumstances [not] of our own choosing," in which we make "our own history."

That led me to an increasing appreciation of contingency and complexity, even irony, in historical action. I went from itching to be part of a group, a school of thought, to wishing, as much as anything, to defy classification, to not be pigeonholed. Along with others, I had become aware that the new social historians, in reacting against the previous generation's singular focus on those who wielded power, had tipped the balance too far by concentrating solely on ordinary people at the local level. In place of our teachers' exaggerated belief in consensus and homogeneity there was now heterogeneity and fragmentation. Rather than a mansion with many rooms, history, as C. Vann Woodward commented, had become scattered suburbs, trailer camps, and a deteriorating central city.

These trends in the history profession also heightened my awareness that we are hardly exempt from the intellectual limitations we see so clearly in our predecessors. I retain my skepticism about claims to "disinterested scholarship" and still believe with E. H. Carr that historians should have "the future in their bones." Yet we can, and should, do better than to write history to vindicate a preconceived judgment about the past or to express a conclusion determined by today's political considerations. History is not a science and will never be perfectly objective. But it is still possible to adhere to the American Historical Association's *Statement on Standards of Professional Historians*, which requires that we acknowledge our own biases and "follow sound method and analysis wherever they may lead."

My interpretation of the known evidence, above all, has led me to keep emphasizing the intrinsic importance of hopefulness to successful social movements—particularly the civil rights movement. I keep coming back to what gives people hope. Like the brass ring on a carousel, I returned again and again in my writings to what Robert Kennedy expressed at the University of Cape Town, South Africa, in 1966:

> It is true that few will have the greatness to bend history itself; but each of us can work to change a small portion of events. . . . It is from those numberless diverse acts of courage and belief that human history is shaped. Each time men and women stand up for an ideal, or act to improve the lot of others, or strike out against injustice, they send a tiny ripple of hope— and crossing each other from a million different centers of energy and daring these ripples build a current which can sweep down the mightiest walls of oppression and resistance.

Even historians can send ripples of hope. Yet history's lessons are not immutable. To understand that interpretations of key events and developments keep changing is to know that we have barely begun a scholarly understanding of civil rights and race relations. As this book of essays demonstrates, historians are grappling with how to tell the story of the civil rights movement, indeed, with what story to tell. Whatever the views of future generations of historians, my wish is that these essays be read, as John Hope Franklin described my *Struggle for Black Equality*, as "a testimonial to the American tradition of courage and determination, [which] bespeaks a clear resolve to move to the next stage, where there is a hope that we can achieve the goals of equality and justice for all." That is more than enough of an achievement for me.

Whatever one thinks of this collection, please do not read it as my valedictory to historical research and writing. I'm still hopeful and vigorously argumentative. I enjoy few things more than a no-holds-barred debate with my closest friends. Challenging one another, saying whatever we think, is our bond. Still irreverent as ever, I aim to rile.

The Preconditions
for Racial Change

Part of a much longer essay that dealt with the sources of the black freedom movement, its evolving ideologies, and the political responses, this excerpt sketching the preconditions for racial change was frequently reprinted and often rebuked. It was written in the early 1970s, when most textbooks commonly ascribed the civil rights movement to the Supreme Court's 1954 ruling in Brown v. Board of Education *that "separate educational facilities are inherently unequal" or to the actions of John F. Kennedy and Lyndon B. Johnson. Instead, I sought to locate the origins and causes of the black freedom struggle in the 1930s and 1940s and to emphasize socioeconomic factors rather than jurists and presidents. Although my looking back to the years before* Brown *eventually helped prod the profession to take a "long" view of the history of the struggle for racial equality and to employ the concept of a "long" civil rights movement, to some, my focus on structural developments appeared to be a denial of black agency. Nothing I've written has given me more trouble. I was assailed by not a few historians for minimizing the importance of individual and collective protest, for reducing African Americans to silent victims, even for erasing blacks from the story. That was hardly my intention. Indeed, the longest section of the original essay dealt with African American activism in the 1960s. Questions remain, moreover, as to the relative importance of, and relationship between, external factors and protest activities. To feed the debate, and perhaps spur some historians to do more contextualizing and less editorializing, what follows is the excerpt most commonly reprinted from "Race Relations: Progress and Prospects," in* Paths to the Present, *ed. James T. Patterson (Minneapolis: Burgess Publishing Co., 1975), 183–227. Reprinted by permission.*

Of the interrelated causes of progress in race relations since the start of the Great Depression, none was more important than the changes in the American economy. No facet of the race problem was untouched by the elephantine growth of the gross national product, which rose from $206 billion in 1940 to $500 billion in 1960, and then in the 1960s increased by an additional 60 percent. By 1970, the economy topped the trillion-dollar mark. This spectacular rate of economic growth produced some 25 million new jobs in the quarter of a century after World War II and raised real wage earnings by at least 50 percent. It made possible the increasing income of blacks, their entry into industries and labor unions previously closed to them, and gains for blacks in occupational status; and it created a shortage of workers that necessitated a slackening of restrictive promotion policies and the introduction of scores of government and private industry special job training programs for Afro-Americans. It also meant that the economic progress of blacks did not have to come at the expense of whites, thus undermining the most powerful source of white resistance to the advancement of blacks.

The effect of economic changes on race relations was particularly marked in the South. The rapid industrialization of the South since 1940 ended the dominance of the cotton culture. With its demise went the need for a vast underclass of unskilled, subjugated laborers. Power shifted from rural areas to the cities, and from tradition-oriented landed families to the new officers and professional workers in absentee-owned corporations. The latter had neither the historical allegiances nor the nonrational attachment to racial mores to risk economic growth for the sake of tradition. The old system of race relations had no place in the new economic order. Time and again in the 1950s and 1960s, the industrial and business elite took the lead in accommodating the South to the changes sought by the civil rights movement.

The existence of an "affluent society" boosted the fortunes of the civil rights movement itself in countless ways. Most obviously, it enabled millions of dollars in contributions from wealthy liberals and philanthropic organizations to pour into the coffers of the NAACP, Urban League, Southern Christian Leadership Conference, and countless other civil rights groups. Without those funds it is difficult to comprehend how the movement could have accomplished those tasks so essential to its success: legislative lobbying and court litigation; nationwide speaking tours and the daily mailings of press releases all over the country; the organization of mass marches, demonstrations, and rallies; constant, rapid communication and traveling over long distances; and the convocation of innumerable public conferences and private strategy sessions.

Prosperity also increased the leisure time of many Americans and enabled them to react immediately to the changing times. The sons and daughters of the newly affluent increasingly went to college. By 1970, five times as many students were in college as in 1940. What they learned helped lead to pronounced changes in white attitudes toward racial discrimination and segregation. Other whites learned from the TV sets in their homes. By the time Lyndon Johnson signed the Voting Rights Act of 1965, some 95 percent of all American families owned at least one television. The race problem entered their living rooms. Tens of millions nightly watched the drama of the Negro revolution. The growing majority of Americans favoring racial equality and justice had those sentiments reinforced by TV shots of snarling police dogs attacking black demonstrators, rowdy white hoods molesting young blacks patiently waiting to be served at a lunch counter, and hate-filled white faces in a frenzy because of the effrontery of little black children entering a previously all-white school.

Blacks viewed the same scenes on their TV sets, and the rage these scenes engendered helped transform isolated battles into a national campaign. Concurrently, the conspicuous display of white affluence on TV vividly awakened blacks to a new sense of their relative deprivation. That, too, aroused black anger. And now something could be done about it. The growing black middle and working classes put their money and bodies on the line. In addition, because the consumer economy depended on consumer purchasing, black demands had to be taken seriously. By 1970, black buying power topped $25 billion, a large enough sum to make the threat of boycotts an effective weapon for social change. Afro-American economic advances also made blacks less patient in demanding alterations in their social status. They desired all the decencies and dignity they believed their full paycheck promised. Lastly, nationwide prosperity contributed to more blacks entering college, which stimulated higher expectations and a heightened confidence that American society need not be static.

Most importantly, changes in the economy radically affected black migration. Cotton mechanization pushed blacks off the farms, and the lure of jobs pulled them to the cities. In 1930, three-quarters of the Afro-Americans lived in or near the rural Black Belt. By 1973, over half the blacks lived outside the South, and nationally, nearly 80 percent resided in urban areas. Indeed, in the two decades prior to 1970, the black population in metropolitan areas rose by more than 7 million—a number greater than the total immigration by any single nationality group in American history. Such a mass migration, in conjunction with prosperity, fundamentally altered the whole configuration of the race problem. First, the issue of race became national in scope. No longer did it affect only one region, and no longer could it be left in the hands of southern whites. Second, it modified the objective conditions of life for blacks and changed their perception of what was right and how to get it. For the first time in American history the great mass of blacks were freed from the confines of a rigid caste structure. Now subject to new formative experiences, blacks developed new norms and beliefs. In the relative anonymity and freedom of the North and the big city, aggression could be turned against one's oppressor rather than against one's self; more educational and employment opportunities could be secured; and political power could be mobilized. Similarly, as expectations of racial equality increased with the size of black migration from the rural South, so the religious faith that had for so long sustained Afro-Americans working on plantations declined. The promise of a better world in the next one could not suffice. The urban black would not wait for his rewards until the afterlife.

Because blacks could vote in the North, they stopped believing they would have to wait. Enfranchisement promised all in this life that religion did in the next. The heavenly city, to put it mildly, was not achieved; but vital legislative and legal accomplishments did flow from the growing black vote. Without the presence of black political power in the North, the demonstrations in the South would not have led to the civil rights laws and presidential actions necessary to realize the objectives of those protesting against Jim Crow in Montgomery, Greensboro, Birmingham, Jackson, and Selma. Although the claim of black publicists that the concentration of northern black votes in the industrial cities made the Afro-American electorate a "balance of power" in national politics was never wholly accepted by either major party, the desire of every president from Franklin Roosevelt to Lyndon Johnson to win and hold the black vote became a factor in determining public policy. And as the Democratic Party became less dependent upon southern electoral votes, and less able to garner them, it had to champion civil rights more in order to win the populous states of the North and Midwest, where blacks were increasingly becoming an indispensable component of the liberal coalition.

The prominence of the United States as a world power further pushed politicians into making race relations a matter of national concern. During World War II millions of Americans became aware for the first time of the danger of racism to national security. The costs of racism went even higher during the Cold War. The Soviet Union continuously undercut American appeals to the nations of Africa and Asia by publicizing American ill treatment of blacks. As the competition between the United States and international communism intensified, foreign policy makers came to recognize racism as the American's own worst enemy. President Harry Truman justified his asking Congress for civil rights legislation squarely on the worldwide implications of American race relations. Rarely in the next twenty years did a plea for civil rights before the Supreme Court, on the floor of Congress, and emanating from the White House fail to emphasize that point. In short, fear forced the nation to hasten the redefining of black status. The more involved in world affairs the United States became, the more imperative grew the task of setting its racial affairs in order.

The rapid growth of nationalistic independence movements among the world's colored peoples had special significance for Afro-Americans. In 1960 alone, sixteen African nations emerged from under white colonial rule. Each proclamation of independence in part shamed blacks in the United States to intensify their struggle for equality and justice, and in part caused a surge of racial pride in Afro-Americans, an affirmation of blackness. The experience of African independence proved the feasibility of change and the vulnerability of white supremacy, while at the same time aiding Afro-Americans to see themselves as members of a world majority rather than as just a hopelessly outnumbered American minority.

The decline in intellectual respectability of ideas used to justify segregation and discrimination similarly provided Afro-Americans with new weapons and shields. The excesses of Nazism and the decline of Western imperialism combined with internal developments in the academic disciplines of anthropology, biology, history, psychology, and sociology to discredit notions of inherent racial differences or predispositions. First in the 1930s, then with accelerating rapidity during World War II and every year thereafter, books and essays attacking racial injustice and inequality rolled off the presses. As early as 1944, Gunnar Myrdal in his monumental *An American Dilemma* termed the pronounced change in scholarship about race "the most important of all social trends in the field of interracial relations." This conclusion overstated the power of the word, but undoubtedly the mountain of new data, theory, and exposition at least helped to erode the pseudo-scientific rationalizations once popularly accepted as the basis for white supremacy.

In such an atmosphere, young blacks could mature without "the mark of oppression." Blacks could safely abandon the "nigger" role. To the extent that textbooks, sermons, declarations by governmental officials, advertising, and movies and TV affirmed the need to transform relationships between the races and to support black demands for full citizenship, blacks could confidently and openly rebel against the inequities they viewed as the sources of their oppression. They could publicly express the rage their parents had been forced to internalize; they could battle for what they deemed their birthright rather than wage war against themselves. Thus, in conjunction with the migration to cities, these new cultural processes helped to produce the "New Negro" hailed by essayists ever since the Montgomery bus boycott in 1956 inaugurated a more aggressive stage in the Afro-American's quest for equality.

In sum, changes in the American economy after 1940 set in motion a host of developments which made possible a transformation in race relations. The increasing income and number of jobs available to blacks and whites, and black migration and social mobility, coalesced with converging trends in politics, foreign affairs, and the mass media to endow those intent on improving race relations with both the resources and the consciousness necessary to challenge the status quo. Objective conditions that had little to do with race in a primary sense thus created a context in which organizations and leaders could press successfully for racial changes. This is not to suggest that individuals do not matter in history or that the civil rights movement did not make an indispensable contribution to progress in race relations. It is, however, to emphasize the preconditions for such an endeavor to prevail. Desire and will are not enough. Significant and long-lasting alterations in society flow neither from the barrel of a gun nor from individual conversions. Mass marches, demonstrations, and rhetoric alone cannot modify entrenched behavior and values. Fundamental social change is accomplished only when individuals seize the moment to mobilize the latent power inherent in an institutional structure in flux.

Beginning in the 1930s, blacks, no longer facing a monolithic white power structure solidly arrayed against them, demanded with numbers and a unity that had never existed before the total elimination of racial inequality in American life. For three decades, the tactics and goals of the movement steadily grew more militant as the organization, protests, and power of blacks jumped exponentially. Each small triumph held out the promise of a greater one, heightening expectations and causing blacks to become ever more anxious about the pace of progress.

The first stage centered on securing the enforcement of the Fourteenth and Fifteenth Amendments. Supported mainly by white liberals and upper-middle-class blacks, the civil rights movement in the 1930s and 1940s relied on publicity, agitation, litigation in the courts, and lobbying in the halls of political power to gain the full inclusion of blacks in American life. Advances came in the legal and economic status of blacks and in the minor social, political, and cultural concessions afforded Afro-Americans in the North, but the all-oppressive system of Jim Crow in the South remained virtually intact.

First in the court system, then in executive actions, and finally in Congress, this unceasing and mounting pressure from the civil rights movement prodded the government consistently in the direction of real racial equality. In the 1930s, the black movement failed to secure its two major legislative goals—anti–poll tax and antilynching laws—but it did manage to get Franklin D. Roosevelt and other members of his official family to speak on behalf of racial justice, to increase the numbers of blacks in government, to establish a Civil Rights Section in the Justice Department, and to ensure blacks a share of the relief and recovery assistance.

The gains during the New Deal, however, functioned primarily as a prelude to the takeoff of the civil rights movement during World War II. The ideological character of the war and the government's need for the loyalty and manpower of all Americans stimulated blacks to expect a better deal from the government; this led to a militancy never before seen in black communities. Membership in the NAACP multiplied nearly ten times; the Congress of Racial Equality, organized in 1942, experimented with various forms of nonviolent direct-action confrontations to challenge segregation; and A. Philip Randolph attempted to build his March-on-Washington Committee into an all-black mass protest movement. In 1941, his threat of a march on Washington, combined with the growth of the black vote and the exigencies of a foreign threat to American security, forced Roosevelt to issue Executive Order 8802 (the first such order dealing with race since Reconstruction), establishing the first President's Committee on Fair Employment Practices (FEPC). And, with increasing firmness, liberal politicians pressed for civil rights legislation and emphasized that the practices of white supremacy brought into disrepute America's stated war aims. Minimal gains to be sure, but the expectations they aroused set the stage for the greater advances in the postwar period. By 1945, Afro-Americans had benefited enough from the expansion in jobs and income, service in the armed forces, and the massive migration to northern cities to know better what they now wanted; and they had developed enough political influence, white alliances, and organizational skills to know how to go about getting their civil rights.

Equally vital, the Supreme Court began to dismantle the separate-but-equal doctrine in 1938. That year, the high court ruled that Missouri could not exclude a Negro from its state university law school when the only alternative was a scholarship to an out-of-state institution. Other Supreme Court decisions prior to World War II whittled away at discrimination in interstate travel, in employment, in judicial and police practices, and in the exclusion of blacks from jury service. During the war, the Court outlawed the white primary, holding that the nominating process of a political party constituted "state action." In other decisions handed down during the Truman presidency, the Supreme Court moved vigorously against all forms of segregation in interstate commerce, decided that states and the federal government cannot enforce restrictive racial covenants on housing, and so emphasized the importance of "intangible factors" in quality education that the demise of legally segregated schooling for students at all levels became a near certainty.

Meanwhile, the Truman administration emerged as an ally of the cause of civil rights. Responding to the growth of the black vote, the need to blunt the Soviet Union's exploitation of the race issue, and the firmly organized campaign for the advancement of blacks, Harry Truman acted where Roosevelt had feared to. In late 1946, the president appointed a Committee on Civil Rights to recommend specific measures to safeguard the civil rights of minorities. This was the first such committee in American history, and its 1947 report, *To Secure These Rights*, eloquently pointed out all the inequities of life in Jim Crow America and spelled out the moral, economic, and international reasons for government action. It called for the end of segregation and discrimination in public education, employment, housing, the armed forces, public accommodations, and interstate transportation. Other commissions appointed by Truman stressed the need for racial equality in the armed services and the field of education. Early in 1948, Truman sent the first presidential message on civil rights to Congress. Congress failed to pass any of the measures he proposed, but Truman later issued executive orders ending segregation in the military and barring discrimination in federal employment and in work done under government contract. In addition, his Justice Department prepared amicus curiae briefs to gain favorable court decisions in civil rights cases, and Truman's rhetoric in behalf of racial justice helped legitimize goals of the civil rights movement. However small the meaningful accomplishment remained, the identification of the Supreme Court and the presidency with the cause of racial equality further aroused the expectations of blacks that they would soon share in the American Dream.

No single event did more to quicken black hopes than the coup de grace to segregated education delivered by a unanimous Supreme Court on May 17, 1954. The *Brown* ruling that separate educational facilities "are inherently unequal" struck at the very heart of white supremacy in the South. A year later, the Court called for compliance "with all deliberate speed," mandating the lower federal courts to require from local school boards "a prompt and reasonable start toward full compliance." The end of legally mandated segregation in education started a chain reaction which led the Supreme Court ever further down the road toward the total elimination of all racial distinctions in the law. For all practical purposes, the legal quest for equality had succeeded: the emphasis on legalism had accomplished its goals. Constitutionally, blacks had become first-class citizens.

But in the decade after the *Brown* decision, the promise of change far outran the reality of it. While individual blacks of talent desegregated most professions, the recessions of the 1950s caused black unemployment to soar and the gap between black and white family income to widen. And despite the rulings of the Supreme Court and the noble gestures and speeches of politicians, massive resistance to desegregation throughout the South proved the rule. This was the context for the second stage of the civil rights movement. When the nation's attempt to forestall integration and racial equality collided with both the Afro-Americans' leaping expectations and their dissatisfaction with the speed of change, blacks took to the streets in a wave of nonviolent, direct-action protests against every aspect of racism still humiliating them.

The New Deal
and Race Relations

None of my scholarly accomplishments has made me more proud than the fact that A New Deal for Blacks, *a slightly revised version of my doctoral dissertation, has been in continuous print for more than three decades and was recently republished by Oxford University Press in a special Thirtieth Anniversary Edition. It was initially praised for presenting a comprehensive account of the many developments, individuals, and organizations that contributed to the emergence of civil rights as a national issue. Those who made major contributions to that end included southern women opposed to lynching, socialists and communists, labor organizers, biological and social scientists, judges and lawyers, clergymen, authors and entertainers, African American protest organizations, a handful of southern liberals, and even some New Dealers. The title of my book was meant to convey (far too imprecisely) that in the 1930s these individuals and organizations planted the seeds of hope that would eventually bear fruit in a successful struggle for racial equality. Instead, it was frequently misconstrued as a claim that the New Deal itself made the quest for racial justice possible or that African Americans received a new and truly equitable deal from the government through its relief and recovery programs or even that Franklin D. Roosevelt's reform efforts highlighted civil rights. Though my larger goal in writing the book—that the profession take a "long" view of the history of the black freedom struggle—has been fully realized, it remains commonplace for many who write about civil rights to see only the negative in the New Deal's and FDR's treatment of African Americans. Such facile judgments are not grounded in the context of the times, of what was feasible at the time. They do not illustrate a historical picture that, like most, is mixed. Thus, I used the occasion of the fiftieth anniversary of the New Deal to make explicit the context of 1930s*

America and how the Roosevelt administration, grappling with hard choices and sometimes inadvertently, brought changes and hopefulness that laid the groundwork for the "Second Reconstruction." The following essay was an outgrowth of a lecture given at a symposium on the significance of the New Deal held at the University of New Hampshire and published as "The New Deal and Race Relations," in Fifty Years Later: The New Deal Evaluated, *ed. Harvard Sitkoff (New York: Alfred A. Knopf, 1985), 93–112. (Also see Harvard Sitkoff, "The Impact of the New Deal on Black Southerners," in* The New Deal and the South, *ed. James Cobb and Michael Namorato [Jackson: University of Mississippi Press, 1984], 117–34.)*

Perhaps no aspect of the New Deal appears more anomalous or paradoxical than the relationship of Afro-Americans and the administration of President Franklin Roosevelt. On the one hand are the facts of pervasive racial discrimination and inequity in the recovery and relief programs, coupled with the evasiveness of New Dealers on civil rights issues. On the other hand, there is the adoration of FDR by blacks and the huge voting switch of Afro-Americans from the party of Lincoln to the Roosevelt coalition between 1932 and 1940. Faced with this enigma, some historians have concluded that Roosevelt gulled blacks in the 1930s, seduced them with rhetoric and gestures that left untouched the actual harm perpetuated by New Deal neglect and political cowardice. Others conjecture that the blacks' positive opinion of Roosevelt in the thirties had little to do with any effort the New Deal made to improve race relations and everything to do with the desperate need of Afro-Americans for the New Deal programs designed to aid the unemployed and the poor, regardless of color. As Congressman Jack Kemp of New York recently surmised: "Hoover offered a balanced budget, and FDR offered buttered bread." Both interpretations have greatly enriched our historical understanding of blacks and the New Deal. Together they give us a more accurate assessment of Roosevelt's shortcomings and his image as a savior. But both interpretations omit the impact of the New Deal on civil rights in the context of the prevailing racial conservatism of the period. However limited and tentative they may seem in retrospect, the New Deal's steps toward racial justice and equality were unprecedented and were judged most favorably by blacks at the time. Their significance is the theme of this essay.

A Raw Deal

Certainly no racial issue or matter had greater priority for blacks in the 1930s than the opportunity to earn a living or to receive adequate relief. The Great Depression devastated Afro-Americans, who were disproportionately mired in farm tenancy or who were the "last hired and first fired" in industry. At the bottommost rungs of the economic ladder, no group was in greater need of governmental assistance simply to survive. Accordingly, every civil rights organization and Afro-American leader scrutinized the various New Deal programs for their material effect on blacks. They found much to condemn. Blacks were never aided to the full extent of their need. New Deal legislation and local administration often resulted in discrimination against blacks or their exclusion from benefits. And, at times, the New Deal augmented the educational, occupational, and residential segregation of Afro-Americans.

However much blacks hoped for a new deal of the cards from Roosevelt, they found the deck stacked against them. The heritage of black poverty and powerlessness brought them into the Depression decade without the wherewithal to overcome at the local level those insisting that they remain the lowest social class or to prevail over their opponents at the national level in a political system granting benefits mostly on the power of the groups demanding them. Largely due to the measures taken by southern state legislatures at the turn of the century to disenfranchise blacks, they could do little to lessen the president's dependence for New Deal legislation and appropriations on the white southerners who held over half the committee chairmanships and a majority of the leadership positions in every congressional session during the thirties. The very ubiquity of the worst depression in American history, moreover, limited the possibility of a major New Deal effort to remedy the plight of blacks. Hard times defined Roosevelt's mandate and kept the pressure on the New Deal to promote the economic recovery of middle-class America rather than to undertake either the long-range reform of the structural bases of poverty or to engage in a protracted effort to vanquish Jim Crow. In addition, the traditions of decentralization and states' rights further undermined the effort of blacks to gain equitable treatment from the New Deal. Despite the laudable intent of many Roosevelt appointees in Washington, those who administered the New Deal at the state and local levels, especially in the South, saw to it that blacks never shared fully or fairly in the relief and recovery projects.

Thus the National Recovery Administration (NRA) quickly earned such epithets as "Negroes Ruined Again," "Negro Run Around," and "Negro Rights Abused." The NRA wage codes excluded those who toiled in agriculture and domestic service—three out of every four employed blacks—and the administrators in Washington connived to accept spurious occupational classifications for black workers, or their displacement by white employees. Denied the benefits of the NRA's effort to raise the labor standards, blacks nevertheless felt the impact of the NRA as consumers by having to pay higher prices for most goods. Similarly, the Agricultural Adjustment Administration (AAA) cotton program achieved about as much for the mass of the nearly 3 million black farm tenants as a plague of boll weevils. The AAA eschewed safeguards to protect the exploited landless black peasantry and acquiesced in the widespread cheating of croppers out of their share of the subsidy to planters, or the wholesale eviction of tenants whose labor was no longer needed. Those who had traditionally oppressed blacks in the South also controlled the local administration of the Tennessee Valley Authority (TVA), and the consequences were the same. Blacks were initially excluded from clerical employment and from living in the TVA's new model town of Norris, Tennessee. Local officials segregated work crews and relegated blacks to the least-skilled, lowest-paying jobs. They refused to admit blacks to TVA vocational schools or to training sessions in foremanship. And, everywhere in the Tennessee Valley, white southern administrators insisted upon Jim Crow housing and recreational facilities, and on segregated drinking fountains and employment offices in the TVA.

The early relief and welfare operations of the New Deal proved to be only marginally more beneficial to blacks. The Civilian Conservation Corps (CCC) allowed local officials to choose the enrollees, and not surprisingly, young black men were woefully underrepresented. They were also, in the main, confined to segregated CCC units and kept out of the training programs that would lead to their advancement. Moreover, despite the laudable intentions of Harry Hopkins, the Federal Emergency Relief Administration and the Civil Works Administration succumbed to the pressure brought by angry whites who thought that blacks were being spoiled by direct relief or were earning more on work-relief than white laborers in private enterprise. New regulations lowered the minimum wages on work-relief and prohibited relief payments from exceeding prevailing wages in a region. They also gave greater discretion to state and local relief officials in the administration of their programs. Consequently, blacks saw both their chances for obtaining relief and the amount of relief drop. Especially in 1933 and 1934, discrimination was rife and blacks depended on the mercy of the lily-white personnel in local relief offices. Similarly, the New Deal's capitulation to racial prejudice became manifest in the refusal to admit blacks in the subsistence homestead program, the failure to prohibit racial discrimination in unions protected by the National Labor Relations Act, the passage of a Social Security Act with enough loopholes to exclude two-thirds of all Afro-American workers in 1935, and the encouragement of residential segregation by the Federal Housing Administration.

Pressure for Change

Gradually, however, counterforces pushed the New Deal toward a more equitable treatment of blacks. A clear demonstration by blacks of their determination to achieve full, first-class citizenship seemed foremost among the interrelated reasons for that transformation. On a scale, and with an intensity, unknown in any previous decade, a host of black advancement and protest organizations campaigned for racial justice and equality. More blacks than ever before marched, picketed, rallied, and lobbied against racial discrimination. They boycotted businesses with unjust racial practices. The National Association for the Advancement of Colored People (NAACP) and the National Urban League adapted to the mood of militance. They forged additional weapons of struggle, developed greater skills and sophistication, and acquired powerful allies and sources of support. New militant organizations such as the National Negro Congress and Southern Negro Youth Congress prodded the more moderate black groups to greater aggressiveness and amplified the volume of the growing movement for black rights. Simultaneously, the Negro vote in the 1930s developed into a relatively sizable and volatile bloc that politicians of both major parties in the North could no longer ignore. A marked upsurge in the number of blacks who registered and voted resulted from the continuing migration of Afro-Americans from the South to the cities above the Mason-Dixon line, and from the new immediacy of government to the life of the common people during the New Deal. Concentrated in the states richest in electoral votes, the black vote began to be ballyhooed as a balance of power in national elections, a swing bloc that would go to whichever party most benefited blacks. Northern big-city Democrats became especially attentive and displayed unprecedented solicitude for black needs. At the same time, the power of the South within the Democratic Party declined, Dixie Democrats prominently joined in the conservative criticism of the New Deal, and racism became identified with fascism. One result was that northern Democrats ceased to support their southern brethren in opposing black rights.

Augmenting these developments, members of the radical Left and the labor movement in the thirties preached the egalitarian gospel to millions of white Americans. Communists and the Congress of Industrial Organizations, in particular, advocated an end to racial discrimination and insisted on the necessity for interracial harmony. Their desire for strong labor unions or class unity, unhampered by racial divisions, propelled them into the forefront of mainly white organizations pressing for civil rights. White southern race liberals, although few in number, joined the fray, stressing the connections between economic democracy in the South and the cause of black rights. What George Washington Cable once called the "Silent South" grew vocal, shattering the image of a white South that was solidly united on racial matters. These trends, in turn, gained from the changes in the 1930s in the academic and intellectual communities. Biologists refuted the doctrines of inherent and irremediable racial differences. Social scientists started to undermine white racism by emphasizing environment rather than innate characteristics, by stressing the damage done to individuals by prejudice, and by eroding the stereotype of the Afro-American as a contented buffoon. A new ideological consensus began to emerge, an American creed of treating all people alike, of judging each person as an individual.

Roosevelt could neither ignore what these occurrences portended nor disregard the strength of the forces arrayed against racial reform. He understood that however much black powerlessness had decreased and white hostility to blacks had begun to diminish, the majority of white Americans still opposed desegregation and equal opportunities for blacks. He knew that to combat the worst depression in the nation's history he needed the backing of the southern Democrats who wanted no modification of traditional racial practices. Roosevelt, the consummate politician and humanitarian, therefore husbanded his political capital on racial matters, doing what he thought was right if it would not cost him dearly. Above all, he avoided an all-out confrontation with those whose support he deemed necessary. Always the fox and never the lion on civil rights issues, Roosevelt nevertheless acted in ways that had the unintended consequence of laying the groundwork for the Second Reconstruction.

A Better Deal for Blacks

After 1934, although Jim Crow remained largely intact, blacks gained a much fairer, but still far from fully adequate, share of New Deal benefits and services. In the CCC the percentage of black enrollees rose from 3 percent in 1933 to 6 percent in 1936, to nearly 10 percent in 1937, and to over 11 percent in 1938. In that same year about 40,000 young blacks were sending $700,000 a month home to their parents and dependents. By the start of 1939, some 200,000 blacks had served in the Civilian Conservation Corps, and when the CCC ended in 1942 the number stood at 350,000. In addition, over 40,000 blacks who had entered the Corps as illiterates had learned to read and write.

The National Youth Administration (NYA) directly aided another 300,000 black youths. Like other New Deal agencies, the NYA accepted segregated projects in the South, employed a disproportionate number of blacks in servile work, and lacked the resources to assist Afro-Americans to the extent their privation required. Yet the fervor of Aubrey Williams, head of the NYA until it ended in 1943, led that agency to hire black administrative assistants to supervise black work in every southern state, to forbid either racial or geographic differentials in wages, and to an insistence that black secondary and college students in every state receive aid at least in proportion to their numbers in the population. The NYA also employed more blacks in administrative posts than any other New Deal program, and Afro-Americans annually received between 10 and 20 percent of NYA's appropriations.

With a zeal similar to that of Williams, Dr. Will Alexander, the chief of the Farm Security Administration (FSA), managed to insure benefits for black farmers that were roughly proportionate to their percentage of farm operators. Overall, blacks received about 23 percent of the New Deal's farm security assistance. This was achieved only because FSA officials in Washington kept constant pressure on local authorities to prevent racial discrimination. But the FSA could never convince Congress to appropriate the funds needed to make more than the slightest dent in the problem of needy and displaced tenant farmers. By 1940, despite its egalitarianism, FSA had placed a mere 1,393 black families on its resettlement communities and had provided tenant purchase loans to only 3,400 blacks. Even this minimal effort, however, earned the FSA a reputation as a "disturber of the peace" and the top place on the southern conservatives' "death list" of New Deal programs.

Equally vigilant on matters of race, Secretary of Interior Harold Ickes, who ran the Public Works Administration (PWA), employed a quota system on government construction projects to root out discrimination against black laborers. Beginning in 1934, the PWA included a clause in all its construction contracts stipulating that the number of blacks hired and their percentage of the project payroll be equal to the proportion of blacks in either the local labor force or the 1930 occupational census. The quota was effective in diminishing discrimination. It led to the admission of hundreds of skilled blacks into previously lily-white southern construction trade unions and resulted in over $2 million, nearly 6 percent of the total payroll to skilled workers, being paid to blacks—a portion considerably greater than that warranted by the occupational census. Similar quota systems would later be adopted by the U.S. Housing Authority, the Federal Works Agency, and the President's Committee on Fair Employment Practices.

Icke's concern for racial fairness also led to the PWA expenditure of over $45 million for the construction and renovation of Afro-American schools, hospitals, and recreational facilities. The nearly $5 million granted for new buildings at black colleges increased their total plant value by more than 25 percent. In addition, the PWA loaned municipalities and states more than $20 million to build and repair scores of schools, dormitories, auditoriums, and gymnasiums for blacks. Of the forty-eight PWA housing projects completed by 1938, fourteen were solely for Afro-Americans and fifteen for joint black-white occupancy. Blacks occupied one-third of all PWA housing units and 41,000 of the 122,000 dwelling units built by the U.S. Housing Authority (USHA). The determination of the PWA and USHA to be racially fair and to meet the black demand for public housing also led them to charge blacks a lower monthly average rent than they did whites and to set a higher maximum family income for blacks than whites as the cutoff for admission to the housing projects.

Likewise, the concern for black welfare of Harry Hopkins was manifest in the constant efforts of officials in the Works Progress Administration (WPA) to forbid racial discrimination by local relief authorities in assigning jobs to the unemployed and in establishing wage rates. Hopkins did not succeed in ending such practices in the South, but as the Urban League proclaimed: "It is to the eternal credit of the administrative offices of the WPA that discrimination on various projects because of race has been kept to a minimum and that in almost every community Negroes have been given a chance to participate in the work program." Indeed, during Roosevelt's second term, roughly 350,000 blacks were employed by the WPA annually, about 15 percent of the total in the work-relief program. For the most part, blacks received their proper job classifications from the WPA, gained the equal wages promised them, and were included in all special projects. Over 5,000 blacks were employed as teachers and supervisors in the WPA Education Program, where nearly 250,000 Afro-Americans learned to read and write. Tens of thousands of blacks were trained for skilled jobs in WPA vocational classes. The Federal Music Project performed the works of contemporary Afro-American composers; featured all-black casts in several of its operas; made a special effort to preserve, record, and publish Negro folk music; and conducted music instruction classes for blacks in more than a score of cities. The Federal Art Project, the Federal Theatre Project, and the Federal Writers' Project also employed hundreds of blacks and made special efforts to highlight the artistic contributions of Afro-Americans.

Blacks, long accustomed to receiving little more than crumbs, largely accepted the New Deal's half a loaf. The continuance of discrimination and segregation appeared secondary to the vital importance of work-relief, public housing, government-sponsored health clinics and infant care programs, NYA employment to keep a child in school, an FSA loan to purchase a farm, or new educational facilities in the neighborhood. Primarily because of the PWA and WPA, the gap between both black unemployment rates and black median family income relative to whites diminished during the 1930s, and the percentage of black workers in skilled and semiskilled occupations rose from 23 to 29 percent.

In no small part because of the myriad New Deal programs that improved the nutrition, housing, and health care available to Afro-Americans, black infant and maternal mortality significantly decreased, and black life expectancy climbed from 48 to 53 years in the 1930s. Over 1 million blacks learned to read and write in New Deal–sponsored literacy classes. Federal funds and New Deal guidelines for the expenditure of those funds also resulted in a lengthening of the school term for blacks and a significant growth in the number of schools for blacks. The percentage of Afro-Americans aged five and eighteen attending school jumped from 60 to 65 percent, and the gap in expenditures per black pupil narrowed from 29 percent of the average for white students in 1930 to 44 percent in 1940. In addition, the average salary paid to black teachers, only one-third of that paid to white teachers in 1930, increased to about one-half in 1940.

Summing up the prevailing Afro-American response to the New Deal efforts to relieve black distress, the *Pittsburgh Courier* editorialized that "armies of unemployed Negro workers have been kept from the near-starvation level on which they lived under President Hoover" by the work provided by the WPA, CCC, PWA, and other federal projects. It acknowledged the unfortunate continuation of racial discrimination and the New Deal's failure to end such practices. "But what administration within the memory of man," the *Courier* concluded, "has done a better job in that direction considering the very imperfect human material with which it had to work? The answer, of course, is none."

Diminishing Racism

Blacks expressed their thankfulness for the uncommon concern the Roosevelt administration showed for their well-being and for the direct material assistance that enabled them to endure the Depression. The very novelty of simply being included — of being considered and planned for—elicited praise in hundreds of letters written to the White House and to New Deal agencies. As a group of black social workers visiting Hyde Park proclaimed: "For the first time Negro men and women have reason to believe that their government does care." That sentiment was bolstered time and again by the battles that Alexander, Ickes, Williams, and other New Dealers waged in pursuit of a more equitable deal for blacks, by their overt disdain for racist attitudes and practices, and by their public championing, in articles and speeches, of the cause of racial justice and equality. Blacks viewed their actions with hope as symbolic of a new high-level governmental disposition to oppose racial discrimination.

Blacks in the 1930s also applauded the success of these New Dealers in enlarging the roster of Afro-Americans working for the government. The number of blacks on the federal payroll more than tripled during the Depression decade. The proportion of black government employees in 1940 was twice what it had been in 1930. In an unprecedented move, the Roosevelt administration hired thousands of blacks as architects, engineers, lawyers, librarians, office managers, and statisticians. This was viewed at the time as "the first significant step toward the participation of Negroes in federal government activity" and as "representing something new in the administration of our national affairs." To ensure further steps, the administration also abolished the Civil Service regulations that had required job seekers to designate their race and to attach a photograph to their application forms. Some New Deal officials desegregated the cafeterias, restrooms, and secretarial pools in their agencies and departments; others highlighted their abhorrence of Jim Crow by having blacks and whites work at adjoining desks.

Roosevelt also reversed two decades of diminishing black patronage. He appointed over 100 blacks to administrative posts in the New Deal. Previous administrations had, at best, reserved a handful of honorific and innocuous positions for loyal Negro party leaders. Roosevelt selected a large number of nonpartisan black professionals and veterans of the civil rights movement and placed them in formal positions of public importance so that both government officers and the Afro-American community regarded their presence as significant. Popularly referred to as the Black Cabinet or Black Brain Trust, these black officials had considerably more symbolic value than actual power. They rarely succeeded in pushing the New Deal further along the road to racial equality than it wished to go. Most of their efforts to win greater equity for blacks were defeated by interest groups that were better able to bring pressure to bear on Roosevelt. But their very being and prominence, Roy Wilkins of the NAACP noted, "had never existed before." This fact alone elicited howls from white southerners that "Negroes were taking over the White House," which was hardly the case. Still, the presence of the Black Cabinet, like Roosevelt's selection of William Hastie as the first Afro-American federal judge in American history, hinted at a New Deal determination to break, however timorously, with prevailing customs of racial prejudice. As Mary McLeod Bethune, director of the NYA's Division of Negro Affairs, emphasized during the thirties, such appointments were not "tokenism" but the essential first steps in making the government aware of black needs and planning policies that would help the race.

The Black Cabinet certainly did raise the level of national awareness of racial issues. The race advisers appointed by Roosevelt articulated the problems of blacks, the ultimate goal of integration, and the specific responsibility of the federal government in the area of civil rights, both within the corridors of the various agencies in which they worked and in the public conferences and reports they generated. "At no time since the curtain had dropped on the Reconstruction drama," wrote Henry Lee Moon of the NAACP, "had government focused as much attention upon the Negro's basic needs as did the New Deal." For example, the NYA convened a three-day National Conference on the Problems of the Negro and Negro Youth in 1937, for the purpose of increasing support for greater governmental assistance to blacks. It was addressed by four cabinet members, half a dozen agency chiefs, and Eleanor Roosevelt. Such a conference would have been inconceivable before the New Deal. As Mary Bethune noted in her opening remarks: "This is the first time in history of our race that the Negroes of America have felt free to reduce to writing their problems and plans for meeting them with the expectancy of sympathetic understanding and interpretation." Even Ralph Bunche, who was perhaps the New Deal's severest black critic, admitted at the end of the 1930s that the New Deal was without precedent in the manner in which it granted "broad recognition to the existence of the Negro as a national problem and undertook to give specific consideration to this fact in many ways."

A New Hope

Roosevelt appointees also stirred the hopes of Afro-Americans by establishing precedents that challenged local white control over blacks. The National Advisory Committee on Education, which was appointed by Roosevelt, called in 1938 for specific guarantees that federal grants to states for education would be spent equitably for black as well as white schooling. No government body had said that before. Less than a decade earlier, in fact, that exact proposition had been overwhelmingly rejected by President Hoover's National Advisory Committee on Education. In fact, only the blacks on the Hoover committee supported it. But during the New Deal, the earlier all-black minority opinion became a part of the official proposal, and the committee's recommendation appeared verbatim with Roosevelt's support in the Harrison-Fletcher-Thomas federal aid to education bill submitted to Congress.

The New Deal, indeed, substantially expanded the scope of the federal government's authority and constricted traditional states' rights. The states' failures to cope with the economic crisis enlarged the responsibilities of the national government, and the New Deal involved the states in joint programs in which the federal government increasingly imposed the standards and goals. This alteration in the system of federalism augured well for black hopes of future federal civil rights actions, as did the emergence of a new conception of positive government, the "powerful promoter of society's welfare," which guaranteed every American a minimally decent economic existence as a matter of right, not charity, and which assumed the role of the protector of weak interests that could not contend successfully on their own.

Roosevelt's appointments to the Supreme Court immediately sanctioned the expansion of federal power over matters of race and strengthened the rights of blacks. After FDR's abortive attempt at "court packing" in 1937, the personnel on the Supreme Court changed swiftly and power passed into the hands of the New Dealers, who articulated a new judicial philosophy which championed the rights of racial and religious minorities and formulated new constitutional guarantees to protect civil rights. As a result, both the number of cases involving black rights brought before the federal courts and the percentage of decisions favorable to black plaintiffs leaped dramatically. What would culminate in the Warren Court clearly began in the Roosevelt Court. With the exception of James Byrnes, Roosevelt's eight appointees to the Court were truly partisans of the cause of civil rights. Together, men who had long been associated with the NAACP and issues of racial justice, such as Felix Frankfurter, Wiley Rutledge, and Frank Murphy, joined with new converts like Hugo Black and William O. Douglas to begin dismantling a century of legal discrimination against blacks. Their decisions in cases involving the exclusion of blacks from juries, the right to picket against discrimination in employment, racially restrictive covenants, inequality in interstate transportation, peonage, disfranchisement, and discrimination in the payment of black teachers and in graduate education signaled the demise of the separate-but-equal doctrine established by *Plessy v. Ferguson* (1896).

Such decisions, according to legal scholar Loren Miller, made the Negro less a *freedman* and more a *free man*. The federalizing of the Bill of Rights left blacks less at the mercy of states' rights. The inquiry into the facts of segregation, rather than just the theory, diminished the possibility of anything racially separate meeting the test of constitutionality. And the expansion of the concept of state action severely circumscribed the boundaries of private discrimination. Perhaps most importantly, the decisions of the Roosevelt Court had a multiplier effect. They stimulated scores of additional challenges to Jim Crow, both in court and out. Fittingly, in 1944, when the Supreme Court struck down the white primary, the only dissenter was Owen Roberts, the sole justice then sitting whom Roosevelt had not appointed.

Eleanor Roosevelt

Although not a presidential appointee, Eleanor Roosevelt certainly made the most of her position as first lady to link the civil rights cause with the New Deal. Working quietly within the administration, at first, Mrs. Roosevelt influenced her husband and numerous agency heads to be more concerned with the special needs of blacks. Gradually her commitment became more open and visible. Functioning as an unofficial ombudsman for blacks, she goaded bureaucrats and congressmen into lessening racial discrimination in federal programs and acted as the main conduit between the civil rights leadership and the higher circles of the New Deal and the Democratic Party. Repeatedly breaking with tradition, Eleanor Roosevelt openly entertained Afro-American leaders at the White House, posed for photographs with blacks, and publicly associated herself with most of the major civil rights organizations and issues. The peripatetic Mrs. Roosevelt spoke out for National Sharecroppers Week, addressed conventions of the Brotherhood of Sleeping Car Porters and National Council of Negro Women, candidly backed the civil rights activities of the American Youth Congress, and frequently pleaded for racial tolerance and fairness in her syndicated newspaper column, published articles, and radio broadcasts.

"Nigger Lover Eleanor," as some whites derided her, squarely placed her authority and prestige behind the drive for civil rights legislation in President Roosevelt's second term. Delivering the keynote address at the first meeting of the Southern Electoral Reform League, she emphasized the necessity for a federal act to end all poll tax requirements for voting. Mrs. Roosevelt also publicly endorsed the quest for antilynching legislation and sat prominently in the Senate gallery during the efforts of northern liberals to invoke cloture and shut off the southern filibuster of the 1938 Wagner–Van Nuys–Gavagan antilynching bill. In the same year Eleanor Roosevelt also helped to organize the Southern Conference for Human Welfare. At its opening session in Birmingham, Alabama, she defied the local segregation ordinance, conspicuously taking a seat on the "Colored" side of the auditorium. White supremacists immediately condemned the first lady's act as "an insult to every white man and woman in the South." But in the Negro press, Eleanor Roosevelt's disdain for Jim Crow was a "rare and precious moment in the social history of America." Further stirring the wrath of white supremacists and gaining the admiration of blacks, Mrs. Roosevelt began to denounce racial discrimination in the defense program. In 1939, she publicly decried the bigotry of the Daughters of the American Revolution when that organization refused to rent its Constitutional Hall for a concert by the famous black contralto Marian Anderson. Mrs. Roosevelt then used her "My Day" newspaper column to explain why she could no longer remain a member of a group practicing such discrimination and, working with her husband and the NAACP, she arranged for Marian Anderson to sing her concert in front of the Lincoln Memorial. Two months later, on behalf of the NAACP, Eleanor Roosevelt officially presented the Spingarn Medal for Freedom to Marian Anderson.

Progress, Not Perfection

Such highly publicized actions of Mrs. Roosevelt, as well as the president's increasingly more egalitarian gestures and rhetoric, had a vital impact on blacks in the 1930s. Although Franklin Roosevelt shied away from any direct challenges to white supremacy, the very fact that he frequently invited blacks to the White House, held conferences with civil rights leaders, and appeared before Afro-American organizations indicated to blacks that they mattered. It was smart. Mindful of political realities, blacks sought progress, not perfection. They understood that no president would act boldly and unyieldingly on black rights until a majority constituency for dramatic change had emerged. Until then, symbolic actions would count, for they played an important role in educating and persuading, in inspiring hope and commitment.

Accordingly, the civil rights leadership and their allies in the 1930s utilized the president's association with the campaigns for anti-lynching and anti–poll tax legislation to mobilize future support. Their public complaints to the contrary, these black rights spokesmen recognized the insurmountable barriers to cloture being voted in the Senate and the necessity for Roosevelt to maintain the backing of the southern leadership in Congress. They knew he would not jeopardize his relief and defense programs for a futile attempt at civil rights legislation. Accordingly, blacks extracted the greatest possible advantages from what the president said and did, however lukewarm and timorous.

On the poll tax, Roosevelt publicly supported the legislative efforts for its abolition. "The right to vote," he declared, "must be open to all our citizens irrespective of race, color, or creed—without tax or artificial restriction of any kind. The sooner we get to that basis of political equality, the better it will be for the country as a whole." In a public letter Roosevelt vigorously endorsed the anti–poll tax movement in Arkansas. At the press conference in 1938 he opposed the use of poll taxes: "They are inevitably contrary to the fundamental democracy and its representative form of government in which we believe." No legislator or informed citizen doubted where the president stood on this matter. In part, this helps to explain why the House of Representatives in 1941 voted to pass an anti–poll tax bill by a better than three-to-one margin.

Similarly, the president aided the civil rights movement on anti-lynching, with both public statements to influence mass opinion and private pressures on the Senate to get it to consider legislation, but Roosevelt would neither place the antilynching bills on his list of "must" legislation nor intervene with the Senate leadership to end the filibusters that doomed the proposals from even coming to a vote. Over a coast-to-coast radio hook-up, early in his administration, Roosevelt denounced lynching as "a vile form of collective murder." Lynch law, he continued, "is murder, a deliberate and definite disobedience of the high command, 'Thou shalt not kill.' We do not excuse those in high places or low who condone lynch law." No president had ever spoken like that before. W. E. B. DuBois, writing immediately afterward in *The Crisis*, observed: "It took war, riot and upheaval to make Wilson say one small word. Nothing ever induced Herbert Hoover to say anything on the subject worth the saying. Even Harding was virtually dumb." Only Roosevelt, DuBois concluded, "has declared frankly that lynching is murder. We all knew it, but it is unusual to have a President of the United States admit it. These things give us hope."

More ambiguously, Roosevelt in 1934 authorized Senators Edward Costigan and Robert Wagner to inform the majority leader "that the President will be glad to see the anti-lynching bill pass and wishes it passed." And in 1935, he requested that the majority leader permit the Senate to consider the bill. The halfheartedness of Roosevelt's support did nothing to avert the inevitable southern filibuster that killed the measure in 1935. Meanwhile, Roosevelt's private encouragement of others to keep up the fight led to a protracted and bitter wrangle over antilynching legislation in 1938. A far cry from the charade of 1935 in which both sides went through the motions, the two-month-long talkathon of 1938 smacked of fratricide. The southern senators overwhelmingly blamed the New Deal for provoking the civil rights issues that alienated the South from the Democratic Party. They pledged to talk as long as necessary to "preserve the white supremacy of America." And they held Roosevelt responsible for having the Senate rules enforced "in a technical manner," for holding night sessions in an attempt to break the filibuster, and for trying to invoke cloture twice.

The result in Congress notwithstanding, black leaders gained significantly from the struggle against lynching and from the president's involvement in the cause. Lynchings declined from a high for the decade of twenty-eight in 1933 to eighteen in 1935, six in 1938, and two in 1939. To ward off federal legislation, most southern states made greater efforts to prevent lynching and enacted their own bills to stop the crime. At the end of the decade, Roosevelt established a special Civil Rights Section of the Justice Department and empowered it to investigate all lynchings that might involve some denial of a federal right. And, in no small part because the public identified the crusade against lynching with the First Family, the campaign for federal legislation attracted new supporters and allies to the black cause who would stay to fight against discrimination in the defense program, segregation in education, and the disfranchisement of Afro-Americans. In this limited regard, the president's pronouncements meant much to blacks. In political language, at least, they were yet another manifestation of Roosevelt's desire to win the allegiance of blacks and to take the steps necessary to retain their loyalty, even at the risk of gradual southern disenchantment with the New Deal.

Roosevelt's overtures in this direction also showed in the series of precedent-shattering "firsts" that he orchestrated in the 1936 campaign. Never before had the Democrats accredited an Afro-American as a convention delegate; in 1936 they accorded thirty blacks that distinction. For the first time, additionally, the national party in 1936 invited black reporters into the regular press box, chose a black minister to offer the convention invocation, selected blacks to deliver the welcome address and one of the speeches seconding Roosevelt's renomination, and placed a black on the delegation to notify the vice president of his renomination. Yet another significant event at the convention occurred when liberals and New Dealers wiped out the century-old rule, utilized by the South as a political veto, which required the Democratic nominee to win two-thirds of the delegates' votes in order to obtain the nomination. The white South recognized the threat and resented the intrusion. And its fears of a future attempt by the New Deal to alter race relations were heightened when Roosevelt pointedly campaigned before black audiences and promised that in his administration there would be "no forgotten races" as well as no forgotten men. Then in the 1940 presidential race, Roosevelt affirmed his desire to include blacks evenhandedly in defense training and employment, promoted the first black to the rank of army brigadier general, and insisted that, for the first time, the Democrats include a specific Negro plank in the party platform, pledging "to strive for complete legislative safeguards against discrimination in government services and benefits."

A New Deal for Blacks: An Assessment

However circumspect this New Deal record seems today, for blacks in the thirties it meant change for the better. The mixture of symbolic and substantive assistance, of rhetoric and recognition, led blacks to cast their ballots overwhelmingly for Roosevelt once the New Deal began. After voting more than 70 percent for Herbert Hoover in 1932, a majority of black voters deserted the Republican Party for the first time in history in 1934, about two-thirds of the Afro-Americans registered in 1936 entered the Roosevelt coalition, and nearly 68 percent of all black voters in 1940 went for FDR. This startling shift in the black vote, more pronounced than that of any other ethnic, racial, or religious group, according to the NAACP came not only because of black "concern for immediate relief, either in jobs or direct assistance," but because of "a feeling that Mr. Roosevelt represented a kind of philosophy of government which will mean much to their cause."

Virtually every civil rights spokesman stressed both the value of new government precedents favorable to blacks and the manner in which the New Deal made explicit the federal government's responsibility in the field of civil rights. Editorials in the black press and journals frequently reiterated that the New Deal had ended the "invisibility" of the race problem and had made civil rights a part of the liberal agenda. Perhaps most importantly, blacks in the thirties lauded the manifold ways in which the New Deal reform spirit ushered in a new political climate in which Afro-Americans and their allies could begin to struggle with some expectation of success. They took heart from the expanding authority of the federal government and the changing balance of power in the Democratic Party, as well as from the overt sympathy for the underprivileged shown by the Roosevelt administration; and they made common cause with fellow sufferers in pressing the New Deal to become even more of an instrument for humane, liberal reform.

These developments did little to change the concrete aspects of life for most blacks in the 1930s. The New Deal failed to end the rampant discrimination against blacks in the North, who were living in ghettos that had turned to slums and who were twice as likely to be unemployed as whites. The Roosevelt administration also failed to enfranchise black southerners, to eradicate segregation, or to elevate the great mass of blacks who remained a submerged caste of menials, sharecroppers, unskilled laborers, and domestics. These facts cannot be gainsaid. The New Deal record on race is replete with failures and timidity, unfulfilled promises, and insufficient effort. The New Deal did not fundamentally transform the economic, legal, or social status of Afro-Americans.

But for the millions of blacks who hung FDR's picture on their walls, who kept voting for Roosevelt and naming their children after him, something vital did begin in the New Deal, breaking the crust of quiescence that had long stifled even the dream of equal opportunity and full participation in American life. The New Deal gave blacks hope. A black newspaper called it "the emergence of a new type of faith." The pervasive despondency that had led several generations of Americans, black and white, to regard the racial status quo as immutable gradually gave way to a conviction that racial reform was possible. The dream that would prove indispensable in the continuing struggle for black equality could at last be dreamt. The barely visible flicker of black hope at the start of the New Deal would shine brightly as the United States mobilized for World War II.

Suggested Readings

This essay is based largely on the research done for Harvard Sitkoff, *A New Deal For Blacks: The Emergence of Civil Rights as a National Issue* (New York, 1978). It also owes much to John B. Kirby, *Black Americans in the Roosevelt Era: Liberalism and Race* (Knoxville, Tenn., 1980), and Raymond Wolters, *Negros and the Great Depres-*

sion: *The Problem of Economic Recovery* (Westport, Conn., 1970). George B. Tindall, *The Emergence of the New South, 1913–1945* (Baton Rouge, 1976) is indispensable, as is Gunnar Myrdal, *An American Dilemma: The Negro Problem and Modern Democracy* (New York, 1944).

For background on the black experience, see John Hope Franklin, *From Slavery to Freedom: A History of American Negros* (New York, rev. ed., 1980), and August Meier and Elliott Rudwick, *From Plantation to Ghetto: An Interpretive History of American Negroes* (New York, rev. ed., 1976). Specific New Deal programs and policies are analyzed in Sidney Baldwin, *Poverty and Politics: The Rise and Decline of the Farm Security Administration* (Chapel Hill, N.C., 1968); Donald H. Grubbs, *Cry from the Cotton: The Southern Tenants Farmers' Union and the New Deal* (Chapel Hill, N.C., 1971); Donald S. Howard, *The WPA and Federal Relief Policy* (New York, 1943); Paul E. Mertz, *New Deal Policy and Southern Rural Poverty* (Baton Rouge, 1978); John A. Salmond, *The Civilian Conservation Corps, 1933–1942: A New Deal Case Study* (Durham, N.C., 1967); and Richard Sterner, *The Negro's Share: A Study of Income, Consumption, Housing and Public Assistance* (New York, 1943).

The role of key individuals is analyzed in Jervis Anderson, *A. Philip Randolph: A Biographical Portrait* (New York, 1973); Andrew Buni, *Robert L. Vann and The Pittsburgh Courier* (Pittsburgh, 1974); Wilma Dykeman and James Stokely, *Seeds of Southern Change: The Life of Will Alexander* (Chicago, 1962); Tamara K. Hareven, *Eleanor Roosevelt: An American Conscience* (Chicago, 1968); Rackham Holt, *Mary McLeod Bethune: A Biography* (New York, 1964); Joseph P. Lash, *Eleanor and Franklin* (New York, 1971); B. Joyce Ross, *J. E. Spingarn and the Rise of the NAACP, 1911–1939* (New York, 1972); and Walter White's autobiography *A Man Called White* (New York, 1948). The following are invaluable for the racial mood of the era and an assessment of the impact of the New Deal: Dan T. Carter, *Scottsboro: A Tragedy of the American South* (New York, 1969); Frank Friedel, *F.D.R. and the South* (Baton Rouge, 1965); Thomas A. Krueger, *And Promises to Keep: The Southern Conference on Human Welfare, 1938–1948* (Nashville, 1967); Rayford W. Logan, ed., *The Attitude of the Southern Press toward Negro Suffrage, 1932–1940* (Washington, D.C., 1940); Morton Sosna, *In Search of the Silent South: Southern*

Liberals and the Race Issue (New York, 1977); Robert L. Zangrando, *The NAACP Crusade against Lynching, 1909–1950* (Philadelphia, 1980); and especially Ralph J. Bunche, *The Political Status of the Negro in the Age of FDR*, Dewey W. Grantham, ed. (Chicago, 1973).

The Detroit Race Riot of 1943

My initial scholarly publication proudly wore my heart on its sleeve. The first of what would be several essays exploring the diverse impacts of the Second World War on civil rights and race relations began with a research trip to Detroit in 1967. I arrived in the Motor City just one week after its massive race riot that summer. What I saw and heard from Detroit blacks, and the contrary views being expressed by many whites, thoroughly influenced my interpretation of the riot that had occurred a quarter of a century earlier. More than just trying to capture the horror of the event that left 25 blacks and 9 whites dead and more than 700 injured, I felt an urgency to emphasize the barriers erected by whites to block blacks' residential and occupational mobility, and I felt the need to attribute black aggressiveness to political militancy rather than criminality—the popular explanation given by most politicians at the time. Likewise, I felt obligated to blame the riot primarily on the many whites who sought to keep "the nigger in his place"—that is, in an inferior economic and social position—and on their leaders in Detroit and Washington who were content with "politics as usual." Along with others in the New Left in the late 1960s, I questioned whether the nation had moved at all along the path toward racial justice, and I used Detroit as a prototype of the residential segregation, unemployment and underemployment, substandard housing, and inferior education that made the United States anything but a land of equality and opportunity. To underscore my political viewpoint, I ended the article with the judgment of an old black woman: "There ain't no North any more. Everything now is South." The essay "The Detroit Race Riot of 1943" was originally published in Michigan History *53 (Fall 1969), 183–206, and is reprinted by permission of the Michigan Historical Commission.*

For the American Negro, World War II began a quarter of a century of increasing hope and frustration. After a long decade of depression, the war promised a better deal. Negroes confidently expected a crusade against Nazi racism and for the Four Freedoms, a battle requiring the loyalty and manpower of all Americans, to be the turning point for their race. This war would be "Civil War II," a "Double V" campaign. No Negro leader urged his people to suspend grievances until victory was won, as most did during World War I. Rather, the government's need for full cooperation from the total population, the ideological character of the war, the constant preaching to square American practices with the American Creed, and the beginning of the end of the era of white supremacy in the world, intensified Negro demands for equality *now*.[1]

Never before in American history had Negroes been so united and militant. Led by the *Baltimore Afro-American, Chicago Defender, Pittsburgh Courier,* and Adam Clayton Powell's *People's Voice* ("The New Paper for the New Negro"), the Negro press urged civil rights leaders to be more aggressive. It publicized protest movements, headlined atrocity stories of lynched and assaulted Negroes, and developed race solidarity. Every major civil rights organization subscribed to the "Double V" campaign, demanding an end to discrimination in industry and the armed forces. The National Association for the Advancement of Colored People (NAACP), National Urban League, National Negro Congress, A. Philip Randolph's March-on-Washington Movement, and the newly organized Congress of Racial Equality joined with Negro professional and fraternal organizations, labor unions, and church leaders to insist on "Democracy in Our Time!" These groups organized rallies, formed committees, supported letter and telegram mail-ins, began picketing and boycotting, and threatened unruly demonstrations. This as well as collaboration with sympathetic whites helped exert pressure on government officials.[2]

The combined effects of exhortation and organization made the Negro man-in-the-street increasingly militant. After years of futility, there was now bitter hope. As he slowly gained economic and political power, won victories in the courts, heard his aspirations legitimized by respected whites, and identified his cause with the two-thirds of the world's colored people, the Negro became more impatient with any impediment to first-class citizenship and more determined to assert his new status. Each gain increased his expectations; each improvement in the conditions of whites increased his dissatisfaction. Still forced to fight in a segregated army supplied by a Jim Crow industrial force, still denied his basic rights in the South and imprisoned in rat- and vermin-infested ghettos in the North, he rejected all pleas "to go slow." At the same time many whites renewed their efforts to keep the Negro in an inferior economic and social position regardless of the changes wrought by the war. Frightened by his new militancy and wartime gains, resenting his competition for jobs, housing, and power, whites sought to retain their cherished status and keep "the nigger in his place." The more Negroes demanded their due, the more white resistance stiffened.[3]

American engagement in a world war, as well as the lack of government action to relieve racial anxiety or even enforce "neutral" police control, made it likely that racial antagonism would erupt into violence. President Roosevelt, preoccupied with international diplomacy and military strategy, and still dependent on southern support in Congress, ignored the deteriorating domestic situation. Participation in the war increased the prestige of violence and its use as an effective way to accomplish specific aims. The psychological effects of war, the new strains and uncertainty, multiplied hatred and insecurity. Many petty irritations—the rationing, shortages, overcrowding, and high prices—engendered short tempers; and the fatigue of long workweeks, little opportunity for recreation, the anxious scanning of casualty lists, the new job and strange city, the need for the noncombatant to prove his masculinity led to heightened tension and the desire to express it violently.[4]

For three years public officials throughout the nation watched the growth of racial strife. Fights between Negroes and whites became a daily occurrence on public vehicles.[5] Nearly every issue of the Negro press reported clashes between Negro soldiers and white military or civilian police. At least seventeen Negroes were lynched between 1940 and 1943.[6] The accumulation of agitation and violence then burst into an epidemic of race riots in June 1943. Racial gang fights, or "zoot-suit riots," broke out in several non-southern cities. The worst of these hit Los Angeles. While the city fathers wrung their hands, white sailors and their civilian allies attacked scores of Negroes and Mexican Americans. The only action taken by the Los Angeles City

Council was to declare the wearing of a zoot suit a misdemeanor. In mid-June, a rumor of rape touched off a twenty-hour riot in Beaumont, Texas. White mobs burned and pillaged the Negro ghetto. War production stopped, businesses closed, thousands of dollars of property was damaged, two were killed, and more than seventy were injured. In Mobile, the attempt to upgrade some Negro workers as welders in the yards of the Alabama Dry Dock and Shipbuilders Company caused 20,000 white workers to walk off their jobs and riot for four days. Only the intervention of federal troops stopped the riot. The President's Committee on Fair Employment Practices then backed down and agreed to let segregation continue in the shipyards.[7]

Nowhere was trouble more expected than in Detroit.[8] In the three years after 1940, more than 50,000 southern Negroes and half a million southern whites migrated to the "Arsenal of Democracy" seeking employment. Negroes were forced to crowd into the already teeming thirty-block ghetto of Paradise Valley, and some fifty registered "neighborhood improvement associations" and the Detroit Housing Commission kept them confined there. Although 10 percent of the population, Negroes comprised less than 1 percent of the city teachers and police. Over half the workers on relief in 1942 were Negro, and most of those with jobs did menial work. Only 3 percent of the women employed in defense work were Negro, and these were mainly in custodial positions. The Negro demand for adequate housing, jobs, recreation, and transportation facilities, and the white refusal to give anything up, led to violence.[9] Early in 1942, over a thousand whites armed with clubs, knives, and rifles rioted to stop Negroes from moving into the Sojourner Truth Housing Project. Fiery crosses burned throughout the city. More than a thousand state troopers had to escort 200 Negro families into the project. Federal investigators warned Washington officials of that city's inability to keep racial peace, and the Office of Facts and Figures warned that "unless strong and quick intervention by some high official, preferably the President, is not taken at once, hell is going to be let loose." Nothing was done in Detroit or Washington. Throughout that year Negro and white students clashed in the city's high schools, and the number of outbreaks in factories multiplied.[10]

In 1943, racial violence in Detroit increased in frequency and boldness. The forced close mingling of Negroes with southern whites on buses and trolleys, crowded with nearly 40 percent more passengers than at the start of the war, led to fights and stabbings. White soldiers battled Negroes in suburban Inkster. In April, a racial brawl in a city playground involved more than a hundred teenagers. Early in June, 25,000 Packard employees struck in protest against the upgrading of three Negro workers.[11] More than 500 Negroes and whites fought at parks in different parts of the city. Negro leaders openly predicted greater violence unless something was done quickly to provide jobs and housing. Walter White of the NAACP told a packed rally in Cadillac Square: "Let us drag out into the open what has been whispered throughout Detroit for months—that a race riot may break out here at any time."[12] Detroit newspapers and national magazines described the city as "a keg of powder with a short fuse." But no one in the city, state, or federal government dared to act. Everyone watched and waited. When the riot exploded, Mayor Edward Jeffries told reporters: "I was taken by surprise only by the day it happened."[13]

The riot began, like those in 1919, with direct clashes between groups of Negroes and whites. Over 100,000 Detroiters crowded onto Belle Isle on Sunday, June 20, 1943, to seek relief from the hot, humid city streets. The temperature was over ninety. Long lines of Negroes and whites pushed and jostled to get into the bathhouse, rent canoes, and buy refreshments. Police continuously received reports of minor fights. Charles (Little Willie) Lyon, who had been attacked a few days earlier for trying to enter the all-white Eastwood Amusement Park, gathered a group of Negro teenagers to "take care of the Hunkies." They broke up picnics, forced whites to leave the park, beat up some boys, and started a melee on the bridge connecting Belle Isle with the city. Brawls broke out at the park's casino, ferry dock, playground, and bus stops. By evening rumors of a race riot swept the island. Sailors from a nearby armory, angered by a Negro assault on two sailors the previous day, hurried to the bridge to join the fray. Shortly after 11:00 P.M. more than 5,000 people were fighting on the bridge. By 2:00 A.M. the police had arrested twenty-eight Negroes and nineteen whites, quelling the melee without a single gunshot.[14]

As the thousands of rioters and onlookers returned home, stories of racial violence spread to every section of Detroit. In Paradise Valley, Leon Tipton jumped on the stage of the Forrest Club, grabbed the microphone, and shouted: "There's a riot at Belle Isle! The whites have killed a colored lady and her baby. Thrown them over a bridge. Everybody come on! There's free transportation outside!" Hundreds rushed out of the nightclub, only to find the bridge barricaded and all traffic approaches to the Isle blocked. Sullen, the mob returned to the ghetto, stoning passing white motorists, hurling rocks and bottles at the police, and stopping streetcars to beat up unsuspecting whites. The frustrations bottled up by the war burst. Negroes—tired of moving to find the promised land, tired of finding the North too much like the South, tired of being Jim-Crowed, scorned, despised, spat upon, tired of being called "boy"—struck out in blind fury against the white-owned ghetto. Unlike the riots of 1919, Negroes now began to destroy the hated white property and symbols of authority. By early morning every white-owned store window on Hastings Avenue in the ghetto had been smashed. There was little looting at first, but the temptation of an open store soon turned Paradise Valley into an open-air market: liquor bottles, quarters of beef, and whole sides of bacon were freely carried about, sold, and bartered.[15]

As the police hesitatingly struggled to end the rioting in the ghetto, rumors of white women being raped at Belle Isle enraged white crowds forming along Woodward Avenue. Unhampered by the police, the mobs attacked all Negroes caught outside the ghetto. They stopped, overturned, and burned cars driven by Negroes. The mob dragged off and beat Negroes in the all-night movies along the "strip" and those riding trolleys. When a white instructor at Wayne University asked the police to help a Negro caught by a white gang, they taunted him as a "nigger lover." The police would do nothing to help.[16] Throughout the morning fresh rumors kept refueling the frenzy, and the rioting grew. The excitement of a car burning in the night, the screeching wail of a police siren, plenty of free liquor, and a feeling of being free to do whatever one wished without fear of police retaliation all fed the appetite of a riot-ready city.[17]

At 4:00 A.M. Detroit Mayor Edward Jeffries met with the police commissioner, the FBI, State Police, and Colonel August Krech, the highest ranking army officer stationed in Detroit. With hysteria growing, and the ability of police to control violence diminishing, most of the meeting involved a discussion of the procedure to be used to obtain federal troops. They agreed that the mayor should ask the governor for troops; the governor would telephone his request to General Henry Aurand, commander of the Sixth Service in Chicago; and Aurand would call Krech in Detroit to order the troops into the city. Colonel Krech then alerted the 728th Military Police Battalion at River Rouge and assured the mayor that the military police would be patrolling Detroit within forty-nine minutes after receiving their orders. Nothing was done to check the plan for acquiring federal troops, and no mention was made of the need for martial law or a presidential proclamation.[18]

When the meeting ended at 7:00 A.M. the police commissioner prematurely declared that the situation was now under control, and federal troops would not be needed. The opposite was true. Negro looting became widespread, and white mobs on Woodward Avenue swelled. Two hours later Negro leaders begged the mayor to get federal troops to stop the riot. Jeffries refused, promising only to talk with them again at a noon meeting of the Detroit Citizens Committee. The mayor would discuss neither the grievances of the Negro community nor how Negroes could help contain the destruction in the ghetto. A half hour later Jeffries changed his mind, telling those in his City Hall office that only federal troops could restore peace to Detroit.[19]

Harry F. Kelly, the newly elected Republican governor of Michigan, was enjoying his first session of the Conference of Governors in Ohio when shortly before 10.00 A.M. he was called to the telephone. Mayor Jeffries described the riot situation to the governor, asserted that the city was out of control, and insisted that he needed more manpower. Kelly responded by ordering the Michigan State Police and state troops on alert. An hour later he telephoned Sixth Service Command Headquarters in Chicago. Believing he had done all that was necessary to get federal troops into the city, Kelly hurriedly left for Detroit. But according to the Sixth Service Command, the governor's call was only about a *possible* request for troops.[20] Thus, the twelve-hour burlesque of deploying federal troops in Detroit began. The War Department and the White House flatly refused to take the initiative. Army officials in Chicago and Washington kept passing the buck back and forth. And both Kelly and Jeffries feared doing anything that might indicate to the voters their inability to cope with the disorder.[21]

After Kelly's call to Chicago, Aurand dispatched his director of

internal security, Brigadier General William Guthner, to Detroit
to command federal troops "in the event" the governor formally
requested them. Military police units surrounding Detroit were put
on alert but forbidden to enter the city. In Washington the top brass
remained busy with conferences on the use of the army taking over
mines in the threatened coal strike. No advice or instructions were
given to Aurand. The Washington generals privately agreed that
Aurand could send troops into Detroit without involving the president or waiting for a formal request by the governor by acting on the
principle of protecting defense production. But the War Department
refused to give any orders to Aurand because it might "furnish him
with a first class alibi if things go wrong."[22]

While the generals and politicians fiddled, the riot raged. With
most of the Detroit police cordoning off the ghetto, white mobs
freely roamed the city attacking Negroes. At noon, three police cars
escorted the mayor into Paradise Valley to attend a Detroit Citizens
Committee meeting. The interracial committee roundly denounced
the mayor for doing too little but could not agree on what should be
done. Some argued for federal troops and others for Negro auxiliary
police. Exasperated, Jeffries finally agreed to appoint 200 Negro auxiliaries. But with no power and little cooperation from the police, the
auxiliaries accomplished nothing. Rioters on the streets continued to
do as they pleased. At 1:30 P.M. high schools were closed, and many
students joined the riot.[23]

Shortly after three, General Guthner arrived in Detroit to tell Kelly
and Jeffries that federal martial law, which could only be proclaimed
by the president, was necessary before federal troops could be called
in. Dumbfounded by this new procedure, the governor telephoned
Aurand for an explanation. Aurand, more determined than ever to
escape the responsibility for calling the troops, confirmed Guthner's
statement. Despite Jeffries' frantic plea for more men, Kelly refused
to ask for martial law: such a request would be taken as an admission
of his failure.[24]

Not knowing what else to do, after almost twenty hours of rioting, Jeffries and Kelly made their first radio appeal to the people of
Detroit. The governor proclaimed a state of emergency, banning the
sale of alcoholic beverages, closing amusement places, asking persons
not going to or from work to stay home, prohibiting the carrying of

weapons, and refusing permission for crowds to assemble. The proclamation cleared the way for the use of state troops but still did not
comply with Aurand's prerequisite for the use of federal troops. Mayor
Jeffries pleaded for an end to hysteria, arguing that only the Axis benefited from the strife in Detroit.[25]

On the streets neither the proclamation nor the plea had any
effect. Negro and white mobs continued their assaults and destruction. The weary police were barely able to restrain whites from entering Paradise Valley or to check the extent of Negro looting. Just as
the mayor finished pleading for sanity, four teenagers shot an elderly
Negro because they "didn't have anything to do." Tired of milling
about, they agreed to "go out and kill us a nigger. . . . We didn't know
him. He wasn't bothering us. But other people were fighting and
killing and we felt like it too."[26] As the city darkened, the violence
increased. At 8:00 P.M. Jeffries called for the state troops. The governor had ordered the force of 2,000 mobilized earlier, but now the
mayor learned that only 32 men were available. At the same time the
mayor was informed that a direct clash between whites and Negroes
was imminent. At Cadillac Square, the police were losing their struggle to hold back a white mob heading for the ghetto. Nineteen different police precincts reported riot activity. Seventy-five percent of the
Detroit area was affected. Sixteen transportation lines had to suspend
operation. The Detroit Fire Department could no longer control the
more than 100 fires. Detroiters entered Receiving Hospital at the rate
of one every other minute.[27]

In Washington, Lieutenant General Brehon Somervell, commander of all army service forces, directed the army's provost marshal,
Major General Allen Guillon, to prepare a presidential proclamation. At 8:00 P.M. Guillon and Somervell took the proclamation to
the home of Secretary of War Henry Stimson. Sitting in the secretary's library, the three men laid plans for the use of federal troops; as
they discussed the situation they kept in telephone contact with the
president at Hyde Park, the governor in Detroit, and General Aurand
in Chicago. Stimson instructed Aurand not to issue the text of the
proclamation until the president signed it. Shortly after nine, Kelly
telephoned Colonel Krech to request federal troops. At 9:20, the governor repeated his appeal to General Aurand. Aurand immediately
ordered the military police units into Detroit, although federal mar-

tial law had not been declared and the president had not signed the proclamation.[28]

As the politicians and generals wrangled over the legality of Aurand's order, 350 men of the 701st Military Police Battalion raced into Cadillac Square to disperse a white mob of over 10,000. In full battle gear, bayonets fixed at high port, the federal troops swept the mob away from Woodward Avenue without firing a shot. The 701st then linked up with the 728th Battalion, which had been on the alert since 4:00 A.M., to clear rioters out of the ghetto. Using tear gas grenades and rifle butts, the military police forced all Negroes and whites off the streets. At 11:30 the riot was over, but the presidential proclamation was still to be signed.[29]

After Aurand transmitted his orders to Guthner, he had called Somervell to get permission to issue the proclamation. Somervell demanded that Aurand follow Stimson's instructions to wait until Governor Kelly contacted the president and Roosevelt signed the official order. Aurand relayed this message to Guthner, but the governor could no be located until the riot had been quelled. Not until shortly before midnight did Kelly call Hyde Park to request the troops already deployed in the city. President Roosevelt signed the proclamation at 11:55 P.M. The Detroit rioters, now pacified, were commanded "to disperse and retire peaceably to their respective abodes." Twenty-one hours had passed since army officials in Detroit first planned to use federal troops to end the riot. More than fifteen hours had been wasted since the mayor first asked for army manpower. Half a day had been lost between the governor's first call to Sixth Service Command and Aurand's decision to send the military police into Detroit. General Guthner sat in Detroit for six hours before deploying the troops he had been sent to command. And it was during that time that most of Detroit's riot toll was recorded: 34 killed, more than 700 injured, over $2 million in property losses, and 100 million man-hours lost in war production.[30]

The armed peace in Detroit continued into Tuesday morning. Five thousand soldiers patrolled the streets, and military vehicles escorted buses and trolleys on their usual runs. Although racial tension remained high, firm and impartial action by the federal troops kept the city calm. Following Aurand's recommendations, Guthner instructed his troops to act with extreme restraint. Each field order ended with the admonition: "Under no circumstances will the use of firearms be resorted to unless all other measures fail to control the situation, bearing in mind that the suppression of violence, when accomplished without bloodshed, is a worthy achievement."[31]

Continued hysteria in the city caused most of Guthner's difficulties. Rumors of new violence and repeated instances of police brutality kept the Negro ghetto seething. Most Negroes feared to leave their homes to go to work or buy food. Guthner persistently urged Commissioner Witherspoon to order the police to ease off in their treatment of Negroes, but he refused. Tales of the riot inflamed Negroes in surrounding communities. A group of Negro soldiers at Fort Custer, 140 miles west of Detroit, tried to seize arms and a truck to help their families in the city. In Toledo, police turned back 1,500 Negroes trying to get rail transportation to Detroit. Muskego, Indiana Harbor, Springfield, East St. Louis, and Chicago reported racial disturbances. Aurand changed his mind about leaving Chicago for Detroit and ordered Sixth Service Command troops in Illinois on the alert.[32]

Unrest and ill feeling continued throughout the week. The city courts, disregarding the depths of racial hostility in Detroit, employed separate and unequal standards in sentencing Negroes and whites arrested in the riot. With little regard for due process of law, the police carried out systematic raids on Negro rooming houses and apartments. Anxiety increased, isolated racial fights continued, repeated rumors of a new riot on July Fourth poisoned the tense atmosphere. Negroes and whites prepared for "the next one." Workmen in defense plants made knives out of flat files and hacksaw blades. Kelly and Jeffries urged the president to keep the federal troops in Detroit.[33]

While the troops patrolled the streets, the search for answers and scapegoats to give some meaning to the outburst began. Adamant that it really "can't happen here," the same liberals and Negro leaders who had warned that white racism made Detroit ripe for a riot now attributed the violence to Axis agents. Telegrams poured into the White House asking for an FBI investigation of German agents in Detroit who aimed to disrupt war production. When the myth of an organized fifth column behind the riot was quickly shattered, liberals accused domestic reactionaries. The KKK, Gerald L. K. Smith, Father Charles Coughlin, Reverend J. Frank Norris, southern congressmen, and antiunion demagogues were all singled out for blame.[34] The NAACP aimed its sights at reactionary Poles who led the battle against decent Negro housing. Conservatives were just as anxious to hold liberals and Japanese agents responsible for race conflict. Martin Dies, chairman of the House Un-American Activities Committee, saw the Japanese-Americans released from internment camps behind the riot. Congressman John Rankin of Mississippi taunted his colleagues in the House who supported the anti–poll tax bill by saying "their chickens are coming home to roost" and asserted that the Detroit violence had been caused by the "crazy policies of the so-called fair employment practices committee in attempting to mix the races in all kinds of employment."[35] Many southerners blamed Negro agitators. Some talked of "Eleanor Clubs" as the source of the riot. "It is blood on your hands, Mrs. Roosevelt," claimed the *Jackson Daily News.* "You have been personally proclaiming and practicing social equality at the White House and wherever you go, Mrs. Roosevelt. In Detroit, a city noted for the growing impudence and insolence of its Negro population, an attempt was made to put your preachments into practice, Mrs. Roosevelt. What followed is now history." A Gallup poll revealed that most northerners believed Axis propaganda and sabotage were responsible for the violence, while most southerners attributed it to lack of segregation in the North. An analysis of 200 newspapers indicated that southern editors stressed Negro militancy as the primary cause, while northern editors accused fifth column subversives and southern migrants new to city ways.[36]

In Detroit the causes and handling of the riot quickly became the central issue of the city politics. The Congress of Industrial Organizations (CIO), Negro organizations, and many civil liberties groups formed an alliance to defeat Mayor Edward Jeffries in November, to get rid of Commissioner Witherspoon, and to demand additional housing and jobs for Negroes. Led by United Auto Workers (UAW) president R. J. Thomas and City Councilman George Edwards, a former UAW organizer, the coalition gained the backing of most CIO locals, the NAACP and Urban League, International Labor Defense, National Lawyers Guild, National Negro Congress, National Federation for Constitutional Liberties, Catholic Trade Unionists, Socialist Party of Michigan, Inter-Racial Fellowship, Negro Council for Victory and Democracy, Metropolitan Detroit Youth Council, Union for Democratic Action, and March-on-Washington Movement. They were supported editorially by the *Detroit Free Press, Detroit Tribune,* and the Negro *Michigan Chronicle.*[37] Throughout the summer the coalition clamored for a special grand jury to investigate the causes of the riot and the unsolved riot deaths.

Michigan's leading Republicans, the Hearst press, and most real estate and antiunion groups opposed any change in the Negro's status. The governor, mayor, and police commissioner, abetted by the obligating Common Council, squelched the pleas for better housing and jobs and a grand jury investigation. Unwilling to make any changes in the conditions underlying the riot, the Republicans made meaningless gestures. The mayor established an interracial committee with no power. After a few sleepy sessions, it adjourned for a long summer vacation. Commissioner Witherspoon refused to allow changes in the regulations to make possible the hiring of more Negro policemen. Instead of a grand jury investigation, the governor appointed his own Fact-Finding Committee of four Republican law officers involved in the handling of the riot. And the Detroit Council of Churches, non-partisan but similarly reluctant to face the issue of white racism, called upon the city to observe the following Sunday as a day of humility and penitence.[38]

A week after the riot, Witherspoon appeared before the Common Council to report on his department's actions. He blamed Negroes for starting the riot and army authorities for prolonging it. The commissioner pictured white mob violence as only "retaliatory action" and police behavior as a model of "rare courage and efficiency." In fact, Witherspoon concluded, the police have been so fair that "some have accused the Department of having a kid glove policy toward the Negro." No one on the council bothered to ask the commissioner why the police failed to give Negroes the adequate protection required by law or how this policy accounted for seventeen of the twenty-five Negroes killed in the riot having been shot by the police.[39] Two days later, Mayor Jeffries presented his "white paper" to the Common Council. He reiterated the commissioner's criticism of the army and praise for the police and added an attack on "those Negro leaders who insist that their people do not and will not trust policemen and the Police Department. After what happened I am certain that some of these leaders are more vocal in their caustic criticism of the Police Department than they are in educating their own people to their responsibilities as citizens." The Common Council heartily approved the two reports. Gus Dorias and William (Billy) Rogell, two Detroit athletic heroes on the council, advocated a bigger ghetto to solve the racial crisis. Councilman Comstock did not think this or anything should be done. "The racial conflict has been going on in the country since our ancestors made the first mistake of bringing the Negro to the country." The conflict would go on regardless of what was done, added Comstock, so why do anything?[40]

Throughout July the accusations and recriminations intensified. Then, as the city began to tire of the familiar arguments, a fresh controversy erupted. When three Negro leaders asked William Dowling, the Wayne County prosecutor, to investigate the unsolved riot deaths, Dowling berated them for turning information over to the NAACP that they withheld from him. He charged the NAACP with being "the biggest instigators of the race riot. If a grand jury were called, they would be the first indicted." The NAACP threatened to sue Dowling for libel, and the county prosecutor quickly denied making the charge. "Why, I like Negroes," he said. "I know what it is to be a member of a minority group. I am an Irish Catholic myself." The next day Dowling again charged an "unnamed civil rights group" with causing the riot. Witherspoon endorsed Dowling's allegation, and the battle flared. "It was as if a bomb had been dropped," said one Negro church leader. "The situation is what it was just before June 21."[41]

In the midst of this tense situation, the governor released the report of his Fact-Finding Committee. Parts I and II, a detailed chronology of the riot and supporting exhibits, placed the blame for the violence squarely on Negroes who had started fights at Belle Isle and spread riot rumors. Content to fix liability on the initial aggressors, the report did not connect the Sunday fights with any of the scores of incidents of violence by whites on Negroes which preceded the fights at Belle Isle. Nor did the report mention any of the elements which permitted some fights to lead to such extensive hysteria and violence, or which allowed rumors to be so instantly efficacious. No whites were accused of contributing to the riot's causes. The sailors responsible for much of the fighting on the bridge, and the nineteen other whites arrested by the police Sunday night, escaped blame. The report emphasized the culpability of the Negro-instigated rumors, especially Leo Tipton's, but let the other rumors remain "lily-white." Although many instances of police brutality were attested and documented, the committee failed to mention them. And while only a court or grand jury in Michigan had the right to classify a homicide as legally "justifiable," the committee, hearing only police testimony, took it upon itself to "justify" all police killings of Negroes.[42]

Part III, an analysis of Detroit's racial problems, completely departed from the committee's aim of avoiding "conclusions of a controversial or conjectural nature." The section on those responsible for racial tensions omitted any mention of the KKK, Black Legion, National Workers League, and the scores of anti-Negro demagogues and organizations openly preaching race hatred in Detroit. Racial tension was totally attributed to Negro agitators who "constantly beat the drums of: 'Racial prejudice, inequality, intolerance, discrimination.'" Repeatedly, the report referred to the Negro's "presumed grievances" and complaints of "alleged Jim Crowism." In the world of the Fact-Finding Committee no real Negro problems existed, or if they did, they were to be endured in silence. Publication of the obviously prejudiced report proved an immediate embarrassment to the governor. Most newspapers and journals denounced it as a "whitewash," and Kelly's friends wisely buried it. The Common Council then declared the riot a "closed incident."[43]

In Washington, too, politics went on as usual. The administration did nothing to prevent future riots or attempt to solve the American dilemma. The problem of responding to the riots became compounded when the same combination of underlying grievances and war-bred tensions which triggered the Detroit riot led to an orgy of looting and destruction in Harlem. Henry Wallace and Wendell Willkie delivered progressive speeches; leading radio commentators called for a new approach to racial problems; and many prominent Americans signed newspaper advertisements urging the president to condemn segregation and racial violence. But the White House remained silent.[44]

In much the same way it had handled the question of segregation in the armed forces and discrimination in defense production, the Roosevelt administration muddled its way through a summer of violence. The four presidential aides handling race relations problems, all southerners, determined to go slow, protect the "boss," and keep the shaky Democratic coalition together, and they fought all proposals for White House action. They politely buried pleas for the president to give a fireside chat on the riots and brushed aside recommendations that would force Roosevelt to acknowledge the gravity of the race problem. The Interior Department's plans for a national race relations commission, and those of Attorney General Francis Biddle for an interdepartmental committee, were shelved in favor of Jonathan Daniels' inoffensive suggestion to correlate personally all information on racial problems. Even Marshall Field's proposal to circulate pledges asking people not to spread rumors and to help "win the war at home by combating racial discrimination wherever I meet it," which appealed to Roosevelt, went ignored. The federal government took only two actions: clarification of the procedure by which federal troops could be called, and approval of J. Edgar Hoover's recommendation to defer from the draft members of city police forces. Like the Republicans in Michigan, the Democrats in the capital occupied themselves with the efficient handling of a future riot rather than its prevention.[45]

With a war to win, Detroit and the nation resumed "business as usual." Negroes continued to be brutalized by the police and to be the "first fired, last hired." In the Senate, the administration killed a proposal to have Congress investigate the riots, and Michigan's Homer Ferguson and Arthur Vandenberg stymied every proposal for Negro housing in Detroit's suburbs. Their constituents continued boasting "the sun never sets on a nigger in Dearborn." Governor Kelly appropriated $1 million to equip and train special riot troops. Mayor Jeffries, running as a defender of "white supremacy," easily won reelection in 1943 and 1945. The lesson from the riot? In the mayor's words: "We'll know what to do next time." Yet southern Negroes continued to pour into Detroit looking for the promised land—only to find discrimination, hatred, a world of little opportunity and less dignity. The dream deferred festered like a sore, waiting to explode. "There ain't no North any more," sighed an old Negro woman. "Everything now is South."[46]

Notes

1. Louis Wirth, *Research Memorandum on the Effect of War on American Minorities* (New York: Social Science Research Council, 1942); Carey McWilliams, "How the Negro Fared in the War," *Negro Digest* 5 (January

1946), 67–74. On Negro militancy see Horace Cayton, "Fighting for White Folks?" *The Nation* 155 (September 26, 1942), 545–52; Roi Ottley, "Negro Morale," *New Republic* 195 (November 10, 1941), 613–15; Charles Williams, "Harlem at War," *The Nation* 156 (January 16, 1943), 86–88; Adam Clayton Powell Jr., *Marching Blacks* (New York: Dial Press, 1945), 3–5, 125–32.

2. "Negro Organizations and the War Effort," report from Special Services Division, April 28, 1942, R.G. 228, Box 427, National Archives. On the Negro press see Roi Ottley, *New World A-Coming* (Boston: Houghton Mifflin, 1943), 268–88.

3. James Davies, "Toward a Theory of Revolution," *American Sociological Review* 27 (February 1962), 5–18; Everett Hughes, "Social Change and Status Protest: An Essay on the Marginal Man," *Phylon* 10 (First Quarter 1949), 58–65; Ralph Bunche, "Conceptions and Ideologies of the Negro Problem," memorandum prepared for the Carnegie-Myrdal Study of the Negro in America, 1940, New York Public Library, 161; Gunnar Myrdal, *An American Dilemma* (New York: Harper & Bros., 1944), 1015–16; letter from Pauli Murray to Marvin McIntyre, June 18, 1943, OF 93C, Roosevelt Papers, Franklin D. Roosevelt Library, Hyde Park, New York.

4. Arthur Waskow, *From Race Riot to Sit-in 1919 and the 1960's* (Garden City, N.Y.: Doubleday, 1966), 220–23; E. L. Quarantelli, "The Nature and Conditions of Panic," *American Journal of Sociology* 60 (November 1954), 267–75; Louis Wirth, "Ideological Aspects of Social Disorganization," *American Sociological Review* 5 (August 1940), 474–75. War tensions in Detroit are described in two "Commentator" columns by W. K. Kelsey in the *Detroit News*, June 22, 1943, 18, and June 25, 1943, 18.

5. Robert Lee Eichorn, "Patterns of Segregation, Discrimination and Interracial Conflict" (unpublished Ph.D. dissertation, Cornell University, 1954), 61–64; Allen Grimshaw, "Urban Racial Violence in the United States: Changing Ecological Considerations," *American Journal of Sociology* 66 (September 1960), 117; *A Monthly News Summary of National Events and Trends in Race Relations* 1 (August 1943), 9–10, cited hereafter as *News Summary*.

6. Nancy and Dwight Macdonald, *The War's Greatest Scandal! The Story of Jim Crow in Uniform* (New York: March-on-Washington Movement, 1943), 2–3; *News Summary* 1 (1943), 7–9; Walter White to Roosevelt, August 13, 18, and 20, 1941, OF 25, Roosevelt Papers; minutes of the Board of Directors, September 8, 1941, NAACP Papers, Library of Congress. Wartime lynchings are listed in Florence Murray (ed.), *The Negro Handbook, 1944* (New York: Current Reference Publications, 1944), 169–72.

7. On racial tensions and rumors of riots see Will Alexander, Oral His-

tory Memoir, typescript in Columbia University Oral History Center, 696–99; minutes of the Board of Directors, May 10 and July 12, 1943, NAACP Papers. On the riots see Chester B. Himes, "Zoot Riots Are Race Riots," *The Crisis* 50 (July 1943), 200–201; Thomas Sancton, "The Race Riots," *New Republic* 109 (July 5, 1943), 9–13; "Summary of a Report on the Race Riots in the Alabama Dry Dock and Shipbuilding Company Yards in Mobile," prepared by the National Urban League, Detroit Urban League Papers, University of Michigan Historical Collections, Ann Arbor. On warnings to Roosevelt and future racial violence see Vito Marcantonio and Philip Murray letters to the president, June 16 and 18, 1943, OF 93C, Roosevelt Papers.

8. "The National Urban League Report of the Detroit Riots," and Walter White, "What Caused the Detroit Riots," both in Detroit Urban League Papers.

9. H. Black, "Restrictive Covenants in Relation to Segregated Negro Housing in Detroit" (unpublished master's thesis, Wayne University, 1947); B. S. Jenkins, "The Racial Policies of the Detroit Housing Commission and Their Administration" (unpublished master's thesis, Wayne University, 1951); Robert Weaver, *Negro Labor: A National Problem* (New York: Harcourt, Brace, 1946), chapter 6; Alfred McClung Lee and Norman Humphrey, *Race Riot* (New York: Dryden Press, 1943), 7, 92–93.

10. Charles S. Johnson, *To Stem This Tide* (Boston: Pilgrim Press, 1943), 50–59; the administration's desire to bury racial problems is seen in a letter from McIntyre to Charles Palmer, January 19, 1942, OF 93, Roosevelt Papers.

11. T. M. Newcomb, *Social Psychology* (New York: Dryden Press, 1950), 596. On the Packard strike see J. F. Scott and G. C. Homans, "Reflections on the Wildcat Strikes," *American Sociological Review* 12 (June 1947), 278–79. According to the Bureau of Labor Statistics, in the three-month period from March 1 to May 31, 1943, 101,995 man-days or 2,466,920 man-hours of war production were lost by hate strikes due to the employment or upgrading of Negro workers. Naomi Friedman Goldstein, *The Roots of Prejudice Against the Negro in the United States* (Boston: Boston University Press, 1948), 49–50.

12. Minutes of the Board of Directors, July 16, 1942, NAACP Papers; *Detroit Free Press*, June 4, 1943, 1, 9, quotes Walter White. Also see press release of John Dancy, June 26, 1943, and memorandum of William Baldwin, July 6, 1943, in Detroit Urban League Papers.

13. A. C. Smith, "The Negro Problem in Detroit," *Detroit News*, October 5, 1942, 1, 4, October 6, 1942, 1, 11, October 7, 1942, 1, 4, October 8, 1942, 1, 4, October 9, 1942, 1, 4; "Detroit Is Dynamite," *Life* 13 (August 17, 1942), 15–23, dismissed by the mayor as "scurrillous" in *Detroit Free Press*, August 17, 1942, 13. Jeffries is quoted in *PM* (New York), June 28, 1943, 3.

14. The description of the riot that follows is based on Brigadier General William Guthner, "Commander's Estimate of the Situation," June 26, 1943, in Publications during the Detroit Race Riots, R.G. 389, National Archives, Alexandria, Virginia; the report of the governor's Fact-Finding Committee, *Committee to Investigate the Riot Occurring in Detroit on June 21, 1943* (Detroit: Dowling, Oscar Olander, J. H. Witherspoon, 1943), by W. Dowling, O. Olander, H. Rushton, and J. Witherspoon, cited hereafter as *Committee to Investigate Riot*; Lee and Humphrey, *Race Riot*; Robert Shogan and Tom Craig, *The Detroit Race Riot: A Study in Violence* (Philadelphia: Chilton Books, 1964).

15. See note 3 and Harold Kingsley, "Memorandum on Detroit Race Disturbance," June 23, 1943, in Detroit Urban League Papers.

16. "Report of Thurgood Marshall, Special Counsel for the N.A.A.C.P., Concerning Activities of the Detroit Police during the Riots, June 21 and 22, 1943," in Jeffries Papers, Burton Historical Collection, Detroit Public Library. According to *The Nation* 157 (July 3, 1943), 4, the police did nothing to interfere with white mobs but were quick to use violence on Negroes attacking white property. Waskow, *Race Riot to Sit-in*, 209–10, emphasizes the importance of "unneutral" police behavior in a race riot.

17. Neil J. Smelser, *Theory of Collective Behavior* (New York: Free Press, 1962), 71–73, 269; G. W. Allport and L. Postman, *The Psychology of Rumor* (New York: Henry Holt, 1947), 33–45, 193–96; and Allen Grimshaw, "A Study in Social Violence: Urban Race Riots in the United States" (unpublished Ph.D. dissertation, University of Pennsylvania, 1959), 114–15.

18. Police Commissioner Witherspoon's Report to the Common Council, June 28, 1943, in OF 93C, Roosevelt Papers.

19. Lee and Humphrey, *Race Riot*, 29–30.

20. "History of the Detroit Race Riot," File No. 333.5, Sixth Service Command, National Archives; and Guthner, "Commander's Estimate No. 1."

21. Robert Lovett to Roosevelt, August 19, OF 93C, Roosevelt Papers.

22. Colonel R. G. Roamer, "Summary of Events in the Detroit Riot," Roamer-Guillon transcript, June 21, 1943, 1:45 P.M.; and Lerch-Roamer transcript, June 21, 1943, 4:45 P.M., all in R.G. 389, National Archives. On the impending coal strike see Stimson Diary, June 21, 1943, Yale University, New Haven, Connecticut.

23. Lee and Humphrey, *Race Riot*, 33–34.

24. Memo from Adjutant General, "Use of Federal Troops at Request of State," July 24, 1943, A.G.O. File 370.6, National Archives; Francis Biddle to Roosevelt, July 15, 1943, and Roosevelt to Biddle and Henry Stimson, July 29, 1943, OF 93C, Roosevelt Papers.

25. *Detroit Free Press*, June 22, 1943, 1.

26. Lee and Humphrey, *Race Riot,* 37–41.

27. General Guthner to Lt. Col. F. W. Reese, August 2, 1943, Detroit Race Riot, R.G. 389, National Archives; *Detroit Free Press,* July 1, 1943, 1.

28. Roamer, "Summary of Events in the Detroit Riot"; Stimson Diary, June 21, 1943; "Memorandum Re Race Riots in Detroit," June 21, 1943, Stimson Papers, Yale University.

29. Aurand to Guillon, July 3, 1943, Detroit Race Riot, R.G. 389, National Archives.

30. Roamer, "Summary of Events in the Detroit Riot"; memo from Brehon Somervell to Stimson, June 22, 1943, WDCSA-370-61 (December 1943), National Archives; and Roosevelt's proclamation, ibid.

31. Guthner, "Commander's Estimate No. 2"; Field Orders No. 1 and No. 2-A; Aurand memorandum to Guthner, "Use of Troops in Connection with the Domestic Disturbance at Detroit, Michigan," June 22, 1943, all in R.G. 389, National Archives.

32. Guthner-Aurand transcript, June 24, 1943; Aurand-Guillon transcript, June 22, 1943; Guthner, "Commander's Estimate No. 2," R.G. 389, National Archives.

33. Guthner, "Commander's Estimate No. 3" and "Commander's Estimate No. 4," R.G. 389, National Archives; and letters from Kelly and Jeffries to the president, OF 93C, Roosevelt Papers.

34. W. J. Norton, "The Detroit Riots—And After," *Survey Graphic* 31 (August 1943), 317; George Beatty, "The Background and Causes of the 1943 Detroit Race Riot," April 14, 1954 (History Department, Princeton University), especially 81–87; Granger to Dancy, June 21, 1943, and National Urban League telegram to Roosevelt, June 23, 1943, both in Detroit Urban League Papers. Also see Stimson Diary, June 22, 1943; Sancton, "Race Riots," 9–13; and the Civil Rights Federation of Detroit newsletter, *Action,* June 23, 1943, Detroit Urban League Papers.

35. Walter White to Frank Murphy, June 30 and September 1, 1943, Frank Murphy Papers, University of Michigan Historical Collections; and the stories on Dies and Rankin in the *New York Times,* June 24, 1943, 12.

36. Stimson Diary, June 24, 1943; Shogan and Craig, *Detroit Race Riot,* 98; the Gallup poll and press analysis are reported in *News Summary* 1 (1943), 19–27.

37. On the formation of the coalition see the *Detroit Free Press,* June 23, 1943, 19, June 28, 1943, 1–2, and June 29, 1943, 19; Lee and Humphrey, *Race Riot,* 54–55; and the scores of resolutions passed by local unions and political associations in the Detroit Urban League Papers and the 1943 Mayor's Papers. On the United Auto Workers' race policies see Benjamin McLaurin, Oral History Memoir, typescript in Columbia University Oral

History Center, 54; and two articles in the Urban League's journal: Louis Martin, "The Negro in the Political Picture," *Opportunity* 21 (July 1943), 104–7, 137–39, and Albert Hamilton, "Allies of the Negro," ibid., 115–17.

38. Earl Brown, "The Truth About the Detroit Race Riot," *Harper's Magazine* 187 (November 1943), 489; *PM* (New York), June 27, 1943, 3–5; for an analysis of police activities, see the report of Thurgood Marshall, July 26, 1943, "Race Riot—Detroit, 1943," R.G. 42, Box 75, folio 1, Michigan Historical Commission Archives, Lansing.

39. "Witherspoon Report." When General Somervell read it he exclaimed: "Now what the hell do we do with a case like that"; Shogan and Craig, *Detroit Race Riot*, 102. Exhibit XII of *Committee to Investigate Riot* also blamed the delay on the army, concluding: "At the time the troops arrived there was actually no violence to suppress." On the brutality of the police see Thurgood Marshall, "The Gestapo in Detroit," *The Crisis* 50 (August 1943), 232–33, 246–47, and note 16.

40. Jeffries' "White Paper" is in the 1943 Mayor's Papers; *Detroit Free Press*, July 1, 1943, 1; Lester Velie, "Housing: Detroit's Time Bomb," *Collier's* 118 (November 23, 1946), 78; Lee and Humphrey, *Race Riot*, 56.

41. Stories in *Detroit Free Press*, July 27, 1943, 1, 3, July 28, 1943, 1–2, 22; Brown, "Truth About Detroit Race Riot," 497; Shogan and Craig, *Detroit Race Riot*, 105–6.

42. *Committee to Investigate Riot*, especially exhibits XVIII and XIX. For a critical analysis see Detroit Chapter of the National Lawyers Guild, "Analysis of Report of Governor's Fact Finding Committee," in 1943 Mayor's Papers.

43. *Committee to Investigate Riot* and editorial survey in *Detroit Free Press*, August 24, 1943, 6; *Time* 42 (August 23, 1943), 20, denounced the report as a "broad whitewash of the city's bumbling, do-nothing administration and incompetent police force."

44. Samuel Battle, Oral History Memoir, typescript in Columbia University Oral History Center, 54–55; Lee and Humphrey, *Race Riot*, 64–70; Walter White, *A Man Called White* (New York: Viking Press, 1948), 230–41; and pleas to the president in OF 4245-G, Roosevelt Papers.

45. The four southern aides were James Byrnes, Jonathan Daniels, Stephen Early, and Marvin McIntyre. On a fireside chat see Daniels to Roosevelt, June 22, 1943, PPF 1820, and John H. Sengstacke to the president, June 29, 1943, OF 93C, both in Roosevelt Papers. Interior Department plans are in Saul Padover to Harold Ickes, June 29, 1943, PSF Ickes, and Ickes to the president, July 15, 16, and 26, 1943, OF 6, Roosevelt Papers. Also see Biddle to Roosevelt, July 15, 1943, OF 93C; Daniels to Roosevelt, July 23, 1943, Daniels to George Haas, July 28, 1943, and Daniels to Howard Odum,

September 1, 1943, in OF 4245-G; and Marshall Field to Roosevelt, July 24, 1943, OF 93C, all in Roosevelt Papers.

46. Henry Lee Moon, "Danger in Detroit," *The Crisis* 53 (January 1946), 12–13, 28–29, and *Balance of Power: The Negro Vote* (Garden City, N.Y.: Doubleday, 1948), 154; Louis Martin, "Detroit—Still Dynamite," *The Crisis* 51 (January 1944), 8–10; Lester Velie, *Collier's* 118 (1946), 76; and John Dancy to Harold Kingsley, October 29, 1943, Detroit Urban League Papers. Riot appropriations are discussed by Charles S. Johnson in *First Annual Report of the Illinois Inter-Racial Commission* (Springfield: Commission on Human Relations, 1944), 37. The Negro woman is quoted in Lee and Humphrey, *Race Riot,* 141. Also see letter from Richard Wright to Senor Frasconi, *Twice a Year* 12–13 (1945), 259–60.

Racial Militancy and Interracial Violence in the Second World War

To many, "Racial Militancy and Interracial Violence in the Second World War" appeared to be merely a variation on the theme of the Detroit race riot article published two years earlier. It was similarly praised by New Leftist historians for describing "the brutality toward and degradation of black soldiers during World War II, the military's refusal to protect its black members from white mobs, and Roosevelt's total disregard for violent race riots. Like Wilson's southern advisers, Roosevelt's southern advisers refused to alleviate or prevent the numerous lynchings and vicious race riots which occurred throughout the country" (Blanche Wiesen Cook, Alice Kessler Harris, and Ronald Radosh, eds., Past Imperfect: Alternative Essays in American History [New York: Alfred A. Knopf, 1973], 237). *Although this was a correct summation of the conditions underlying the riots, what went largely misunderstood or ignored at the time was the extent to which this later essay stressed the stifling, stunting effect of wartime racial violence on black militancy. The riots forced black organizations and newspapers to urge the struggle out of the streets and into the courtroom. Winning white allies and promoting better race relations superseded hopes for an all-black mass direct-action movement. Despite this change, attributing black wartime gains to aggressive militancy won favor among the New Left generation of historians. It became commonplace to describe the Second World War as the watershed in the black freedom struggle and to ascribe that pivotal event to wartime African American militancy. I still don't think so. Let the debate go on. "Racial Militancy and Interracial Violence in the Second World War" first appeared in* Journal of American History 58 (December

1971), 661–81, and is reprinted by permission of the Organization of American Historians.

World War II opened a quarter of a century of increasing hope and frustration for the black man. After a decade of depression, the ideological character of the war and the government's need for the loyalty and manpower of all Americans led blacks to expect a better deal from President Franklin D. Roosevelt. With a near unanimity rare in the Negro community, civil rights groups joined with the Negro press and influential, church, labor, and political leaders to demand "Democracy in Our Time!"[1] Individuals and organizations never before involved in a protest movement found it respectable, even expedient, to be part of the new militancy in the black community.[2] The war stimulated racial militancy, which in turn led to increased interracial violence that culminated in the bloody summer of 1943. Negro leaders then retreated, eschewing mass movements and direct action in favor of aid from white liberals for their congressional and court battles. While many of the goals of the early war years remained, the mood and tactics became increasingly conservative.[3] Paradoxically, the wartime violence which summoned forth the modern civil rights movement, enlisting in the struggle scores of liberal organizations and tens of thousands of whites previously blind or indifferent to American racism, also smothered the embryonic black movement for equality by tying it ever more closely to liberal interracialism, which all too easily accepted the appearance of racial peace for the reality of racial justice. By the end of the war two trends emerged which would shape the course of the next two decades. Jim Crow had stumbled badly enough to heighten the aspirations of many Negroes that they would soon share the American Dream; and leadership in the battle for civil rights had been taken over by various communist-front organizations, labor unions, religious groups fighting intolerance, and social scientists making a career of studying race relations.[4]

At the beginning of this war, unlike World War I, few Negro leaders asked blacks to close ranks and ignore their grievances until the war ended.[5] Rather, the very dependency of the government on the cooperation of the Negro intensified his demand for civil rights. "If we don't fight for our rights during this war," said one Harlem leader, "while the government needs us, it will be too late after the war."[6]

Memories of the false promises of World War I stirred a reader of the *Amsterdam-Star News* to write: "Remember, that which you fail to get now you won't get after the war."[7] Some Negro columnists openly advocated a prolonged war as the best hope for destroying the racial status quo. And the Negro press proclaimed the "time ripe for a new emancipation" and mobilized a "Double V" campaign to fight fascism and racism both abroad and at home.[8]

The Negro press headlined evidence of blacks excluded from defense jobs, blood plasma segregated by the Red Cross, abused Negro soldiers, and white hostility and violence. Circulation increased 40 percent as the Negro newspapers, functioning primarily to foster race solidarity and prod increasing militancy, campaigned to embarrass America's war for democracy by publicizing America's Jim Crow policies and practices.[9] Membership in the National Association for the Advancement of Colored People (NAACP) multiplied nearly ten times during the war, and the number of its chapters tripled.[10] The Congress of Racial Equality, organized in 1942, experimented with nonviolent action to end segregation in the North and stimulated students at Howard University and interracial groups in various cities to begin sitting-in and experimenting with other forms of direct confrontation.[11] To "demand the right to work and fight for our country," A. Philip Randolph labored to build his March-on-Washington Committee into an all-black mass protest movement.[12] Even Negro fraternal, business, and professional societies collaborated in the battle against oppression on the home front. Everywhere he turned, the urban black found new Negro organizations enlisting in the crusade and new leaders and journals exhorting him to demand equality. Each concession wrested from the government and every sign of the weakening of white supremacy added new converts, made fundraising easier, and stimulated greater confidence and higher hopes.[13]

The establishment of the United Nations, the anti-imperialistic pronouncements of government officials, and a steady stream of articles, books, letters, and speeches—especially those of Pearl S. Buck, Eleanor Roosevelt, Wendell Willkie, and Henry Wallace—disputing the scientific basis of racism and urging America to practice what it preached further augmented the militancy of black America.[14] The attempt to educate the public to stop discrimination and end prejudice reached its peak in 1944 with the publication of Gunnar Myrdal's

An American Dilemma. Eschewing the socioeconomic explanations popularized by American Marxists in the 1930s, Myrdal described the race problem as a moral problem for white America, brought about by the collision between the American Creed's promise of equality and liberty and the denial of them to the Negro. Woefully underestimating the extent and depth of American racism, Myrdal optimistically predicted that Americans would resolve their dilemma by ending discrimination and segregation.[15]

The growth of Negro political power also stimulated hope for change. The steady migration of blacks to the North and the return, after 1938, of many white Republicans to their traditional voting habits prematurely led Negro leaders to believe that Franklin D. Roosevelt could be persuaded to support civil rights.[16] He refused to do so in 1940, but Willkie's strong bid for the Negro vote and the inclusion of a solid civil rights plank in the Republican platform forced the president to approve an antidiscrimination clause in the Selective Service Act, promote Colonel Benjamin O. Davis as the first Negro brigadier general, and appoint William Hastie as civilian aide to the secretary of war and Colonel Campbell Johnson as executive assistant to the director of Selective Service. Black political pressure also opened the way for new Reserve Officers' Training Corps units in Negro colleges and an air force aviation school for blacks at Tuskegee.[17] These actions barely affected black life in America, but as possible first steps to be lengthened as the Negro vote grew in the North, they showed Negro leaders the power of the vote and the need for coordinated efforts. Moreover, the fact that President Roosevelt did respond, if only with gestures, increased black expectations. But the paucity of the response further clarified the disparity between Negro goals and gains—between democratic myths and realities.[18]

The experience of living in Jim Crow America led the Negro to be acutely conscious of his deprivations and impatient with all impediments to first-class citizenship. Magazines and newspapers at the beginning of the war charted his plummeting morale and increased assertiveness.[19] Only a few blacks, mainly the followers of Leonard Robert Jordan's Ethiopia Pacific League and Elijah Muhammad's Temple of Islam, actually flirted with treason; many simply, but loudly, held their loyalty in check.[20] A Harlem doctor driving through Manhattan with a large sign on his car reading, "IS THERE A

DIFFERENCE? JAPS BRUTALLY BEAT AMERICAN REPORTER GERMANS BRUTALLY BEAT SEVERAL JEWS AMERICAN CRACKERS BRUTALLY BEAT ROLAND HAYES & NEGRO SOLDIERS,"[21] expressed the bitterness of countless others, as did the black college student who asked: "The Army jim-crows us. The Navy lets us serve only as messmen. The Red Cross refuses our blood. Employers and labor unions shut us out. Lynchings continue. We are disfranchised, jim-crowed, spat upon. What more could Hitler do than that?"[22] NAACP responded to the new mood by repeatedly comparing Hitlerism with American racism and urging its followers: "Now Is the Time Not to Be Silent."[23]

The changing of signs on hiring gates from "No Help Wanted" to "Help Wanted, *White*," most stirred the militancy of lower-class blacks. After being first-fired during the Depression, they now found themselves last-hired, discriminated against in government training programs, excluded from many unions, and forced into the dirtiest and lowest paying jobs. To make matters worse, as the Depression in white America officially ended, the federal government drastically slashed welfare appropriations despite the fact that most blacks remained unemployed or underemployed.[24] Negro leaders established new committees and attended conferences requesting action, but their polite, formal protests and negotiations failed to budge President Roosevelt or the nation's leading industrialists and unions.[25]

As black discontent deepened, the established civil rights groups turned to mass protest meetings and picketing.[26] At the same time, Randolph issued a call for 10,000 blacks to march on Washington to demand federal action on job discrimination. Throughout the spring of 1941 the March-on-Washington Committee mobilized lower-class blacks never previously recruited by any Negro organization. As his movement grew, NAACP, Urban League, and a score of staid, old-line Negro associations and leagues that had always shunned direct action hastily boarded Randolph's bandwagon.[27] Randolph kept countering presidential indifference by threatening to raise the number of angry marching blacks to 50,000 and then 100,000. A week before the scheduled march Franklin Roosevelt capitulated, agreeing to issue an executive order establishing the first President's Committee on Fair Employment Practices (FEPC) in exchange for cancellation of the embarrassing march on the nation's capital.[28] Although neither the original order nor the authority of FEPC ever fully met

Negro expectations, President Roosevelt's action buoyed the most optimistic hopes of Negro organizations for further federal assistance. Similarly, the March-on-Washington Movement's apparent success in stirring thousands of blacks never before touched by the civil rights movement and in threatening the government with direct action graphically demonstrated the potential of mass black militancy.[29] The *Chicago Defender*, which in February labeled Randolph's proposal as "the miracle of the century," heralded the death of "Uncle-Tomism" and the new age of mass protest in July.[30]

To oppose discrimination in the armed services and the lack of black combat units, the two most bitterly resented aspects of American racism during the war, some young blacks publicly refused induction.[31] Various individuals and organizations such as the Chicago Conscientious Objectors Against Jim Crow tried to fight military segregation and racial quotas in the courts.[32] Countless other blacks just never showed up for examination or induction. Those who served often did so sullenly. "Here lies a black man killed fighting a yellow man for the glory of a white man," became a popular saying of black draftees.[33] In Harlem, a white draft board member noted: "When colored draftees came to the board for induction last year, I used to give them a little patriotic talk to make them feel good. But they didn't. They only laughed at me. Now I bow my head as they come in for their induction."[34]

The publicized denigration of blacks in the armed services caused both frustration and militant protest. Army policy at the beginning of the war strictly limited the quota of Negroes to be inducted and rigidly confined them to noncombatant units. Naval policy excluded them from the marines and coast guard and restricted blacks to being messboys in the navy.[35] While political pressure and war manpower needs slowly forced the armed services to move from exclusion to segregation to token integration, the great mass of blacks served throughout the war in service units commanded by white officers. They trained in segregated base camps, mostly in the South, and found themselves barred or Jim Crowed by USO, service centers, theaters, and post exchanges.[36] Most bases even provided segregated chapels; the sign listing the schedule of religious services at one camp post read: "Catholic, Jews, Protestants, and Negroes."[37] Blacks who protested were harassed and intimidated; those who persisted in their opposition were transferred, placed in the stockade, or dishonorably discharged.[38]

The most chafing practice of the army, however, was its refusal to protect Negro servicemen off the post and its use of white military police to control blacks. Throughout the South a Negro in uniform symbolized "a nigger not knowing his place."[39] White bus drivers habitually refused to transport blacks to and from their bases. White military police enforced Jim Crow seating restrictions, and off-base bars and restaurants used them to keep blacks out. To avoid friction with the local community, base commanders continuously enjoined blacks to obey the local customs of segregation and some even prohibited blacks from securing leave.[40] Little wonder that blacks equated army law with "white" law. Many blacks responded with cynicism and despair, and the War Department regularly received reports on the low morale of the Negro soldier and accounts of black suicides, mental "crack-ups," desertions, and AWOLs due to discrimination and racist brutality.[41]

Other blacks responded by fighting back. Racial friction, sporadic conflict, and finally outright rioting became commonplace at nearly every army base in the South, many in the North, and even at a few in Australia, England, and the South Pacific.[42] As the experiences of war shattered the Negroes' illusions about white sincerity and destroyed their fear of white authority, "thousands of spontaneous and individual rebellions went unrecorded and unnoticed." Although the War Department systematically suppressed most evidence of black revolt and labeled most of the deaths due to race battles as combat fatalities or "motor vehicle accidents," army statisticians nevertheless reported an unusually high number of casualties suffered by white officers of Negro troops and at least fifty black soldiers killed in race riots in the United States.[43]

In 1941, army authorities found a black private, arms and legs bound, lynched at Fort Benning. Brutality by the military police in Fayetteville, North Carolina, led to a pitched gun battle with black soldiers. Forty-three blacks went AWOL to escape the harassment and terrorization by whites in Prescott, Arizona. Black soldiers at Fort Bragg, Camps Davis and Gibbon, and Jackson Barracks fought white soldiers and police.[44] Although complaints and protests from Negro soldiers, chaplains, NAACP, and National Lawyers Guild poured into the War Department and White House, neither would publicly respond.[45] The quantity and intensity of racial violence at military bases accelerated in 1942. The attempt by a military policeman to arrest a drunken black soldier in Alexandria, Louisiana, sparked a race riot that resulted in the shooting of 28 Negroes and the arrest of nearly 3,000.[46] Other race riots broke out in New Orleans; Vallejo, California; Flagstaff and Phoenix, Arizona; Florence, South Carolina; Fort Dix, New Jersey; and the air force training school in Tuskegee.[47] The War Department even refused to intervene when Beaumont, Texas, city policemen clubbed and shot a black soldier and when a Negro army nurse was brutally beaten and jailed for defying Jim Crow seating arrangements on a Montgomery bus.[48]

Stories of race riots at Camps Stewart and Shelby, Forts Bliss and Benning, and March Field dominated the front pages of the Negro press along with accounts of southern peace officers killing black soldiers. Numerous bases reported Negroes wrecking post facilities and off-base restaurants that refused to serve them. Accounts of Negro soldiers going "over the hill" and battling with white military police increased dramatically. The growing fear of retaliatory violence by blacks led the governor of Mississippi to request the War Department to move Negro regiments out of his state and forced officers at some southern bases to order the removal of firing pins from the rifles of Negro servicemen.[49] Finally, after a bitter summer of violence, the War Department officially acknowledged the existence of a serious morale problem among Negro troops and urged all white officers to treat blacks with the utmost care and diplomacy.[50]

The tensions and violence within the military mirrored the mushrooming conflict on the home front. Both blacks and whites blamed the other for racial problems and both self-righteously sought advantage in the crisis of war. Many whites intensified their efforts to keep the Negro "in his place," regardless of the changes wrought by the war.[51] Each new protest against discrimination was seen as a sign of Negro disloyalty, and many feared that "the more they get the more they want." The more Negroes demanded their rights, the more white resistance stiffened, which led blacks to become even more impatient with second-class citizenship and determined to assert themselves.[52] The increasing competition between the races and the many petty irritations of war—the rationing, shortages, overcrowding, and high prices—engendered frustration, supersensitivity, and belligerency. The fatigue of long workweeks with little opportunity for recreation, the anxious scanning of casualty lists, the apprehension over a new job and a strange city, and the desire of noncombatants to prove their masculinity all fed the boiling racial cauldron.[53]

Government officials at all levels feared intervening in this explosive situation, contenting themselves with vague appeals to national unity. President Roosevelt, preoccupied with diplomacy and military strategy and deeply dependent on southern support in Congress for his postwar foreign policy, let two southern aides, mobilization director James Byrnes and political secretary Marvin McIntyre, handle most racial matters.[54] Symptomatic of its approach to bury racial problems deeply as possible—a mixture of blindness, patchwork compromise, and faith that good public relations could gloss over prior errors—the White House refused to do anything to prevent the riot by white Detroiters to keep Negroes from entering the Sojourner Truth Public Housing Project. Warned well in advance of the trouble brewing, McIntyre sought only to avoid letting the conflict be publicized.[55] After the riot, the Office of Facts and Figures noted that unless strong and quick intervention by some high official, preferably the president, was not taken at once, disorders would follow.[56] The president did nothing. With little government action to relieve racial anxiety or enforce new norms, whites and blacks moved closer toward violence.[57]

The intensification of interracial rancor prompted various forms of violence, including lynchings.[58] Less dramatic, more immediately affecting the racial climate, were the almost daily fights and incidents on public vehicles. Most involved Negro soldiers from the North refusing to honor southern racial etiquette and southern white migrants to the North refusing to mingle closely with blacks on the overcrowded buses, trolleys, and trains of industrial cities. Verbal abuse, shovings, slappings, and stabbings became everyday happenings, signifying the heightened racial animosity.[59]

The chaos, despair, and frustration arising from the Negro's resentment of the slow pace of racial progress and his accelerating hope for a better day, plus the bewilderment and anger of whites determined to maintain the racial status quo—expressed in and nurtured by three years of racial friction and conflict—exploded in an epidemic of interracial violence in 1943. The Social Science Institute at Fisk University reported 242 racial battles in forty-seven cities.[60] Throughout the North, juvenile delinquency increasingly turned into racial gang fights. Italo-American and Negro teenagers fought week-long battles in Newark and Philadelphia, while black and Polish gangs battled in Buffalo and Chicago.[61] Other racial gang fights were reported in Cambridge, Massachusetts, and Brooklyn.[62] The worst of these "zoot-suit" riots occurred in Los Angeles. A mob of over 1,000 whites, mainly sailors and soldiers, freely roamed the city attacking and stripping zoot-suited blacks and Mexican Americans while the city police, shore patrol, and military police looked the other way. Making no attempt to inquire into the causes of the riot, the Los Angeles City Council further stirred racial emotions by ordering the arrest for "vagrancy" of those who had been beaten and by declaring the wearing of a zoot suit a misdemeanor.[63]

In mid-June, the Christian American Association of Texas spread a rumor that a Negro had raped a young white mother in Beaumont. A white mob of over 3,000, mainly workers from the Pennsylvania Shipyard fearing that FEPC would give their jobs to blacks, stomped through the Negro ghetto burning, pillaging, and terrorizing those in their path. War production stopped, businesses closed, thousands of dollars of property was damaged, one black and one white died, and more than seventy-five people were injured. Only a declaration of martial law and the swift, impartial action of the combined forces of local and state police, volunteers, and Texas Rangers quelled the riot.[64] In Mobile, the attempt to upgrade twelve Negro workers as welders in the yards of the Alabama Dry Dock and Shipbuilders Company caused 20,000 white workers to walk off their jobs and riot for four days. The League for White Supremacy, organized in 1942 to thwart the FEPC demand to end discrimination in the shipyards, had been agitating for a year unhindered by either company or union officials. It answered the company's decision to comply with FEPC policy by spreading a rumor that a black worker had just killed a white woman. While plant guards and local police looked on, gangs of whites attacked Negro workers with crowbars and wrenches and then rioted throughout the city. Only the belated entrance of federal troops finally stopped the riot, and FEPC backed down and agreed to the continuation of segregation in the shipyards.[65] Similar fears of Negro economic competition led to a series of hate strikes against the hiring of black workers in Maryland, Michigan, New York, and Ohio and a violent battle between blacks and whites in the Sun Shipbuild-

ing Yard at Chester, Pennsylvania.[66] A white walkout stopped Phila-
delphia's transportation system for a week when the city hired eight
Negroes as trolley motormen, and a group of blacks in New Iberia,
Louisiana, were driven out of town for setting up a welding school for
Negroes—"the white people didn't want the colored folks to learn to
be anything but sharecroppers and servants."[67]

Other cities beset by rumors of impending racial violence began
taking extraordinary precautions to prevent riots. In Washington, the
federal government worked behind the scenes with local Negro leaders and the municipal police force to keep a demonstration against the
Capital Transit Company for refusing to hire black bus drivers from
turning into an open race war.[68] A score of other cities hastily secured
reinforcements for local police to avert rumored riots and instituted
interracial committees, curfews, cancellation of leaves for local servicemen, and prohibitions on liquor.[69] While columnists publicly
pondered the "threat of a domestic Pearl Harbor," racial rumors swept
the nation.[70] Loose talk of Negro troops seizing the *Queen Mary* in a
mutiny, of "Eleanor Clubs" (where Negro domestics organized a boycott and vowed to get "every white woman in her kitchen by Christ-
mas"), of Disappointment Clubs (where blacks pledged to harass
white women by promising to come to cook or clean on certain days
and then not showing up), combined with tales of shovers, pushers,
and bumpers clubs, whose members plotted to devote one day every
week to walking in crowded areas and shoving whites, and rumors of
blacks buying guns and a white counteroffensive against "uppity, out
of line Negroes," kept many cities on edge.[71]

No city expected racial trouble more than Detroit, and none did
less to prevent it. Forced to accommodate the more than 50,000 southern Negroes and 500,000 whites rushing into the city for employment
in defense industries, with severe shortages of housing, recreation,
and transportation and an overabundance of agitators and extremists
of every color and persuasion, Detroit, the "Arsenal of Democracy,"
seethed with racism and hatred.[72] Racial clashes in schools, play-
grounds, and factories, fights on buses and trolleys, and cross burnings
throughout the city became accepted everyday occurrences.[73] The
city was described as "a keg of powder with a short fuse."[74] When the
riot finally exploded, Detroit's mayor told reporters: "I was taken by
surprise only by the day it happened."[75]

The riot began when thousands of Detroiters, seeking relief from the hot, humid city streets, crowded into the amusement park on Belle Isle on Sunday, June 20. Small fights all through the day combined with rumors of a race war erupted into a riot on the bridge connecting the park with the city. News of the riot spread swiftly to every section of Detroit.[76] In the crowded ghetto, blacks, tired of moving to find the Promised Land, tired of finding the North too much like the South, tired of being Jim Crowed, struck out against "whitey" and his property and symbols of authority. Black mobs stoned passing motorists, hurled rocks and bottles at the police, stopped streetcars to beat up unsuspecting whites, and smashed and looted many of the white-owned stores in the ghetto.[77] White mobs, unhampered by the police, retaliated on all Negroes caught in white sections.[78] Throughout the melee, fresh rumors sustained the frenzy. Tales of babies killed and women raped served to justify the violent expression of old hatreds, while the excitement of a car burning in the night, the screeching wail of an ambulance siren, plenty of looted liquor, and a feeling of being free to do whatever one wished without fear of police reprisal fed the riotous appetite of the angry city.[79]

While the city and state officials feared to act or ask for help and appeared unable to control the violence, and the White House and War Department refused to intervene, the riot raged.[80] By Monday evening, nineteen police precincts, covering 75 percent of the Detroit area, reported riot activity. Most transportation lines had suspended operation, and the fire department could no longer control the city's fires. Injured rioters and spectators were entering hospitals at the rate of one every other minute.[81] By the time federal troops finally arrived late Monday evening, Detroit's riot toll recorded 34 killed, more than 700 injured, over $2 million in property losses, and 100 million man-hours lost in war production.[82] Only the continued presence of soldiers patrolling the streets and armed military vehicles escorting buses and trolleys on their usual runs kept the continuing racial hysteria from erupting again. Throughout the summer anxiety increased, isolated racial fights continued, and rumors of blacks and whites collecting knives and guns for "the next one" heightened the tense atmosphere.[83]

Less than two months later, despite the extensive efforts of New York officials to maintain racial calm, a rumor of a Negro soldier killed

by a white policeman triggered the same combination of deep grievances and war-bred tensions that had sparked the Detroit riot into an
orgy of looting and destruction in Harlem.[84] The protest against discrimination and segregation, unemployment and restricted housing,
police brutality, mistreatment of black soldiers, and the white-owned
rat- and vermin-infested black ghetto led to the death of 5 Negroes,
500 injuries, and an estimated $5 million of property damaged.[85]
Once the rumor of another police killing swept through Harlem, Walter White, executive secretary of NAACP, wrote, "blind, unreasoning
fury swept the community with the speed of lightning." The young
and the poor, goaded by the white-owned property they were powerless to possess, suddenly smashed the plate-glass windows of stores on
all the main avenues in the ghetto, and "the Bigger Thomases of New
York passed like a cloud of locusts over the stores of Harlem."[86]

Shocked by the extent of racial violence in the summer of 1943,
and without a program to do anything about it, liberals and Negro
leaders looked to the White House for leadership.[87] But President Roosevelt remained silent. Having been nurtured and elevated to power
by the southern-dominated and -oriented Democratic Party, he followed the century-old tradition of successful Democratic politicians
by studiously avoiding interference with a state's right to control racial
issues. Although Eleanor Roosevelt and some of the liberals in his
administration cautiously urged him to support civil rights, the president continued to let his southern assistants—Byrnes, McIntyre, press
secretary Stephen T. Early, and General Edwin "Pa" Watson, his military aide and secretary—handle all racial matters. They viewed civil
rights issues as a danger to the fragile Democratic coalition as well
as an unwarranted intrusion on the president's precious time, and
the so-called Negro balance of power as far more expendable than
southern votes in Congress. Consequently, they blocked all proposals
for White House action and shuffled off complaints to David Niles,
Jonathan Daniels, and FEPC—the Wailing Wall for minorities, virtually powerless to act but handy as a safety valve.[88] Secretary of War
Henry L. Stimson and Secretary of the Navy Frank Knox took an even
more standpat attitude on racial questions than Roosevelt's advisers.
Both viewed the civil rights issue as an impediment to the war effort
with which no compromise should be made. Both accepted notions
of Negro inferiority and of black agitators, not even supported by

their own people, unfairly taking advantage of a nation in the midst of war.[89] Even some of the president's liberal advisers, such as Harry Hopkins, failed to see civil rights as a major issue. Following Franklin Roosevelt's lead in replacing "Dr. New Deal with Dr. Win-the-War," they shelved their zeal for social reform for a new standard: "will it help to win the war? if not, the hell with it!"[90]

Moreover, the president would not respond affirmatively to the racial crisis because the congressional elections of 1942 increased his dependence on the southern Democrats and because the new pressures from the black community offended his sense of paternalism. With the Democrats receiving less than half the total major party vote for the first time since 1932, and the Republicans gaining forty-seven seats in the House, the southern bloc in Congress rode high, encouraging Roosevelt to weaken FEPC and pigeonhole all racial issues.[91] At the same time, the black demand for immediate change hampered his hope for a wartime consensus. To Roosevelt, the Negro always remained an unfortunate ward of the nation—to be treated kindly and with charity as a reward for good behavior. Nothing in his political past prepared him for the new black assertiveness. Throughout his administration he had worked with the conservative followers of Booker T. Washington in the South and the reliable Negro machine politicians of the North.[92] Despite the significant change in temper in the black community, Roosevelt continued to rely for advice on Negro matters on an elite coterie which included Lester Granger of the National Urban League; Dr. James Shepard, president of the North Carolina College for Negroes; Lester Walton, the minister to Liberia; and such prominent southern white liberals as Daniels, Mark Ethridge, Frank Graham, and John Temple Graves. Steeped in the politics of gradualism, these men did little to help the president understand why blacks supported NAACP and the March-on-Washington Movement or why civil rights required new initiatives from the White House. They reinforced his inclination to avoid antagonizing southern politicians and to act only when he had a clear mandate from the people, and then only for the simplest, least fundamental solution.[93]

Maintaining an official silence throughout the summer of 1943, the administration hoped to defuse the racial issue by adhering to its standard policy of patronage, public gestures, and public relations. The president's aides first buried all pleas for a fireside chat on the

riots and then killed plans to have Congress investigate the disorders.[94] Franklin Roosevelt's advisers then shelved all proposals for a
governmental race relations commission in favor of the inoffensive
appointment of Daniels to correlate personally all information on
racial problems.[95] Even Marshall Field's innocuous plan to circulate
pledges asking people not to spread rumors and to help "win the war at
home by combating racial discrimination wherever I meet it," which
the president liked, went unheeded.[96] Instead, new government films
and press releases emphasized the recent gains of Negroes, and the
government acted to handle future riots more efficiently by clarify-
ing the procedure for calling in federal troops and approving Federal
Bureau of Investigation director J. Edgar Hoover's recommendation
to grant draft deferments to members of urban police forces.[97] The
following year Hoover announced his plan to round up the communist agitators causing racial unrest.[98]

The American Left however, did little to press a new racial policy on the White House. Most communist sympathizers continued to
subordinate Negro rights to demands for a second front, and liberals,
fearing continued violence, urged the Negro "to go slow," work with
white allies, and avoid precipitating a white reaction.[99]

Social scientists who had earlier supported the more militant
black leaders now began to work to divert aggression and control violence.[100] Scores of liberal organizations that had never before cared
about the race problem suddenly awoke to the realization that they
had to do something. Interracialism became an overnight fad: by the
end of 1943 more than 100 local, state, and national commissions "to
promote better race relations" had been established.[101] But since most
of the liberals enlisting in the crusade for civil rights considered other
issues more important, the committees floundered, doing nothing to
attack the basic causes of racial unrest. Under the banners of ethnic
democracy, interracial cooperation, and a more scientific understanding of group prejudice, most of the committees did little but broaden
the channel of communication between Negro and white leaders, set
up rumor-control bureaus, and institute training sessions for police
on human relations and effective handling of rioters.[102] Despite
some worthy intentions, the committees functioned mainly as a buf-
fer between blacks and their local government and widened the gap
between bourgeois Negro leaders and the urban masses.[103] The more

white liberals joined the movement, the more intent Negro leaders became in holding their support by being accommodating, respectable, and a part of the larger progressive coalition. By the end of the war, interracialism had become the dominant tactic of the civil rights movement, while the committees which had spawned it, content to beget more committees, more surveys, and more reports, quietly faded away.[104]

The fear of continued violence by lower-class blacks and of an even greater period of violence after the war, like that following World War I, along with the emergence of interracialism, had a stunting effect on Negro militancy. Although the single greatest Negro victory since the Civil War, Executive Order 8802, had come because of an uncompromising, independent all-black effort, most of the old-line Negro leadership now retreated from their earlier militancy and began to entrust white liberals with the job of winning the Negro his rights.[105] Some did so because of their apprehension about controlling the aroused black masses of their jealousy of newly organized black groups, and some because they believed a minority without allies could never be successful once the war ended.[106] Moreover, the wartime prosperity of the Negro middle class demanded a movement that would conserve these gains, rather than one that might undo the progress made. Accordingly, by the end of 1943, almost all the Negro fraternal, labor, and professional groups once prominent in the militant battles against Jim Crow in the armed services and defense work were supporting legislation for a permanent FEPC and "Hold Your Job" campaigns.[107] The once angry Negro press, regularly featuring full-page advertisements for war employment, directed much of their critical fire toward "irresponsible" blacks advocating sit-ins and civil disobedience.[108] And NAACP, the largest and richest of the Negro civil rights organizations, increasingly urged its chapters to get the movement out of the streets and into the courtroom and voting booth and to back the national office in its support of an anti–poll tax bill, an aid to education bill, and an increase in Social Security coverage.[109]

In 1944 and 1945 the number of racial incidents declined, convincing many of the value of moderation. Negro and liberal leadership equated the decrease in interracial violence and the vocal support of whites with racial progress. Gradual reform, through legislation and court decisions, became the order of the day; capitalizing on the conscience of white America, the major tactic; and integration, the most sought objective.[110] Without any support from the established organizations and newspapers, the March-on-Washington Movement slowly faded away. With it went Randolph's hope for an all-black, mass direct-action movement—an organization of the masses, built on racial pride, that would force the white majority to heed the demands of black America. Following the lead of the NAACP, Randolph turned his energies to building up the Negro vote and campaigning for a permanent FEPC.[111] Other Negro leaders exhorted blacks to mind their manners, be patient, and support liberal organizations.[112] Every week, it seemed, some new program of intercultural education or interracial goodwill or another council on unity and amity appeared.[113] Not since the Civil War period had Negroes heard so many whites talking about freedom and racial justice; never before were so many journals and radio programs featuring items on race relations.[114] Civil rights had become respectable, and as whites flocked into the movement, their views and needs predominated. The old Negro fighters for equality were quietly relegated to secondary and token positions. Meanwhile, the talk of a new day coming grew louder and louder, convincing many that it was just around the corner while hiding from most Americans the fact that little or nothing was actually being done to eradicate the basic causes of racial inequality. But the masses of lower-class blacks did not have to be reminded of what the *Boston Globe* told its readers: "We have read about it. We have talked about it. We have held meetings and appointed committees and had more talk. We have passed the buck in all our talk. We blame the home, blame the schools, blame the police, blame the war. But what have we done—except talk?"[115]

Notes

1. "Negro Organizations and the War Effort," report from Special Service Division, April 28, 1942, Records of the Committee on Fair Employment Practice, RG 228 (National Archives); "Recent Factors Increasing Negro-White Tension," Special Service Division memorandum, Nov. 2, 1942, Records of the Office of Government reports, RG 44 (National Archives); Roy Wilkins to Walter White, March 24, 1942, Stephen J. Spingarn Papers (Harry S. Truman Library, Independence, Mo.); *New York Times*, Jan. 10, 1942.

2. Richard M. Dalfiume, *Desegregation of the U.S. Armed Forces: Fight-*

ing on Two Fronts 1939–1953 (Columbia, Mo., 1969), 123n; Benjamin McLaurin, "Memoir," 36 (Oral History Collection, Columbia University); Charles S. Johnson, *To Stem This Tide: A Survey of Racial Tension Areas in the United States* (Boston, 1943), 131–39; Howard W. Odum, "Social Change in the South," *Journal of Politics* 10 (May 1948), 247–48.

3. Herbert Garfinkel, *When Negroes March: The March on Washington Movement in the Organizational Politics for FEPC* (Glencoe, 1959), 144; Adam Clayton Powell Jr., *Marching Blacks: An Interpretive History of the Rise of the Black Common Man* (New York, 1945), 172. See also Rayford W. Logan, ed., *What the Negro Wants* (Chapel Hill, N.C., 1944).

4. Lester B. Granger, "A Hopeful Sign in Race Relations," *Survey Graphic* 33 (Nov. 1944), 455–56; "To Minimize Racial Conflict: Committees to Work on Human Relationships," *American Century* 60 (Jan. 1945), 80. See also Harold Cruse, *The Crisis of the Negro Intellectual* (New York, 1967), 163–64, 207–9, 299, 324, 534–35; "Education for Racial Understanding," *Journal of Negro Education* 13 (Summer 1944).

5. Lester M. Jones, "The Editorial Policy of Negro Newspapers of 1917–18 as Compared with That of 1941–42," *Journal of Negro History* 29 (Jan. 1944), 24–31.

6. Charles Williams, "Harlem at War," *Nation* 156 (Jan. 16, 1943), 88.

7. Quoted in Roi Ottley, *"New World A-Coming": Inside Black America* (Boston, 1943), 314.

8. George S. Schuyler, "A Long War Will Aid the Negro," *Crisis* 50 (Nov. 1943), 328–29, 344; *Pittsburgh Courier*, Oct. 5, 1940, Feb. 14, 1942; *Chicago Defender*, Dec. 13, 1941, March 14, 1942; *Norfolk Journal and Guide*, March 21, May 2, 1942; and "Government Blesses Separatism," *Crisis* 50 (April 1943), 105.

9. Ralph N. Davis, "The Negro Newspapers and the War," *Sociology and Social Research* 27 (May–June 1943), 373–80; P. L. Prattis, "The Role of the Negro Press in Race Relations," *Phylon* 7 (Third Quarter 1946), 273–83; Thomas Sancton, "The Negro Press," *New Republic* 108 (April 26, 1943), 557–60; Ernest E. Johnson, "The Washington News Beat," *Phylon* 7 (Second Quarter 1946), 127.

10. Charles R. Lawrence, "Negro Organizations in Crisis: Depression, New Deal, World War II" (doctoral dissertation, Columbia University, 1953), 103; Roy Wilkins, "Memoir," 83–88 (Oral History Collection, Columbia University); Report of the Department of Branches, April 14, 1941, NAACP Papers (Manuscript Division, Library of Congress).

11. Garfinkel, *When Negroes March*, 135–37; George M. Houser, "We Say No to Jim Crow," *Fellowship* 11 (April 1945), 61–63; *Core: A Brief History* (New York, 1949).

12. A. Philip Randolph, "Why Should We March?" *Survey Graphic* 31 (Nov. 1942), 488–89; A. Philip Randolph, "Keynote Address to the Policy Conference of the March on Washington Movement," in Francis L. Broderick and August Meier, eds., *Negro Protest Thought in the Twentieth Century* (Indianapolis, 1965), 201–10.

13. Raymond Hatcher to John Dancy, Feb. 1, 1943, Detroit Urban League Papers (University of Michigan Historical Collections, Ann Arbor); Roscoe E. Lewis, "The Role of Pressure Groups in Maintaining Morale among Negroes," *Journal of Negro Education* 12 (Summer 1943), 464–73; Thomas Sancton, "Something's Happened to the Negro," *New Republic* 108 (Feb. 8, 1943), 175–79; Howard W. Odum, *Race and Rumors of Race: Challenge to Crisis* (Chapel Hill, N.C., 1943), 32–38.

14. Horace R. Cayton, "The Negro's Challenge," *Nation* 157 (July 3, 1943), 10–12; Carey McWilliams, *Brothers under the Skin* (Boston, 1943), 17–20.

15. Gunnar Myrdal, with the assistance of Richard Sterner and Arnold Rose, *An American Dilemma: The Negro Problem and Modern Democracy*, 2 vols. (New York, 1944); Carl N. Degler, "The Negro in America—Where Myrdal Went Wrong," *New York Times Magazine* (Dec. 7, 1969), 152, 154, 160. Also see Charles S. Johnson, "The Present Status of Race Relations in the South," *Social Forces* 23 (Oct. 1944), 27–32.

16. *Pittsburgh Courier*, June 29, 1940.

17. Will Alexander, "Memoir," 360 (Oral History Collection, Columbia University); *Pittsburgh Courier*, July 6, Aug. 24, 1940; Nancy and Dwight Macdonald, *The War's Greatest Scandal: The Story of Jim Crow in Uniform* (New York, 1943), 13–14; Henry L. Stimson Diary, Oct. 25, 1940, Henry L. Stimson Papers (Yale University Library).

18. *Pittsburgh Courier*, Nov. 2, 1940; White to Franklin D. Roosevelt, Nov. 4, 1940, PPF 1336, Franklin D. Roosevelt Papers (Franklin D. Roosevelt Library, Hyde Park).

19. *Washington Post*, March 26, 1944; Horace R. Cayton, "Negro Morale," *Opportunity: Journal of Negro Life* 19 (Dec. 1941), 371–75; Kenneth B. Clark, "Morale of the Negro on the Home Front: World Wars I and II," *Journal of Negro Education* 12 (Summer 1943), 417–28; P. L. Prattis, "The Morale of the Negro in the Armed Services of the United States," ibid., 355–63.

20. Roi Ottley, "A White Folks' War?" *Common Ground* 2 (Spring 1942), 28–31; Alfred McClung Lee, "Subversive Individuals of Minority Status," *Annals of the American Academy of Political and Social Science* 223 (Sept. 1942), 167–68; George Martin, "Why Ask 'Are Negro Americans Loyal?'" *Southern Frontier* 2 (Feb. 1942), 2–3.

21. Ottley, *"New World A-Coming,"* 306–7.

22. Walter White, "What the Negro Thinks of the Army," *Annals of the American Academy of Political and Social Sciences* 223 (Sept. 1942), 67.

23. "Nazi Plan for Negroes Copies Southern U.S.A.," *Crisis* 48 (March 1941), 71; "Now Is the Time Not to Be Silent," ibid., 49 (Jan. 1942), 7; memorandum to NAACP State Branches, Dec. 12, 1941, NAACP Papers.

24. Garfinkel, *When Negroes March,* 17–21.

25. Robert L. Vann to Roosevelt, Jan. 19, 1939, June 13, 1940, OF 335; White to Roosevelt, March 13, 1941; and Edwin Watson to White, April 8, 1941, OF 93, Roosevelt Papers; McLaurin, "Memoir," 64–65, 295–96. Among the committees formed were the *Pittsburgh Courier's* Committee on Participation of Negroes in the National Defense Program; Adam Clayton Powell Jr.'s Temporary National Protest Committee on Segregation; John A. Davis' Citizens Non-Partisan Committee for Equal Rights in National Defense; Committee on Negro Americans in War Industries, established by Phelps-Stokes Fund; and the Committee on Discrimination in Employment.

26. *Pittsburgh Courier,* Jan. 25, 1941; Walter White, *A Man Called White: The Autobiography of Walter White* (New York, 1948), 186–87; Florence Murray, ed., *The Negro Handbook* (New York, 1942), 72.

27. McLaurin, "Memoir," 36, 299; Lester B. Granger, "The President, the Negro, and Defense," *Opportunity: Journal of Negro Life* 19 (July 1941), 204.

28. A. Philip Randolph to Roosevelt, May 29, 1941; Watson to Roosevelt, June 14, 1941, OF 93, Roosevelt Papers; McLaurin, "Memoir," 300–305.

29. Dalfiume, *Desegregation of the U.S. Armed Forces,* 118–22.

30. *Chicago Defender,* Feb. 8, June 28, 1941; Williams, "Harlem at War," 87.

31. McWilliams, *Brothers under the Skin,* 33–34; Dwight MacDonald, "The Novel Case of Winfred Lynn," *Nation* 156 (Feb. 20, 1943), 268–70.

32. Minutes of the Board of Directors, Sept. 9, 1940, NAACP Papers; *Chicago Defender,* Jan. 11, 18, 1941; *PM,* July 18, 1942.

33. Edwin R. Embree, *Julius Rosenwald Fund: Review for the Two-Year Period 1942–1944* (Chicago, 1944), 2.

34. Earl Brown and George Leighton, *The Negro and the War* (New York, 1942), 8.

35. War Department press release, Sept. 16, 1940, OF 93; confidential memorandum from Steve Early to Watson, Sept. 19, 1940, PPF 2538, Roosevelt Papers; NAACP press releases, May 8, July 31, 1942, NAACP Papers; Ulysses Lee, *United States Army in World War II: Special Studies: The Employment of Negro Troops* (Washington, 1966), 21–87.

36. Lucille B. Milner, "Jim Crow in the Army," *New Republic* 110 (March 13, 1944), 339–42; "Jim Crow in the Camps," *Nation* 156 (March 20, 1943), 429.

37. W. Y. Bell Jr., "The Negro Warrior's Home Front," *Phylon* 5 (Third Quarter 1944), 272.

38. Macdonald and Macdonald, *The War's Greatest Scandal*, 9–12; Dwight MacDonald to editors, "The Case of Alton Levy," *Nation* 157 (Nov. 6, 1943), 538; "The Social Front," *Monthly Summary of Events and Trends in Race Relations* 1 (Nov. 1943), 9.

39. "Negroes in the Armed Forces," *New Republic* 109 (Oct. 18, 1943), 542–43.

40. Milner, "Jim Crow in the Army," 339–42; "Personalities on the Spot," *Monthly Summary of Events and Trends in Race Relations* 1 (Sept. 1943), 26.

41. Bell, "The Negro Warrior's Home Front," 276–77. Also see Grant Reynolds, "What the Negro Soldier Thinks," *Crisis* 51 (Nov. 1944), 352–54.

42. Lee, *United States Army*, 348–79.

43. Charles E. Silberman, *Crisis in Black and White* (New York, 1964), 62–64.

44. Minutes of the Board of Directors, Sept. 8, 1941, NAACP Papers; Macdonald and Macdonald, *War's Greatest Scandal*, 2; Powell, *Marching Blacks*, 144; *Pittsburgh Courier*, Jan. 31, 1942.

45. White to Roosevelt, Aug. 13, 18, 20, 1941, OF 25; Ira Lewis to Roosevelt, Aug 19, 1941; Gloster Current to Roosevelt, Sept. 26, 1941, OF 93, Roosevelt Papers; *Chicago Defender*, Aug. 30, 1941.

46. *Southern Frontier* 3 (Feb. 1942), 1; *Washington Post*, March 26, 1944.

47. Macdonald and Macdonald, *War's Greatest Scandal*, 2–3; Powell, *Marching Blacks*, 144–45; *New York Times*, April 4, 1942.

48. McWilliams, *Brothers under the Skin*, 39; Randolph to Roosevelt, Aug. 1, 1942; Marvin McIntyre to Randolph, Aug. 6, 1942, OF 93, Roosevelt Papers.

49. Minutes of the Board of Directors, May 10, 1943, NAACP Papers; *Chicago Defender*, June 12, 19, 1943; *Pittsburgh Courier*, June 19, 1943; Florence Murray, ed., *The Negro Handbook 1944: A Manual of Current Facts, Statistics and General Information Concerning Negroes in the United States* (New York, 1944), 225; Powell, *Marching Blacks*, 145; "The Social Front," *Monthly Summary of Events and Trends in Race Relations* 1 (Aug. 1943), 8–9.

50. "Negroes in the Armed Forces," 544.

51. "White Attitudes toward Negroes," Report from OWI, Bureau of Intelligence, Aug. 5, 1942, Records of the Office of Government Reports, RG 44; "Race Tension and Farm Wages in the Rural South," Agriculture Department, Sept. 22, 1943, in OF 4245, Roosevelt Papers; Odum, *Race and Rumors of Race*, 7–8, 25, 42–43, 47–50; "Cities, North and South: A Reconnaissance Survey of Race Relations," *Monthly Summary of Events and Trends in Race Relations* 1 (Oct. 1943), 11–12.

52. Pauli Murray to McIntyre, June 18, 1943, OF 93C, Roosevelt Papers; Sancton, "Something's Happened to the Negro," 175–79.

53. Arthur I. Waskow, *From Race Riot to Sit-in, 1919 and the 1960s: A Study in the Connections between Conflict and Violence* (Garden City, 1966), 220–23; Walter G. Muelder, "National Unity and National Ethics," *Annals of the American Academy of Political and Social Science* 244 (March 1946), 10.

54. Roosevelt to Edwin Embree, March 16, 1942, OF 93, Roosevelt Papers; McIntyre to Roosevelt, March 2; James Byrnes to McIntyre, March 9, 1943, Records of the War Manpower Commission, RG 211 (National Archives); I. F. Stone, "Capital Notes," *Nation* 156 (Jan. 23, 1943), 115.

55. McIntyre to C. F. Palmer, Jan. 19, 1942, OF 93, Roosevelt Papers; *NAACP Annual Report*, 1942, 22–23, NAACP Papers. See also McIntyre to Roosevelt, Dec. 11, 1942, OF 4245-G, Roosevelt Papers, for McIntyre's attitudes toward racial protest.

56. Quoted in *PM*, June 28, 1943.

57. Bucklin Moon, *The High Cost of Prejudice* (New York, 1947), 60–61.

58. Jessie Parkhurst Guzman, ed., *Negro Year Book: A Review of Events Affecting Negro Life 1941–1946* (Tuskegee, 1947), 307–9; Murray, ed., *Negro Handbook 1944*, 169–72.

59. A. L. Foster to Dancy, June 10, 1943, Detroit Urban League Papers; Robert Lee Eichorn, "Patterns of Segregation, Discrimination and Interracial Conflict" (doctoral dissertation, Cornell University, 1954), 61–64; Allen Grimshaw, "Urban Racial Violence in the United States: Changing Ecological Considerations," *American Journal of Sociology* 66 (Sept. 1960), 117. See also "The Social Front," *Monthly Summary of Events and Trends in Race Relations* 1 (Sept. 1943), 9; Odum, *Race and Rumors of Race*, 113–31.

60. *Monthly Summary of Events and Trends in Race Relations* 1 (Jan. 1944), 2; Thomas Sancton, "The Race Riots," *New Republic* 109 (July 5, 1943), 9–13; *Michigan Chronicle*, July 3, 1943.

61. White to Frank Murphy, June 30, 1943, Frank Murphy Papers (University of Michigan Historical Collections); *Monthly Summary of Events and Trends in Race Relations* 1 (Aug. 1943), 1.

62. Embree, *Julius Rosenwald Fund*, 6.

63. "Zoot-Suit War," *Time* 41 (June 21, 1943), 18–19; Chester B. Himes, "Zoot Riots Are Race Riots," *Crisis* 50 (July 1943), 200–201; Carey McWilliams, "The Zoot-Suit Riots," *New Republic* 108 (June 21, 1943), 818–20.

64. "The Social Front," *Monthly Summary of Events and Trends in Race Relations* 1 (Aug. 1943), 6; Sancton, "The Race Riots," 10–11.

65. "Summary of a Report on the Race Riots in the Alabama Dry Dock and Shipbuilding Yards in Mobile," National Urban League, Detroit Urban League Papers; *Washington Post*, July 20, 1943.

66. "The Industrial Front," *Monthly Summary of Events and Trends in Race Relations* 1 (Aug. 1943), 4–5; ibid. (Oct. 1943), 5; White, *A Man Called White*, 224–25; *New York Times*, Aug. 5, 1943.

67. "The Industrial Front," *Monthly Summary of Events and Trends in Race Relations* 2 (Aug.–Sept. 1944), 6–7; Embree, *Julius Rosenwald Fund*, 3.

68. Alexander, "Memoir," 167–68; minutes of the Board of Directors, May 10, 1943, NAACP Papers.

69. Minutes of the Board of Directors, July 12, 1943, NAACP Papers; *Monthly Summary of Events and Trends in Race Relations* 1 (Aug. 1943), 7–8.

70. Thomas Sancton, "Trouble in Dixie: I. The Returning Tragic Era," *New Republic* 108 (Jan. 4, 1943), 11–14; Thomas Sancton, "Race Fear Sweeps the South," ibid. (Jan. 18, 1943), 81–83; Alexander, "Memoir," 696–99.

71. Odum, *Race and Rumors of Race*, 67–89, 96–103; Embree, *Julius Rosenwald Fund*, 4; Johnson, "The Present Status of Race Relations in the South," 29.

72. Walter White, "What Caused the Detroit Riots"; "The National Urban League Report of the Detroit Riots," Detroit Urban League Papers.

73. Minutes of the Board of Directors, July 16, 1942, NAACP Papers; John Dancy press release, June 26, 1943, William Baldwin memorandum, July 6, 1943, Detroit Urban League Papers.

74. *Detroit News*, Oct. 5–9, 1942; "Detroit Is Dynamite," *Life* 13 (Aug. 17, 1942), 15–23.

75. *PM*, June 28, 1943.

76. Alfred McClung Lee and Norman D. Humphrey, *Race Riot* (New York, 1943); Robert Shogan and Tom Craig, *The Detroit Race Riot: A Study in Violence* (Philadelphia, 1964); Harvard Sitkoff, "The Detroit Race Riot of 1943," *Michigan History* 53 (Fall 1969), 183–206.

77. Harold Kingsley, "Memorandum on Detroit Race Disturbance," June 23, 1943, Detroit Urban League Papers.

78. "Report of Thurgood Marshall, Special Counsel for the NAACP, Concerning Activities of the Detroit Police During the Riots, June 21 and

22, 1943," Mayor's Papers (Burton Historical Collection, Detroit Public Library).

79. Neil J. Smelser, *Theory of Collective Behavior* (New York, 1962), 71–73, 269.

80. Colonel R. G. Roamer, "Summary of Events in the Detroit Riot"; Roamer-Lerch transcript, June 21, 1943, Records of the Office of the Provost Marshal General, RG 389 (National Archives).

81. William Guthner to F. W. Reese, Aug. 2, 1943, ibid.; *Detroit Free Press*, July 1, 1943.

82. Sitkoff, "The Detroit Race Riot of 1942," 192–96; White, *A Man Called White*, 226–27.

83. William Guthner, "Commander's Estimate of the Situation," Nos. I–IV, Records of the Office of the Provost Marshal General, RG 389; Fiorello La Guardia to Roosevelt, June 27, 1943, OF 93C, Roosevelt papers.

84. White, *A Man Called White*, 233–41; Margaret Marshall, "Some Notes on Harlem," *Nation* 157 (Aug. 21, 1943), 200–202.

85. Harold Orlansky, *The Harlem Riot: A Study in Mass Frustration* (New York 1943); Powell, *Marching Blacks*, 171–72.

86. Walter White, "Behind the Harlem Riot," *New Republic* 109 (Aug. 16, 1943), 220–22.

87. Vito Marcantonio to Roosevelt, June 16, 1943; Philip Murray to Roosevelt, June 18, 1943; Douglas Horton to Roosevelt, June 27, 1943, OF 93C, Roosevelt Papers.

88. Malcolm MacLean to McIntyre, Feb. 24, 1942; Jonathan Daniels to Roosevelt, Sept. 28, 1944; and Frank Boykin to Watson, OF 93; David Niles to Daniels, Sept. 8, 1943; and A. V. Boren to Early, May 19, 1944, OF 4245-G, Roosevelt Papers. See also Helen Fuller, "The Ring Around the President," *New Republic* 109 (Oct. 25, 1943), 563–65; "The Negro in Industry," ibid. (Oct. 18, 1943), 539; Joseph P. Lash, *Eleanor Roosevelt: A Friend's Memoir* (Garden City, 1964), 160, 217.

89. Stimson to Roosevelt, Feb. 16, 1942, OF 18, Roosevelt Papers; Stimson Diary, Sept. 27, Oct. 22, 23, 1940, June 18, 1941, May 12, 1942, June 23, 24, 1943, Stimson Papers.

90. Quoted in Arthur Krock, "Memoir," 86 (Oral History Collection, Columbia University).

91. Ed Pauley to Roosevelt, Dec. 14, 1942, PPF 1820, Roosevelt Papers; James A. Wechsler, "Pigeonhole for Negro Equality," *Nation* 156 (Jan. 23, 1943), 122; "The Jim Crow Bloc," *New Republic* 108 (Feb. 22, 1943), 240–41.

92. Roosevelt to George Foster Peabody, March 22, 1935, Dec. 12, 1935, PPF 660; Roosevelt to McIntyre, June 7, 1941, PPF 1248, Roosevelt Papers.

See also Henry Stimson memorandum on consultants on Negro affairs, Feb. 18, 1943, Stimson Papers; Mary McLeod Bethune, "My Secret Talks with F. D. R.," *Ebony* 4 (April 1949), 42–51.

93. Mark Ethridge to Early, Aug. 20, 1941; Daniels to Samuel Rosenman, Sept. 9, 1943, OF 93; Daniels to Roosevelt, Sept. 24, 1943; and Daniels to Watson, Sept. 11, 1944, OF 4245-G, Roosevelt Papers. See also Thomas Sancton, "A Southern View of the Race Question," *Negro Quarterly: A Review of Negro Life and Culture* 1 (Fall 1942), 197–200; John Temple Graves, "It's the Direction That Counts," *Southern Frontier* 3 (April 1942), 2–3.

94. Many pleas for a presidential statement on the riots are in OF 93, Roosevelt Papers. Henry Wallace wanted the congressional plan to investigate the riots stopped because it "was bad from the standpoint of the 1944 election." Wallace to Roosevelt, July 7, 1943, PPF 1820, Roosevelt Papers. See also Roosevelt to Byrnes, Aug. 13, 1943, OF 88, ibid.

95. Harold L. Ickes to Roosevelt, July 15, 16, 26, 1943, OF 6; Francis Biddle to Roosevelt, July 15, Aug. 19, 1943, OF 93C; Biddle to Daniels, July 27, 1943; Daniels to Roosevelt, July 23, 1943; Daniels to Bishop Haas, July 28, 1943, OF 4245-G; Saul K. Padover, memorandum, June 29, 1943, PPF 1820, ibid.

96. Marshall Field to Roosevelt, July 24, 1943, OF 93C, ibid.

97. Biddle to Roosevelt, July 15, 1943, OF 93C; and Daniels to Haas, Sept. 8, 1943, OF 4245-G, ibid.

98. J. Edgar Hoover to Daniels, Aug. 22, 1944, OF 4245-G, ibid.

99. See essays by Willard S. Townsend and Doxey A. Wilkerson in Logan, ed., *What the Negro Wants*, 163–92, 193–216; and James Boyd, "Strategy for Negroes," *Nation* 156 (June 26, 1943), 884–87.

100. Gordon W. Allport, ed., "Controlling Group Prejudice," *Annals of the American Academy of Political and Social Science* 244 (March 1946). See Arnold M. Rose, *Studies in Reduction of Prejudice: A Memorandum Summarizing Research on Modification of Attitudes* (Chicago, 1947); Goodwin Watson, *Action for Unity* (New York, 1947); Robert C. Weaver, "A Needed Program of Research in Race Relations and Associated Problems," *Journal of Negro Education* 16 (Spring 1947), 130–35; Robin M. Williams Jr., *The Reduction of Intergroup Tensions: A Survey of Research on Problems of Ethnic, Racial, and Religious Group Relations* (New York, 1947); Donald Young, "Techniques of Race Relations," *Proceedings of the American Philosophical Society* 91 (April 1947), 150–61; and, in general, the work of Louis Wirth and his students at the Committee on Education, Training and Research in Race Relations at the University of Chicago.

101. *Monthly Summary of Events and Trends in Race Relations* 1 (Jan. 1942), 2.

102. Embree, *Julius Rosenwald Fund*, 13–14; "Liberals and the Future," *New Republic* 111 (Sept. 11, 1944), 310; *Monthly Summary of Events and Trends in Race Relations* 1 (Sept. 1943), 1–2; *Monthly Summary of Events and Trends in Race Relations* 1 (Dec. 1943), 2; Rebecca Chalmers Barton, *Our Human Rights: A Study in the Art of Persuasion* (Washington, 1955), 13.

103. A. A. Liveright, "The Community and Race Relations," *Annals of the American Academy of Political and Social Science* 244 (March 1946), 106–7.

104. Langston Hughes, "Down under in Harlem," *New Republic* 110 (March 27, 1944), 404–5; Albert W. Hamilton, "Allies of the Negro," *Opportunity: Journal of Negro Life* 21 (July 1943), 115–17; Lester B. Granger, "Victory through Unity," ibid. (Oct. 1943), 148.

105. Sancton, "A Southern View of the Race Question," 199; Granger, "A Hopeful Sign in Race Relations," 455–56. Of the fourteen contributors to Logan's *What the Negro Wants*, only W. E. B. DuBois dissented from the general view that Negroes must avoid extralegal tactics and ally themselves with labor and liberals to secure first-class citizenship from the government.

106. Minutes of the Board of Directors, Sept. 14, 1942, NAACP Papers; *Monthly Summary of Events and Trends in Race Relations* 1 (Oct. 1943), 2; McWilliams, *Brothers under the Skin*, 42–43.

107. "Programs of Action on the Democratic Front," *Monthly Summary of Events and Trends in Race Relations* 2 (Nov. 1944), 105; "Negro Women Organize for Unity of Purpose and Action," *Southern Frontier* 4 (Dec. 1943), 2; Alvin E. Dodd, "Negro Employment Opportunities—during and after the War," *Opportunity: Journal of Negro Life* 23 (April–June 1945), 59–62; E. Franklin Frazier, *Black Bourgeoisie* (Glencoe, 1957), 49–50.

108. Garfinkel, *When Negroes March*, 144; Pauli Murray, "A Blueprint for First Class Citizenship," *Crisis* 51 (Nov. 1944), 358–59.

109. Wilkins to Rev. E. S. Hardge, Dec. 19, 1944; minutes of the Board of Directors, Dec. 14, 1943, NAACP Papers. See also "Negroes Fight on Four Major Fronts," *Southern Frontier* 5 (Jan. 1944), 1–2.

110. "Racial Tensions Seem Easier," *Christian Century* 61 (Aug. 30, 1944), 988; "To Minimize Racial Conflicts: Committees to Work on Human Relationships," *American Century* 60 (Jan. 1945), 80.

111. *New York Times*, July 4, 1943; Randolph to Wilkins, Jan. 31, 1944, NAACP Papers; Garfinkel, *When Negroes March*, 145–46; Cruse, *Crisis of the Negro Intellectual*, 208–9.

112. "The National Urban League Establishes Department of Public Education," *Opportunity: Journal of Negro Life* 22 (Oct.–Dec. 1944), 184; "Negro Leader Supports White Liberals," *Southern Frontier* 6 (Nov. 1945), 2;

Charles S. Johnson, "The Next Decade in Race Relations," *Journal of Negro Education* 13 (Summer 1944), 442–44; Wilkins to White, Dec. 28, 1944, NAACP Papers. Significantly, White broke a thirty-five-year-old NAACP tradition of staying out of electoral politics by campaigning for Senator Robert Wagner. *New York Times*, Oct. 14, 1944.

113. Philip L. Seman, "Inter-Faith—Inter-Race," *Monthly Summary of Events and Trends in Race Relations* 2 (Aug.–Sept. 1944), 22; "Programs of Action on the Democratic Front," ibid. (Dec. 1944), 135; "Programs of Action on the Democratic Front," ibid. (Jan. 1945), 165–69.

114. "In the daily press and on the air," wrote Horace Cayton, "the Negro is getting more attention than he has enjoyed since the old Abolitionist days. And there is a growing awareness on the part of labor that the Negro problem requires action. In normal conditions all these things would be considered gains for the Negro. But they are *sporadic and unintegrated* and are insufficient to counteract the apparent inability of the government to set up a comprehensive plan." Quoted in McWilliams, *Brothers under the Skin*, 46–47. See also Liveright, "The Community and Race Relations," 106; "Institutes of Race Relations," *Monthly Summary of Events and Trends in Race Relations* 2 (Aug.–Sept. 1944), 57–58; "The Negro: His Future in America: A Special Section," *New Republic* 109 (Oct. 18, 1943), 535–50.

115. *Boston Globe*, Aug. 19, 1944. See also June Blythe, "Can Public Relations Help Reduce Prejudice?" *Public Opinion Quarterly* 11 (Fall 1947), 342–60.

African American Militancy in the World War II South

Another Perspective

"African American Militancy in the World War II South: Another Per-spective" developed from a lecture I gave in 1995 at the University of Southern Mississippi's second Charles W. Moorman Symposium, "World War II and the American South: The War that Drove Old Dixie Down." It was one of several talks I gave on the fiftieth anniversary of the end of World War II in which I sought to recognize the importance of the war's transformations in American life and world affairs to the later civil rights movement yet, contrary to what had become almost a cliché by then, to de-emphasize militant black behavior. Extending and sharpening the argument I presented in "Racial Militancy and Interracial Violence in the Second World War," this reconsideration underscores both the war's constraints on combative protest and the discontinuity between wartime activism and the freedom struggle of the 1960s. I concluded my effort to present a subtler and more com-plex treatment of African American wartime behavior than I had for-merly depicted by stating: "The status and protest cognition of southern blacks in 1945, their organizations, leadership, language, and strate-gies for reform were neither exactly the same nor fundamentally differ-ent than they had been in 1940. The goals considered a distant dream in the 1930s had not suddenly appeared attainable. The traditional tactics of African American protest groups had not suddenly become unacceptable, nor had new, more disruptive ones come into widespread use." In sum: "Those militantly fighting for change in the 60s would not look to the agenda and actions of World War II blacks and racial orga-nizations as models to emulate." It is one thing, I believe, to recognize

forerunners or acknowledge antecedents and quite another to posit one long, continuous movement stretching back further and further in time so that, in the end, little or nothing distinguishes one era or decade from another. There is, of course, no finality, no absolutes, in my interpretations in this essay and the others I have written. The scholarship on the civil rights movement has, and should have, no end. And the beat goes on, the beat goes on. "African American Militancy in the World War II South: Another Perspective" was originally published in Remaking Dixie: The Impact of World War II on the American South, *ed. Neil R. McMillen (Jackson: University Press of Mississippi, 1997), 70–92.*

It is now commonplace to emphasize the Second World War as a watershed in the African American freedom struggle, as a time of mass black militancy, and as the direct precursor to the civil rights protest movement of the late 1950s and 1960s. Even most textbooks today dramatize the wartime bitterness of African American protests against racial discrimination in the defense industry and the military and highlight the phenomenal growth of the National Association for the Advancement of Colored People (NAACP) and the beginnings of the Congress of Racial Equality (CORE), which practiced direct-action civil disobedience to desegregate places of public accommodation. They quote the sardonic statement, supposedly popular during the war, of a black man, just drafted, who seethed: "Write on my tombstone—Here lies a black man, killed fighting a yellow man, for the protection of a white man." The individual military experience of a Jackie Robinson or a Medgar Evers is portrayed as representative of the turning point for African Americans as a whole, and virtually all devote the lion's share of space on blacks in the war to A. Philip Randolph's March-on-Washington Movement. Commonly described as the foremost manifestation of wartime mass black militancy, and singularly credited with forcing a reluctant President Franklin Roosevelt to issue Executive Order 8802 banning racial discrimination in defense and government employment, the March-on-Washington Movement is invariably pictured as the forerunner of the later black freedom struggle's tactics and strategy. Most accounts also assert that the African American press during World War II was militantly demanding in a way it had never before been and that the black masses, who actively, aggressively, even violently confronted Jim

Crow, were yet far more militant. The war years, in sum, are depicted as a time when mass militancy became characteristic of the African American, when blacks belligerently assaulted the racial status quo, and when this watershed in black consciousness and behavior ignited the Negro revolution that would later blaze.[1]

Perhaps. Maybe. It is comforting to think that the destructiveness of mass warfare can have redeeming virtues; it is good to have fore-bears to admire and emulate. But if by a watershed in militancy we mean a crucial turning point in the aggressiveness of black actions, a far greater combativeness than previously exhibited, then the evidence to prove this argument conclusively has yet to appear, and major questions concerning this interpretation remain unanswered. This is especially so concerning the South, particularly the rural South, where most African Americans continued to live during World War II. Total war did, of course, generate major ruptures and upheavals in American life. Japan's sudden attack on the U.S. Pacific Fleet at Pearl Harbor on December 7, 1941, evoked a widespread wave of patrio-tism and national purpose. Few Americans, black or white, dissented from the war spirit, intensified by media publicity and government-orchestrated campaigns to rally 'round the flag. Support for the war effort placed a premium on loyalty and unity. Even those who wished to protest had to tread carefully.

The angry demonstrations by African Americans against racial discrimination in the defense industry and in the armed services, the flurry of petitions and protests, so common in 1940 and 1941, dimin-ished after the United States entered the war and received decreasing attention as the war dragged on. In fact, the most militant editorials in the Negro press, the virulent threats by African American protest lead-ers and protest organizations, the indignant portents of black disloy-alty or of tepid support by blacks for the Allied cause, almost without exception came before Pearl Harbor, before the United States entered the war. Prewar actions are not instances of wartime militancy.[2]

Indeed, soon after the attack on Pearl Harbor, Edgar G. Brown, director of the National Negro Council, telegraphed President Roo-sevelt that all African Americans pledged 100 percent loyalty to the United States. The National Urban League promised total support for the war effort. The Southern Negro Youth Congress raised money for defense bonds, sponsored an Army Welfare Committee to establish a USO Center for Negroes, and created its own Youth V for Victory Committee. W. E. B. DuBois and A. Philip Randolph spoke at "Victory Through Unity" conferences. Father Divine donated a hotel to the navy, and Paul Robeson traveled to training camps to entertain the troops. Dr. Charles Drew, whose research made blood transfusions possible, proclaimed that the priority of all Americans, "whether black or white, is to get on with the winning of the war," despite the scientifically unwarranted decision of the Red Cross to segregate the blood of black and white donors. Joe Louis promised the entire profits of his next two fights to the army and navy relief funds. Langston Hughes wrote plays for the War Writers Board and jingles for the Treasury Department. Josh White sang "Are You Ready?" promising to batter the Japanese "ratter till his head gets flatter," and Doc Clayton sounded a call for revenge in his "Pearl Harbor Blues." African Americans working in Hollywood formed a Victory Committee, headed by Hattie McDaniel. Richard Wright, who had earlier denounced American involvement in the war, immediately offered his literary services to the government for "the national democratic cause," and African Americans in the Communist Party hierarchy sought to aid the war effort by ordering that the attacks on racism in the script for the Broadway play based on Wright's *Native Son* be toned down.[3]

The first issues of the Negro press after Pearl Harbor proclaimed in banner headlines "Mr. President, Count on Us," and "The Black Tenth Is Ready." Major newspapers that had once excoriated DuBois for penning his First World War "Close Ranks" editorial now repeated his very imagery to restate his plea that Negroes put aside their special grievances for the duration. The *Norfolk Journal and Guide* called upon African Americans to "close ranks and join with fervent patriotism in this battle for America." "The hour calls for a closing of ranks, for joining of hands, not for a widening of the racial gap," echoed the *Chicago Defender*. The *California Eagle* promised to shift its campaign from full citizenship rights to full citizenship duties. A study of twenty-four Negro newspapers in the first several months of the war found that only three harped on the grievances and complaints of African Americans; the other twenty-one stressed the necessity of racial cooperation to avenge Pearl Harbor and the common goal of both blacks and whites of defeating the United States' foreign enemies. Columnists who before the attack on Pearl Harbor had accentuated the similarities between Nazism and American racism stressed their differences after Pearl Harbor; essayists who had trumpeted that the "Black Yanks Are Not Coming" changed their tune to the "Need to Do Everything to Win the War." And the Negro Newspaper Publishers Association, at its first meeting after the entry of the United States into the war, unanimously pledged its unequivocal loyalty to the nation and to the president.[4]

In marked contrast to the First World War, the Post Office Department did not suppress black publications in World War II, the Negro press suffered no special censorship restraints, and there were only a few short-lived bans on African American newspapers at army and navy installations. Even Patrick Washburn, whose research most extensively emphasizes the threat of suppression, states that by June 1942 consideration of this had ended. By then, the opening of hiring gates to blacks had quelled militant political activity, adds Herbert Garfinkel: "The fighting bite had gone out of the Negro protest."[5]

Only a tiny, numerically insignificant number of African Americans initially opposed the entry of the United States into the war, and an even smaller number maintained such opposition. But even the actions of these few should not automatically be equated with wartime racial militancy. Some blacks had sincere religious objections to war; some were truly pacifists. And those that did base their opposition on the racial discrimination and segregation rampant in the armed services and had the support of some mainstream African American groups and newspapers, like the Conscientious Objectors Against Jim Crow, disappeared with American entry into the war. But whatever the reasons, there were only thirty-three black conscientious objectors in 1941, less than 2 percent of the total number of COs, and only 166 in the following four years. Between 1941 and 1946, when over 1,154,000 blacks joined the military, just 2,000 African Americans went to prison for not complying with the Selective Service Act. Most were members of the Ethiopian Pacific Movement, the Pacific Movement of the Eastern World, and the Nation of Islam. Hardly supported by those in the forefront of the freedom struggle, those groups opposing the drafting of African Americans were labeled "the lunatic fringe" by A. Philip Randolph, referred to as "agents of fascism" by the *Chicago Defender,* and described as "Japanese agents" by the black journalist Roi Ottley. Moreover, the almost infinitesimal number of

African American "conscientious objectors, delinquents and evaders or seditionists" during World War II, concluded a study of the wartime selective service system, was "little short of phenomenal," given the extent of racism in American society. As Lester Granger of the National Urban League maintained throughout the conflict, African Americans want "full partnership in the war," they "desire to assume full citizenship responsibilities." Apparently agreeing, a higher proportion of blacks volunteered for service, despite discrimination and segregation in all the branches of the armed forces, and a lower proportion sought to evade service than did whites or did African Americans in the First World War.[6]

Equally telling, the Negro press during the war continually downplayed or denounced as "fools and fanatics," as "crackpots and starry-eyed cultists who are without influence or intelligence," those few African Americans who refused induction. Dissociating "the traitors" from the mass of loyal blacks, the Negro press admonished African Americans that patriotic service to the nation was the path to eventual equality. Not a single mainstream African American newspaper, organization, or spokesperson supported draft resistance by blacks. In the most publicized case, that of Winfred W. Lynn, who refused induction to protest segregation in the military, no Negro newspaper or black rights group backed him. Not only did the leading protest organization, the NAACP, refuse to aid Lynn, but its most prominent attorney, Thurgood Marshall, went to the American Civil Liberties Union and pleaded that they not take Lynn's case. They did not. Similarly, when Edgar B. Keemer, a black physician in Detroit, refused induction because the navy would not accept African Americans as doctors, no major black organization would take his case.[7]

Instead of militant protest, the dominant theme of African American organizations and journals during the Second World War was that patriotic duty and battlefield bravery would lead to the Negro's advancement. The notion that blacks would gain from the war, not as a gift of white goodwill but because the nation needed the loyalty and manpower of African Americans, had been sounded in every one of America's previous armed conflicts, and it continued to reverberate throughout World War II. "War may be hell for some," columnist Joseph Bibb exulted, "but it bids fair to open up the portals of heaven for us." Whites will respond positively to the needs of African

Americans if Negroes do their part as 100 percent loyal Americans, declared Lester Granger. In order for African Americans to benefit later they must fight for the United States now, "segregation and Jim Crowism to the contrary notwithstanding," announced the *New York Age*. Full participation in the defense of the nation, claimed the *Baltimore Afro-American*, is the path to eventual equality. And the NAACP declared the slogan for its mid-1942 convention to be "Victory Is Vital to Minorities."[8]

In this vein, African Americans took up the call of the *Pittsburgh Courier* for a "Double V" campaign. Originating with a letter to the editor from James G. Thompson of Wichita, Kansas, who sought to join the army "to take his place on the fighting front for the principles which he so dearly loved," the *Courier* urged blacks to "fight for the right to fight" because wartime performance would determine postwar status. Opposing the war effort, or sitting on the sidelines, argued the *Courier*, would be the worst possible course for blacks to follow. Rather than calling for a massive attack on the Jim Crow system, the *Courier* added, African Americans must join in the defense of their country. "The more we put in," argued columnist J. A. Rogers, "the more we have a right to claim." That notion was restated in hundreds of ways, as the *Courier* and the Negro press overall harped on the necessity of African Americans serving fully and faithfully so that they could prove their patriotism and later gain concessions. With cause, the Socialist Workers' Party denounced the Double V as "a cover for unqualified support of the war." Yet even a fight for the right to fight could be misunderstood, and the space devoted to the Double V in the *Courier* declined by half between April and August 1942. By the end of 1942 the Double V campaign had been wholly superseded by less ambiguous, more positive declarations of African American patriotism, and the *Courier* would go on to urge black soldiers to "insist on combat duty." "The most significant achievement of the Negro press during this crisis, in our estimation," bragged African American publishers in 1944, "lies in the fact that the Negro newspapers have brought home to the Negro people of America that this is their war and not merely 'a white man's war.'"[9]

However much the great majority of African Americans desired the end of racial discrimination and segregation in American life, only a minority thought that their fight for rights should take precedence over defeating Germany and Japan, and far fewer flirted with militant protests that might be considered harmful to the war effort. Thus A. Philip Randolph's March-on-Washington Movement, generally depicted as the epitome of mass black militancy during the war, truly held center stage in the Negro community only for a few months in 1941, before American entry into the war, and then gradually withered away. Shunned as "unpatriotic" by many of the mainstream Negro organizations and newspapers that had earlier supported it, Randolph's group labored in vain to rebut accusations of employing the "most dangerous demagoguery on record" and of "Marching Against the War Effort." Polls in the Negro press during 1942 revealed a steady diminution of black support for a march on Washington to demand a redress of grievances. When Randolph called for mass marches on city halls in 1942, no blacks marched. When he called for a week of nonviolent civil disobedience and noncooperation to protest Jim Crow school and transportation systems in 1943, a poll indicated that more than 70 percent of African Americans opposed the campaign, and no blacks engaged in such activities. And when he called upon the masses to come to his "We Are Americans, Too!" conference in Chicago in the summer of 1943, virtually no blacks other than members of his Sleeping Car Porters Union attended. By then, as Randolph admitted, the March-on-Washington Movement was "without funds." Unable to pay the rent for an office or for the services of an executive secretary, the organization existed only on paper.[10]

Randolph's brief shining moment had passed quickly. The March-on-Washington Movement ended with Randolph having never led a wartime mass march or a civil disobedience campaign. When he described the program of his organization in Rayford Logan's *What the Negro Wants* (1944), Randolph barely discussed mass militant protests. Instead, most of his essay was devoted to attacking American communists, to explaining why racial change in the South must be gradual and piecemeal, and to advocating race relations committees that would take the necessary measures to prevent or stop race riots. Quite at odds with the image of the wartime Randolph in most current accounts, his wartime agenda for the March-on-Washington Movement in fact differed little from that of the NAACP. Randolph, moreover, devoted the greatest amount of his time and energy during the war to criticizing discrimination within the American Federation of Labor and heading the National Council for a Permanent Fair Employment Practices Commission, a traditional legislative lobby which never advocated mobilizing the masses and which was controlled by an elite group of mainly white New York socialists and labor leaders. Penning the moribund March-on-Washington Movement's epitaph in 1945, Adam Clayton Powell Jr. described it as an "organization with a name that it does not live up to, an announced program that it does not stick to, and a philosophy contrary to the mood of the times." Its former headquarters in Harlem had already been converted into a bookshop.[11]

The Congress of Racial Equality suffered much the same fate as the March-on-Washington Movement during the war, but it did so in relative obscurity. The white media barely mentioned it, and the Negro press did so even less. A tiny interracial, primarily white, elite group of pacifist and socialist followers of A. J. Muste, CORE mainly engaged in efforts to counter discrimination in places of public accommodation and recreation in northern cities, where those practices were already illegal. It did little to try to desegregate schools and housing, to expand job opportunities for African Americans, or to influence civil rights legislation, and its wartime efforts proved negligible. Because its dozen or so local chapters took to heart the reconciliatory aspects of Gandhian nonviolence, the vital importance of changing the consciousness of those engaged in racist practices, few of its Christian pacifist members went beyond negotiations to direct action in the streets. CORE's hopes of becoming a mass, broad-based movement lingered as only a dream during the war, and blacks at Howard University and in St. Louis who, independent of each other, thought they were inventing the sit-in in 1944 did not even know that CORE, too, sought to employ the tactics of the CIO's famous "sitdown" strikes in the fight against Jim Crow. Faced with public apathy, unstable chapters, and a budget of less than $100 a month for its national office, CORE did not even contemplate entering the upper South until 1947, when eight blacks and eight whites decided to test the compliance with the Supreme Court's 1946 ruling in the Irene Morgan case, declaring segregation in interstate carriers unconstitutional. Even then, CORE would not try to establish a chapter in the South for another decade.[12]

The NAACP, on the other hand, saw its membership grow from 50,556 and 355 branches in 1940 to over half a million and more than 1,000 branches in 1946. Yet it essentially remained middle class in orientation and bureaucratic in structure, abhorring radical tactics and adhering to a legalistic approach that did not countenance collective action. This was especially so in the South, the site of three-quarters of the new wartime branches. None of the southern branches sanctioned confrontations, direct action, or extralegal tactics. Ella Baker, who visited local chapters of the NAACP throughout the wartime South, first as an assistant field secretary of the association and then as its national director of branches, never ceased hectoring the national office that most of those branches were little more than social clubs with no interest whatsoever in pursuing local protests. Thurgood Marshall also chafed at the reluctance of the southern branch officers to attack Jim Crow and their tendency to devote themselves solely to teacher-salary equalization suits. Such suits "aroused little excitement, even in the Deep South," maintains George B. Tindall: "The tedious pace, the limited results, the manifest equity of the claim" muted white alarm. And that suited the NAACP's southern leadership of black academics, businessmen, and ministers just fine. The issue of inequitable salaries for Negro public school teachers would remain their top priority even in the immediate postwar years. The pursuit of traditional objectives by restrained tactics remained the hallmark of the association in the South. As they had in the 1930s, the wartime southern branches lobbied and litigated against the poll tax, the white primary, and lynching and requested a more equitable share of educational facilities and funds.[13]

Continuity also characterized the work of the seven southern affiliates of the National Urban League. They held firm to their social work orientation and to their reliance on negotiations to expand employment, recreational, and housing opportunities for African Americans. Such matters as African American juvenile delinquency and family disorganization took precedence over the fight for equal rights. Their wariness toward demonstrations and protests reflected their fear of losing funding from the Community Chest and local philanthropies, their faith in being able to make progress by working in conventional channels, and their hostility toward the NAACP—which they viewed as a competitor for financial contributions. Confrontation and disruption, even harsh talk, did not fit the Urban League's pursuit of gradual and limited racial change. When Benjamin Bell, the newly appointed executive secretary of the Urban League in Memphis, angered white politicians and businessmen by denouncing Jim Crow, the national office quickly replaced him with someone more compliant.[14]

Much as southern black leaders did not support direct-action protests or forthright attacks on segregation during the war, the editorials of southern Negro newspapers rarely echoed the demands for racial equality of those in the North. Several African American newspapers in the South followed the wartime lead of the *Savannah Tribune* in discontinuing the practice of reprinting editorials from northern black newspapers. Most of the southern Negro press had never done so, and they continued, as did most southern black church and community leaders during the war, to stay on the sidelines of the civil rights struggle, to advocate upright behavior and individual economic advancement within the existing order, and to preach paternalism and "civility." Even when calling for "fair play" or an end to disfranchisement, they did so in a manner that posed no clear and present danger to white supremacy. Lest criticism be construed as unpatriotic, they accentuated African American loyalty and contributions to the war effort above all else. Surveying the Negro press in Mississippi during the war, Julius Thompson concluded: "Submission to the system was the watchword."[15]

True to form in wartime Dixie, the leaders of the South Carolina African American Democratic and Republican clubs both declared that the Negro wants only "a man's chance"—not integration or social equality. And when a young black applied to the all-white College of Charleston in 1944, the local NAACP repudiated him, accusing him of an "exaggerated ego." The opinion studies of African Americans conducted during the war continued to reveal significant attitudinal differences between blacks in the South and in the North. One mid-1943 survey indicated that just 13 percent of southern blacks expressed dissatisfaction with wartime employment opportunities, as opposed to 32 percent of northern blacks; that only 10 percent of African Americans in the South complained about the treatment of blacks in the armed forces, versus 19 percent in the North; and that a mere 3 percent of southern blacks were bothered about social discrimination, compared with 14 percent of northern African Americans. Yet another poll reported in the Negro press claimed that only one out of ten southern blacks felt that segregation should be attacked during the war. Other polls noted that blacks in Memphis did not care as much about civil rights issues as did those in New York, and while a majority of African Americans, both North and South in 1943, did not think that the March-on-Washington Movement would accomplish any good, in Atlanta only one in five blacks thought African Americans would benefit from Randolph's proposed protest.[16]

Despite the many transformations and upheavals triggered by the war, there would be no mass militancy in the World War II South. There, proportionately, fewest blacks joined the NAACP or supported Randolph's March-on-Washington Movement, much less CORE or the National Negro Congress. The bitterness and resentment toward the pervasive color line, which flared occasionally in sporadic acts of aggression or passive disobedience and more frequently in covert "gum-beating" or "taking it out in talk," were largely held in check by a sense of impotency and insecurity, which cautious southern African American leaders did little to combat. Indeed, many such spokespersons, like the Committee of 100 in Mississippi, preferred a separate black community, however unequal, as the base for their careers and profits. Many of the African American educators and teachers, often the mainstay of the NAACP's southern branches, particularly feared the loss of their positions as a consequence of attacking and eliminating the segregated public school systems. Consequently, not until 1950 would the NAACP Board of Directors adopt a resolution stating that all future education cases would seek "education on a nonsegregated basis and that no relief other than that will be acceptable." Until then, separate-but-really-equal remained the long-standing goal of its Dixie affiliates. And the preferred strategy continued to be working within the South's biracial system, meeting behind the scenes to seek improvements on the black side of the color line—that line which not only separated the races but determined rights and modes of conduct, and sustained subordination and exclusion, as well.[17]

The Negro leaders who met secretly in Durham, North Carolina, on October 20, 1942, purposefully excluded northern African Americans to avoid agitation of the segregation issue. That ruse and the initial suggestion for their meeting had come from Jessie Daniel Ames of the Commission on Interracial Cooperation and the Association of Southern Women for the Prevention of Lynching. A white reformer and adversary of the NAACP who insisted that the status of African Americans could be improved within the separate-but-equal framework, Ames believed that the key to her goal was cooperation by the "better class" of southern whites and blacks. She found an ally in Gordon B. Hancock. The president of Virginia Union College in Richmond, Hancock was a black moderate who sought to build bridges between the races while conserving a separate African American community. He agreed to organize a conclave of like-minded black educators and editors, men who would draft a statement of "minimum advances," a "Southern Charter for Race Relations" that would, as Ames urged, "avoid bringing in segregation, white supremacy and other loaded ideas." The seventy-five black professionals who assembled in Durham were eager to reduce racial tensions and prevent racial violence and at the same time to appear assertive enough to forestall being supplanted by northern black firebrands. Accordingly, their "A Basis for Interracial Cooperation and Development in the South," better known as the Durham Manifesto, formally opposed the principle of compulsory segregation but deemed it "both sensible and timely" to defer that thorny matter for the present. Rather than a call to arms to battle Jim Crow, its rallying cry was for improved race relations in the South—"not only a moral matter, but a practical necessity in winning the war." In a most conciliatory tone, it reiterated demands for African American voting rights and an end to the mistreatment of blacks by police; for equality of access to public services, the armed forces, and educational and employment opportunities; and for a federal antilynching law. "No case was made against segregation," charged Benjamin Mays, the president of Morehouse College who had pleaded in vain for an unequivocal denunciation of this "basic evil in the South."[18]

The some 100 white liberals—the "other" South, the largely "invisible" South—who met in Atlanta on April 8, 1943, to respond to the Durham resolutions, as well as the additional 200 who later signed their conference statement, similarly, tepidly sidestepped the central issue of segregation and all that it implied. Having to contend with rotten borough legislatures, entrenched conservative machines, one-party politics, and truncated electorates, these journalists and academics had long perfected the art of caution and evasion on racial issues lest the white masses be "enraged into resistance." Wartime changes, uncertainties, and fears accentuated this tendency, and seeking safe middle ground, they equated and damned those they considered the irresponsible extremists at both ends of the spectrum: A. Philip Randolph and the racist Mississippi congressman John Rankin, the NAACP and the Ku Klux Klan. To counter the equally small bands of those described as "Negro agitators" and "white rabble-rousers," the southern liberals agreed to a statement effused with visions of fair play and mutual cooperation, yet one that depicted Jim Crow laws as "intended to minister to the welfare and integrity of both races." Insisting that solutions to the race problem must "be found in evolutionary methods and not in ill-founded revolutionary movements which promise immediate solutions," they envisioned racial reform without ending Jim Crow. Because the Durham Manifesto is "so free from any suggestion of threat and ultimatum, and at the same time shows such good will," the white southerners proclaimed, "we gladly agree to cooperate."[19]

These similar commitments to gradualism and moderation became the basis for a biracial meeting of representatives from both conferences in Richmond on June 16, 1943, and then, in Atlanta on August 14, the founding of the Southern Regional Council (SRC). Primarily a vehicle for antimilitant southern journalists and educators, the SRC sought a liberalization of race relations without fundamental change. It wanted trade unions and businesses to act fairly toward African Americans, supported the President's Committee on Fair Employment Practices (FEPC) and the anti–poll tax bill, favored improving the living conditions of minorities, and approved of experimental racially mixed units of volunteers in the army and navy—but not desegregation in the South. It would not publicly condemn segregation until 1949. When chastised by Lillian Smith for this failure, the council's wartime executive director replied that the SRC preferred "to capture the foothills" rather than "storming distant peaks." Booker T. Washington would have approved.[20]

Lillian Smith also had harsh words for the Southern Conference for Human Welfare (SCHW), which she quit because it too refused to oppose segregation during the war. Instead, the SCHW resolved to work "toward the development of the friendliest of relations" between the races. The title of its new magazine, *Southern Patriot*, reflected its wartime priorities, as did the many articles and editorials beating the drums of war and stressing the necessity of racial unity for victory. Essentially mirroring the overall de-emphasis of civil rights by the Left, and unlike the prewar SCHW, which had conducted its annual meetings without segregating the races and had loudly trumpeted its support for civil rights, the SCHW devoted its wartime energies to "Win the War" rallies, to abolishing the poll tax—by keeping it from being identified as a racial issue—to denouncing Roosevelt's domestic opponents as "traitors," and to promoting labor unionization, particularly by the Congress of Industrial Organizations (CIO). The SCHW would not even hire its first black field representative until after the war.[21]

Nor did the SCHW criticize the CIO's wartime acceptance, in the main, of a biracial unionism which acquiesced in Jim Crow meetings of its southern locals and in their selection of union representatives. Dependent upon the CIO for financial support, the SCHW did nothing to oppose discriminatory job classification systems and racial wage differentials in the majority of plants the CIO organized in the South. The fear of losing the support of white workers, who far outnumbered black unionists in almost all of the unions organized by the CIO in the South, meant no commitment to racial equality, no attacks upon traditional racial etiquette and practices, no fight against segregation by the majority of southern CIO affiliates. Anticommunist CIO leaders, particularly prominent in the South, regarded racial integration and communism as related, pernicious evils; and leftist unionists, in the main, contested racism neither within their ranks nor in the larger southern society, for the same antifascist reasons that they zealously promoted the no-strike pledge and advocated speedups and incentive pay to maximize production. Consequently, the CIO in the wartime South, despite the portentous pronouncements of its national officers and its Committee to Abolish Discrimination, essentially left intact the color line pervading both shop floor and union life—as did the American Federation of Labor, which had a larger southern membership than the CIO. Nevertheless, few southern liberals or leftists dissented from the notion that the union card was the most effective way to undermine white supremacy. With few exceptions, the once more racially radical elements of the Popular Front in the South either ceased to exist during the war or subordinated all matters to victory abroad. Commonwealth College expired, and the Southern Tenant Farmers Union barely managed to stay alive as it changed names. Myles Horton's Highlander Folk School retreated from its integrationist practices to concentrate on training labor union organizers, and Howard Kester dissolved his revolutionary Committee on Economic and Racial Justice and sought fulfillment in the Fellowship of Southern Churchmen's battle against materialism and modernity. Both the Southern Negro Youth Congress and the National Negro Congress folded their tents in various southern states, and neither organization would be in existence when the 1940s ended.[22]

Even more so than their counterparts in the CIO, African American communists soft-pedaled their censure of racism in the United States during the war. Executing an about-face from the period of the Nazi-Soviet Pact, when they took the lead in exposing Jim Crow in the armed forces, the communists opposed efforts by blacks to embarrass the military after Germany invaded the Soviet Union in June 1941. They even sought to prevent African American legal challenges against discrimination from coming before the courts. The party's wartime policy was to do nothing that might erode the unity necessary for prosecuting the war. Ben Davis vigorously denounced both the March-on-Washington Movement and the NAACP for placing the interests of blacks above the need for "national unity, maximum war production, and the highest possible morale in the armed forces." Having opposed civil disobedience by blacks and mass protests against racism, and having defended the military against its civil rights critics, Davis confessed after the war that he had "often lost sight of" the black liberation struggle. Communist leader and social scientist John Williamson later concurred. "Neglect of the problems of the Negro people," Williamson wrote, "and the cessation of organizing efforts in the South undoubtedly slowed the pace of the freedom movement which arose later."[23]

As did most black communists, Georgian Angelo Herndon and his *Negro Quarterly* followed Earl Browder's wartime policy of refraining from public censure of Jim Crow. Its articles and editorials downplayed racial militancy, emphasized the need for patriotic unity, dispelled the "dangerous fallacy" that this is "a white man's war," and subordinated all racial issues to victory over fascist aggression. Similarly, chapters of the National Negro Congress metamorphosed into

Negro Labor Victory Committees; Southern Negro Youth Congress cadres mainly worked within NAACP and CIO affiliates to promote victory abroad; and local party members in St. Louis hounded that city's March-on-Washington Movement and accused it of "disrupting the war effort" when it attempted to organize a demonstration to get more blacks jobs in defense plants. The response of the *Daily Worker* to the race riot in Detroit was to condemn the NAACP for making such a fuss and to urge everyone to get back to work quickly. Such actions and the many articles written by James Ford, Ferdinand Smith, Doxey Wilkerson, and Max Yergan insisting that black protest must remain subordinate to the drive for victory even led the leftist *Negro Digest* to publish a debate entitled "Have the Communists Quit Fighting for Negro Rights?" Symptomatic of the Left's preoccupation with wartime unity and concomitant abhorrence of potentially divisive racial issues, Adam Clayton Powell Jr. went so far as to suggest that the NAACP change its name to the National Association for the Advancement of Common People.[24]

With the Left neither prodding them to greater militancy nor challenging them for leadership and membership, mainstream black and interracial organizations tacked to starboard. Many new interracial committees had been established to prevent or control outbreaks of racial violence, the predictable consequence of increasing black hopefulness and the forceful insistence of whites to maintain the racial status quo, and these committees decried black assertiveness as much as white intransigence in their efforts to contain conflict. Rumors of race warfare, of African Americans forming "pushing clubs" and stockpiling ice picks, of "Eleanor Clubs" and blacks "taking over" white women, however unsubstantiated, were rife throughout the wartime South—so much so that the Julius Rosenwald Fund financed the Institute of Social Studies at Fisk University to prepare a study of racial friction areas. Clearly, both talk of violent retaliation and racial violence did occur. But whether sporadic African American belligerency and the apprehensions of those whose views appeared in print during the war constitute a watershed in militant black protest remains problematic. African American and white American soldiers had also repeatedly clashed in the First World War, and Bigger Thomas was not a product of World War II. "Multiply Bigger Thomas twelve million times," Richard Wright had written well before American entry into the war, "and you have the psychology of the Negro people."[25]

Moreover, although the interracial violence within the armed forces is often cited as evidence of wartime black militancy, the largest number of violent clashes on military installations occurred in 1941, prior to the United States' entry into the conflict, and these were primarily instigated by whites against individual blacks. During the war itself, racial strife crested in mid-1943 and then rapidly receded. For the entire period of America's involvement in the war, less than a score of the hundreds of military camps in the United States and abroad reported racial brawls, and many of those had nothing directly to do with African American protests or racist conditions. With a critical mass of a million black servicemen, several hundred thousand of whom had been raised in the North, one may wonder why there were so relatively few outbreaks of violence given the conditions they had to endure during the war. While a relative handful responded to segregation, inferior training and facilities, officers calling them "niggers," and brutal control by hostile military police by attacking whites, others resorted to forms of covert hostility, to violence against other blacks, and to extraordinary efforts to prove their worth. Still others expressed no dissatisfaction with their lot. Only 15,000 joined the NAACP, the organization most vocally critical of the insensitivity of the War Department toward the problems of black GIs. Surveys during the war indicated that only a minority of blacks in the army opposed separate post exchanges, and more African Americans favored racially segregated units than integrated ones. Although some wished to let "the whites fight their own war," many times more thought that the war was as much their affair as anybody else's and served eagerly and proudly, leaving those not considered fit enough or too old to serve to express their disappointment.[26]

Especially after mid-1943, the Negro press, sensing the explosive potential of the race problem, downplayed the remaining incidents of racial violence in the military that transpired, hailed the achievements of African American servicemen, and castigated those blacks who defied military authorities. When the navy court-martialed fifty blacks for refusing to report to work in Port Chicago on San Francisco Bay following an accidental explosion that killed 300 African American seamen, the *Defender* insisted that blacks should obey military orders, whatever the circumstances. "None of us condones disobedience of military orders," opined the *Courier*, "no matter how unjust an order may appear to be." And the *Journal and Guide* added: "No right thinking person can excuse desertion, disobedience, mutiny." The Negro press expressed the same editorial views when four African American WACs were court-martialed following their refusal to do the dirtiest jobs at a military hospital in Fort Devons, Massachusetts. Summing up the sentiment of the Negro press and leadership toward the actions of the black women, the *People's Voice* claimed that "no matter how serious the provocation, they should not have defied military discipline."[27]

The Second World War, as well, failed to ignite the widespread racial rioting by African Americans seen in the 1917–1919 or 1964–1968 periods. Despite the legitimacy of African American aspirations and disillusionment with minimal changes during the war, despite the rising level of both expectations and frustrations, and despite the expansion of settings that brought blacks and whites into close contact and thus possibly into conflict, there were far fewer clashes in the Second World War than in those two other periods. Civilian African Americans during World War II rarely initiated attacks on whites, rarely responded in kind, rarely fought back. Commentators during the war, in fact, singled out the 1943 riot in Detroit, in which 25 blacks and 9 whites died and more than 1,000 were injured, as the sole truly race riot of the period. The two riots in the South, in Mobile and Beaumont in June 1943, now often cited as manifestations of black militancy, resulted from white resistance and hatred, not black aggression. In Mobile, the attempt by FEPC officials to have the Alabama Dry Dock and Shipbuilding Company upgrade 12 of its 7,000 African Americans holding menial positions at the yard to racially mixed welding crews caused white workers to go on a rampage, assaulting and injuring some 50 blacks and forcing the FEPC to back down and accept traditional Jim Crow arrangements in all work assignments. Likewise, in Beaumont, opposition to black aspirations at the Pennsylvania Shipyards sparked a false rumor that a black worker had raped the wife of a white employee and led to six hours of rioting by whites that injured several hundred African Americans and destroyed parts of Beaumont's black ghetto. The Negro press described both outbreaks as white pogroms against defenseless African Americans who neither resisted nor retaliated violently.[28]

That same summer, when a false rumor of a black soldier being killed by a white patrolman ignited Harlem blacks to plunder more than a thousand white-owned stores in the ghetto, African American leaders and columnists with virtually a single voice repudiated the looters as criminal "hotheads," lauded the New York police for quickly quelling the rampage, and maintained that the "orgy of vandalism" was not a race riot! The *Courier* opined that "the prepondering majorities of law-abiding American colored people are deeply downcast and humiliated" by the irresponsible disorder of a minority of blacks in Harlem, and an opinion poll revealed that fewer than one in three Harlem residents thought the riot justified. The NAACP's *Crisis* compared the disorder in Harlem "to a Southern lynch mob." Adam Clayton Powell Sr. blamed the disorder on "criminal subhuman savages" who wanted something for nothing rather than wanting to right racial wrongs. His son agreed. Adam Clayton Powell Jr., whose image had changed from the Great Depression man on the picket line to the war booster selling bonds at "victory rallies," emphatically insisted that the "wanton violence" was wrong, had not accomplished anything, and "was not a race riot." "I don't think it's a race riot," added Richard Wright. "I had the feeling it was a spontaneous outburst of anger, stemming mainly from the economic pinch."[29]

Langston Hughes similarly gave an economic explanation for the wearing of zoot suits by young black males—another supposed sign of racial militancy, of black self-determination, of a subversive response to white oppression. Depression kids who had too little in the 1930s, wrote Hughes in 1943, loved the excesses of material in the outfit: "It made them feel good to go to extremes. In the light of the poverty of their past, too much becomes just enough for them. A key chain six times too long is just enough to hold no keys." However understandable as a sign of young blacks' economic yearning, the zoot suit and all manifestations of disrespectful or antisocial behavior received little but condemnation during the war from those considered to be the voices of the black community. They denounced zoot suits as synonymous with bad conduct and those who wear them as strutting fools. "Zoot suits no more represent the Negro than watermelons, dice, switch-blades, or muggings," claimed the *Defender* in one of its editorials beseeching African Americans not to wear them. Rather than flaunt behavior that confirmed white stereotypes, African American editors and civic leaders advised blacks to buy war bonds, plant victory gardens, do their utmost to spur war production, and serve bravely in the armed forces in order to qualify for equal rights. The two most-read Negro newspapers, the *Chicago Defender* and *Pittsburgh Courier*, carried numerous articles lecturing blacks on their manners and morals, their loud clothes and loud talk. The African American publisher of the *Cincinnati Union* proposed adding to the Double V a third V for "victory over ourselves." He instructed his black readers that "as long as we tolerate and condone among ourselves public misconduct, impoliteness, spendthrift habits, slovenliness, uncleanliness, we need never hope to attain the standards that white American citizenship endorses, the rights that the U.S. Constitution accords." In Cleveland the Vanguard League, which had led militant protests by blacks in the 1930s, conducted a wartime Good Conduct Campaign. Emphasizing the necessity of African Americans being respectable to gain the respect of whites, it displayed posters and handed out cards to those in the black neighborhoods it considered guilty of misconduct, proclaiming: "Watch your conduct on the streetcars," "Fix that door; cut that grass; pull those weeds," and "Zoot suits, the mark of irresponsibility."[30]

The many African American ministers, educators, and civic leaders who served on the some 200 interracial committees established after the Detroit race riot went still further in demanding a "piping down on stentorian drives for equality" and in importuning blacks to behave properly. Mindful of the "practical wisdom of gradual adjustment in dealing with the race problem in the South," the Richmond Ministerial Union adopted resolutions on interracial cooperation which put a lid on potential militancy. So did the Nashville Committee of 50, the Portsmouth, Virginia, Council of Racial Amity, the Birmingham Good Neighbor Club, the Memphis Council for Americanism, the Washington D.C. Citizens' Committee on Race Relations, and the Baltimore and St. Louis mayors' commissions on race relations. All functioned as impartial mediators to minimize tensions, not as advocates for black rights.[31]

Throughout the last two years of the war, the moderate interracial committees set the tone and dominated the discourse on racial matters in the United States. Blunting confrontation and allaying conflict became their strategy and goal. In the South, which had 14 percent of the new interracial committees, more time was spent on requests for more frequent garbage removal in African American neighborhoods and for the hiring of black policemen to patrol those segregated enclaves than on any other matters. Virtually all sought to foster goodwill by initiating interracial contacts and exchanges among students. Many set up rumor-control bureaus and hired consultants in human relations. Race relations suddenly became a cottage industry: interracial committees begat commissions against bigotry, which begat councils for unity; there would be more than a thousand such groups dealing with tolerance for minorities by 1948. In return for not directly attacking racial discrimination and segregation, they had the support of such newly organized national groups as the Race Relations Division of the American Missionary Association, the American Friends Race Relations Committee, the American Jewish Congress Commission on Community Interrelations, and the American Council on Race Relations. Given the backing of such prestigious company and the official status many of the commissions had by virtue of being municipal agencies, as well as the endorsement of leading African Americans, promoting tolerance became voguish in 1943. Brotherhood Week supplanted protests against white supremacy.[32]

With so many former allies in the fight for equal rights now counseling "go slow," most African American advocates of aggressive tactics to achieve fundamental racial change either trimmed their sails or foundered. Battling Hitler largely terminated the encouragement to black assertiveness that had been supplied in the 1930s by the communists, militant labor union activists, and supportive progressive government officials, and by the beliefs and sympathies spurred by the reform liberalism of the Great Depression–New Deal era. During the 1930s, at least ten cities had experienced NAACP-supported school boycotts protesting segregation. To demand employment, African Americans, with the support of major community leadership, had mounted sustained campaigns of picketing and boycotting retail establishments in at least thirty-five cities, including Atlanta, Baltimore, Durham, Houston, Memphis, New Orleans, and Richmond. In Charlotte, Greensboro, and Norfolk, as well as in Chicago, Philadelphia, and New York, blacks had sat-in at relief bureaus, conducted rent strikes, and led mass hunger marches. They had engaged in direct-action protests against racial discrimination at restaurants, hotels, beaches, and theaters in both the South and the North. In comparison, there was only one boycott against school segregation during the war, in Hillburn, New York, and not another one in the South until 1951; there were just a handful of direct-action protests against Jim Crow in public accommodations, primarily by the largely white CORE in Chicago and Denver; and there were no sustained boycotts or mass demonstrations against job discrimination in World War II. As Meier and Rudwick state in the only study to enumerate African American protest activities: the Depression—not the war—is the "watershed in Afro-American direct action." Militant black activism in the 1930s "achieved a salience in black protest that would not be equalled or surpassed until the late 1950s and 1960s." Indeed, they conclude, there "was less actual use of direct action tactics during World War II than in the 1930s"; the number of protest "demonstrations declined sharply during World War II compared to the 1930s"; and, overall, "the amount of direct action was minor compared to the Depression era."[33]

These facts do not in the least suggest that African Americans wanted equal rights any less in 1944 than in 1937 or that blacks during the war complacently accepted second-class status. Discontent is ever present among those who are discriminated against and oppressed. Indeed, as has been amply described, the war against Hitlerism intensified the civil rights consciousness of the New Deal years, raised the expectations of blacks considerably, and had a significant impact on American racial opinions, especially in heightening perceptions of the discrepancy between the democratic ideals of the United States and its undemocratic racial practices. But compared to the Depression decade, and far more to the 1960s, blacks in World War II faced greater resistance to change in a milieu less hospitable to disruptive protests, with reduced internal wherewithal and external support. The constraints imposed by a nation at war, the dwindling resources for sustained confrontation, and the genuinely patriotic response of most African Americans to the dangers their nation faced all inhibited militant protest activity. The NAACP, which had faced challenges throughout the 1930s from more radical, contentious African Americans urging direct action against Jim Crow, for all practical purposes now became the civil rights movement.

The largest and most influential of the black rights organizations, and far more so in 1945 than in 1940, the NAACP during the war gained the support of many of its former leftist critics such as Ralph Bunche, E. Franklin Frazier, and W. E. B. DuBois, who rejoined the association in 1944 as its director of special research. That year, the NAACP's Supreme Court victory in the white-primary case legitimized and gave yet further impetus to its legal-redress campaign. Litigation, always important to the NAACP, now became the keystone of its strategy. Its battle against racism would be fought by lawyers, not the black masses. At the same time, the NAACP became evermore a part of, and bound by, the liberal-labor Democratic coalition, campaigning against the poll tax and lynching and for federal aid to education and an increase in Social Security coverage, but avoiding direct assaults on Jim Crow. With prominent white liberals, as well as A. Philip Randolph and other African American leaders, the NAACP also made the drive for a permanent FEPC a major priority after the war, and close cooperation with the American Jewish Congress and like-minded reform groups who supported NAACP cases with "friends of the court" briefs its main modus operandi.[34]

The most widely noted (if not actually read) wartime book on racial matters, Gunnar Myrdal's authoritative *An American Dilemma* (1944), gave its imprimatur to the NAACP strategy. It judged the NAACP the most effective of all black protest groups, celebrated the success of its legal campaign, and presented a moderate agenda for action almost identical to the NAACP's. Instantly hailed as a "classic," rarely criticized outside the recalcitrant white South, *An American Dilemma* warned against the folly of black militancy in the South, accentuated the role of white liberal allies in the campaign for racial equality, and insisted that the key struggle was the moral one within the white conscience—and not a struggle for power between the races. Myrdal's placid prognosis fit the needs of a moderate African American leadership dreading racial conflict or challenges to its own hegemony within black America, and it set the tone and the premises of action by the civil rights movement in the postwar decade.[35]

As LeRoi Jones would later write, "the psychological hypothesis which informed the Negro's attitude toward America in the mid-forties" was that by relying on legal redress, education, and collaboration with white liberals, blacks would achieve their aspiration: equality of opportunity. And hardly any black intellectuals or leaders dissented.

Across the spectrum from W. E. B. DuBois to George Schuyler, from Richard Wright to Dean Charles H. Thompson to E. Franklin Frazier, African Americans initially lauded *An American Dilemma* and approved of its pragmatic tactics and strategy as the course for blacks to follow. The fourteen southern and northern, conservative, moderate, and radical black contributors to Howard University historian Rayford Logan's landmark *What the Negro Wants* (1944) further implanted and legitimated Myrdalian means and ends in civil rights thought by giving an African American stamp of approval to Myrdal's meliorist approach to the race problem.[36]

While now seen by some as a major break with previous African American thinking, largely because of W. T. Couch's intemperate reaction and defense of segregation in his "Publisher's Introduction," most of the contributors to Logan's compendium took pains to emphasize that what Negroes wanted closely matched Myrdal's rank order of discriminations. What blacks especially desired, equal economic opportunity, whites could easily accept; what blacks least cared about, intermarriage and miscegenation, whites emphatically resisted. Scorning the contention that blacks wanted entree into the drawing rooms of whites, Logan's contributors all stipulated that blacks wanted the same political rights and economic opportunities possessed by other citizens—no more and no less than what African Americans had traditionally wanted. Charles H. Wesley of Wilberforce College underlined this point by entitling his essay "The Negro Has Always Wanted the Four Freedoms." The goals of blacks for equality remain the same, wrote Doxey A. Wilkerson for the Left. "Negroes are demanding nothing new," added the NAACP's Roy Wilkins: equal rights had been the goal of the NAACP since 1909. But neither Wilkins nor any of the others issued a call to arms against the southern Jim Crow system. Believing that it could not be gained "in the near future," Logan favored "the eventual abolition of public segregation." Wesley placed the end of segregated education in the category of "ultimate, long-range proposals" rather than "immediately approximate ones." Sterling Brown, chastising both southern African American leaders who think segregation too deeply rooted ever to be eradicated and those in the North who "believe it can be easily uprooted by speeches and governmental decree," concluded that it must be "eventually abolished"—but not "overnight." A. Philip Randolph also counseled that the racist barriers "in the Southern section of the country cannot be abolished overnight and that they must be approached in terms of the conditions of the racial climate of the community." With still less bravado, Gordon B. Hancock advised blacks to concentrate on eradicating prejudice, not segregation, and to make the most of separation, "gaining strength for the long tomorrow," rather than exhausting their "energies struggling for integration." So did the Tuskegee Institute's Frederick D. Patterson, claiming that blacks prefer to live among their own race and that they need to make the most of segregated opportunities. Neither the conservative Leslie Pinckney Hill of Cheyney College nor the CIO's Willard Townsend and the Communist Party's Doxey Wilkerson even addressed the issue of segregation.[37]

Logan's contributors also urged blacks not to attempt to take advantage of the war to gain their rights. The Negro must "unconditionally" support the war effort and do nothing to hinder a rapid and total Allied victory said Wilkerson. "The Negro race in America must give to the nation its unreserved allegiance" stated Hill. "Even at the cost of the preservation of the status quo," intoned Brown, "this is still the Negro's war." And Logan affirmed: "We have no wish to obstruct the war effort." To that end, none of the fourteen contributors advocated mass marches or protest boycotts. While Wilkerson groused that it would be a grave mistake for "Negroes to organize mass struggles as Negroes" rather than place their faith in President Roosevelt, Townsend averred that the organized labor movement was the medicine for complete recovery from "the Negro problem."[38]

Most emphatically and specifically, however, the southern black contributors affirmed solutions that harkened back to Booker T. Washington. Hancock advised self-help and vocational education. Decrying radical protests, Patterson called for "sound, practical and realistic programs" that recognized the limitations of blacks, employed "the most feasible methods," and aimed at slow, steady improvement in African American life. Hill, claiming that no protest strategy "that produces racial hatred and antagonism can advance the common good," proposed that blacks gain the indulgence of whites by demonstrating "strong personal self-control, good manners," respect for law, obedience to authority, and "faith in the proved leaders and spokesmen of both races." And Langston Hughes suggested replacing Jim Crow with a system of first-, second-, and third-class transportation that would "let the whites who wish to do so ride in coaches where few Negroes have the funds to be." Neither a militant call to arms nor an innovative strategy for black advancement, *What the Negro Wants,* like Myrdal's *An American Dilemma,* concentrated more on eradicating white prejudice and avoiding racial conflict than on storming the ramparts of racial discrimination and segregation.[39]

Militant protest never entirely abated during the war, but it never assumed dominance in either black strategy or action. To the extent that it is now possible to gauge the amount and strength of the rupture, or the transformation, in civil rights protest activities, World War II does not appear to be a watershed. Change, of course, occurred. But in a limited manner. The status and protest cognition of southern blacks in 1945, their organizations, leadership, language, and strategies for reform were neither exactly the same nor fundamentally different than they had been in 1940. The goals considered a distant dream in the 1930s had not suddenly appeared attainable. The traditional tactics of African American protest groups had not suddenly become unacceptable, nor had new, more disruptive ones come into widespread use. Why? In part, because the nearly million young black men who might have been expected to be in the forefront of more militant forays against racist practices had been uprooted from their communities to serve in an armed forces which cramped organized protests. In part, because the optimism of African Americans for postwar progress, induced by the sudden prosperity of those who left mule and plow or domestic work for a job in a defense plant and by the din of democratic propaganda during the war, mitigated against a radical turn in practices. And, certainly in part, because wartime America proved an infertile ground for the seeds of protest planted in the 1930s. The needs of war came first. Period. The domestic unity, as well as manpower and production efficiency, required for victory took precedence over all else, for the Roosevelts and for virtually every prominent African American, labor leader, white liberal, and progressive proponent of civil rights. And if that meant holding the color line, defusing conflicts, eschewing confrontation for compromise, well, the expected rewards for African Americans would come after the war. Furthermore, social, economic, and demographic alterations, no matter how vast or rapid, in and of themselves do not generate mass movements for social change by the aggrieved or oppressed.

The resources for sustained mass confrontations with the Jim Crow system in the South were gestating but still embryonic, and the political climate that would facilitate rather than inhibit militant collective action had not yet emerged. The war had driven old Dixie downward, but not down and out.

The hopes of some, and the dire warnings of others, "that a New Negro will return from the war" willing to fight and die rather than accept the traditional structure of white dominance in southern society, proved premature. Indeed, it appears that many of those southern African Americans most "modernized" by military service soon left the South in the greatest numbers to pursue their individual ambitions in northern cities or reenlisted in the armed forces, depleting the pool of potential southern black activists. The insurgent struggle for racial justice to come in the South would eventually draw sustenance from the many fundamental transformations in American life and world affairs catalyzed by the Second World War, but that mass movement would hardly be just an extension, a continuation, of previous civil rights reform efforts. Those militantly fighting for change in the 1960s would not look to the agenda and actions of World War II blacks and racial organizations as models to emulate.

Notes

1. Especially important in promulgating this viewpoint are Richard M. Dalfiume, "The 'Forgotten Years' of the Negro Revolution," *Journal of American History* 55 (June 1968), 90–106, and *Desegregation of the U.S. Armed Forces* (Columbia, Mo., 1969), esp. 105–13, 122–23; Peter Kellogg, "Civil Rights Consciousness in the 1940s," *The Historian* 42 (Nov. 1979), 18–41; Richard Polenberg, *War and Society: The United States, 1941–1945* (New York, 1972), 99–130; Harvard Sitkoff, "The Detroit Race Riot of 1943," *Michigan History* 53 (Fall 1969), 183–206, and "Racial Militancy and Interracial Violence in the Second World War," *Journal of American History* 58 (Dec. 1971), 661–81; and Neil A. Wynn, *The Afro American and the Second World War* (New York, 1975), esp. 99–121. Their views of a wartime racial crisis owe much to Charles S. Johnson and associates, *To Stem This Tide: A Survey of Racial Tension Areas in the United States* (Boston, 1943).

2. Lee Finkle, *Forum for Protest: The Black Press during World War II* (Rutherford, N.J., 1975), 222; P. L. Prattis, "The Role of the Negro Press in Race Relations," *Phylon* 7 (Third Quarter, 1946), 274; Thomas Sancton,

"The Negro Press," *New Republic*, April 26, 1943, 560; Sterling A. Brown, "Out of Their Mouths," *Survey Graphic* 31 (Nov. 1942), 480–83.

3. Saunders Redding, "A Negro Looks at War," *American Mercury* (Nov. 1942), 585–92; Edgar T. Rouzeau to Franklin Roosevelt, Feb. 24, 1942, OF 93, Roosevelt Papers, Franklin D. Roosevelt Library; Finkle, *Forum for Protest*, 113–14, 205; Robin D. G. Kelley, *Hammer and Hoe: Alabama Communists during the Great Depression* (Chapel Hill, N.C., 1990), 218; *New York Times*, Dec. 8, 10, 14, 1941; *Opportunity* 20 (Oct. 1942), 296, and 21 (Oct. 1943), 147; Byron R. Skinner, "The 'Double V': The Impact of World War II on Black America" (Ph.D. diss., University of California–Berkeley, 1978), 30–31; LeRoi Jones, *Blues People: Negro Music in White America* (New York, 1963), 178; Paul Oliver, *The Meaning of the Blues* (New York, 1960), 278–85; *New York Age*, May 16, 1942; William Pickens, "The Democracy of War Savings," *Crisis* 49 (July 1942), 221; Richard Wright to Archibald MacLeish, Dec. 21, 1941, Office of Facts and Figures, RG 208, National Archives; *Daily Worker*, Dec. 13, 1941.

4. *Baltimore Afro-American* and *Savannah Tribune*, Dec. 13, 1941; *Norfolk Journal and Guide* and *Chicago Defender*, Dec. 20, 1941; *California Eagle*, Dec. 13, 1941; Ernest Johnson, "The Negro Press Reacts to War," *Interracial Review* 15 (March 1942), 39–41; Ralph N. Davis, "The Negro Newspapers and the War," *Sociology and Social Research* 27 (March–April 1943), 373–78; *Crisis* 48 (March 1941), 71; Revels Cayton, "The Yanks Are Not Coming," *Chicago Defender*, Nov. 25, 1939; Max Yergan and Joseph Bibb columns in *Chicago Defender*, Dec. 27, 1941; Adam Clayton Powell Jr., "Is This a White Man's War?" *Common Sense* 2 (April 1942), 111; "Publishers Pledge Support to President during Crisis," *Pittsburgh Courier*, June 13, 1942.

5. Walter White, *A Man Called White* (New York, 1948), 207–8; Florence Murray, "The Negro and Civil Liberties during World War II," *Social Forces* 24 (Dec. 1945), 211; Patrick S. Washburn, *A Question of Sedition: The Federal Government's Investigation of the Black Press during World War II* (New York, 1986); Herbert Garfinkel, *When Negroes March: The March on Washington Movement in the Organizational Politics for FEPC* (Glencoe, Ill., 1959), 109.

6. *Chicago Defender*, Jan. 11, 18, 1941; George Q. Flynn, "Selective Service and American Blacks during World War II," *Journal of Negro History* 69 (Winter 1984), 14–25; A. Philip Randolph, "Pro-Japanese Activities among Negroes," *The Black Worker* (Sept. 1942), 4; *Chicago Defender*, Jan. 16, 1943; Roi Ottley, *New World A'Coming* (New York, 1943), 327–43; U.S. Selective Service System, *Special Groups* (Washington, D.C., 1953), vol. I, 51; Lester Granger in *Opportunity* 21 (April 1943), 2.

7. *Pittsburgh Courier*, Aug. 18, 1942; George Martin, "Why Ask 'Are Negro Americans Loyal?'" *Southern Frontier* 2 (Feb. 1942), 2–3; Louis Martin, "Fifth Column among Negroes," *Opportunity* 20 (Dec. 1942), 358–59; Finkle, *Forum for Protest*, 150–54; Redding, "A Negro Looks at War"; J. A. Rogers column, *Pittsburgh Courier*, July 4, 1942; *Militant*, June 19, 1943.

8. Joseph D. Bibb, "We Gain by War," *Pittsburgh Courier*, Oct. 10, 1942; *New York Amsterdam News*, March 20, 1943; *New York Age*, Nov. 7, 1942; *Baltimore Afro-American*, Nov. 7, 1942; Earl Brown column in *New York Amsterdam News*, Jan. 8, 1944; George Schuyler, "A Long War Will Aid the Negro," *Crisis* 50 (Nov. 1943), 328–29; *Crisis* 49 (Aug. 1942), 264–65; *Crisis* 50 (Sept. 1943), 268. Also see Bureau of Intelligence, Office of Facts and Figures, "Survey of Intelligence Materials No. 14," March 16, 1942, and "Special Intelligence Report No. 38," May 22, 1942, RG 44, National Archives.

9. *Pittsburgh Courier*, Jan. 31, Aug. 8, 1942, Feb. 27, 1943, and June 10, 1944; Rogers column and George Rouzeau column, *Pittsburgh Courier*, July 4, 1942, Jan. 1, 1944; Finkle, *Forum for Protest*, 9–10, 60; Johnson, *To Stem This Tide*, 105; V. V. Oak, "What of the Negro Press?" *Saturday Review of Literature* 26 (March 6, 1943), 45–46; Alain Locke, "The Unfinished Business of Democracy," and Edwin R. Embree, "Negroes and the Commonweal," *Survey Graphic* 31 (Nov. 1942), 455–59, 491–94; St. Clair Drake and Horace Cayton, *Black Metropolis: A Study of Negro Life in a Northern City*, 2nd ed. (New York, 1962), 748; Albert Parker column, *Militant*, April 4, 1942; "Negro Morale," *Crisis* 49 (April 1942), 111; Washburn, *A Question of Sedition*, 98, 131–32; "Publishers at the White House," *Michigan Chronicle*, Feb. 19, 1944.

10. Office of Facts and Figures, "The Negro Looks at the War," 1942, RG 44, National Archives; Morris Milgram to Walter White, Dec. 1, 1942, NAACP Papers, Library of Congress; *Pittsburgh Courier*, Oct. 17, 1942, Jan. 2, 23, April 24, July 10, 1943; *California Eagle*, July 15, 1943; *Chicago Defender*, July 3, 1943; Garfinkel, *When Negroes March*, 134–38; Paula F. Pfeffer, *A. Philip Randolph, Pioneer of the Civil Rights Movement* (Baton Rouge, 1990), 80–83.

11. Ellen Tarry, *The Third Door: The Autobiography of an American Negro Woman* (New York, 1955), 193; Rayford Logan, ed., *What the Negro Wants* (Chapel Hill, N.C., 1944), esp. 148; Eight Point Program of March-on-Washington Movement and Relationship of NAACP to March-on-Washington Movement, in Board of Directors' minutes, Sept. 14, 1942, and A. Philip Randolph and Rev. Dr. Allan Knight Chalmers to Roy Wilkins, Feb. 29, 1944, NAACP Papers; Adam Clayton Powell Jr., *Marching Blacks* (New York, 1945), 159. Louis Kesselman, *The Social Politics of FEPC: A Study in*

Reform Pressure Movements (Chapel Hill, N.C., 1948), 222, describes Randolph during the war as a "political butterfly," flitting from one cause to another but never staying long enough to accomplish his goals.

12. George M. Hauser, *Erasing the Color Line* (New York, 1945); Bayard Rustin, "The Negro and Non-Violence," in *Down the Line: The Collected Writings of Bayard Rustin* (Chicago, 1971), 8–12; Helen Buckler, "The CORE Way," *Survey Graphic* 35 (Feb. 1946), 2; August Meier and Elliot Rudwick, *CORE: A Study in the Civil Rights Movement, 1942–1968* (New York, 1973), 20–39, and "The Origins of Nonviolent Direct Action in Afro-American Protest," in *Along the Color Line: Explorations in the Black Experience* (Urbana, Ill., 1976), 347–50.

13. Marjorie McKenzie column, *Pittsburgh Courier*, July 25, 1942; Dorothy Autrey, "The National Association for the Advancement of Colored People in Alabama, 1913–1952" (Ph.D. diss., University of Notre Dame, 1985), chap. 10; Charles M. Payne, *I've Got the Light of Freedom: The Organizing Tradition and the Mississippi Freedom Struggle* (Berkeley, Calif., 1995), 90; David R. Colburn, *Racial Change and Community Crisis: St. Augustine, Florida, 1877–1980* (New York, 1985), 8, 22; Earl Lewis, *In Their Own Interests: Race, Class, and Power in Twentieth-Century Norfolk, Virginia* (Berkeley, Calif., 1991), 188; Thurgood Marshall to Roy Wilkins, Oct. 28, 1947, Marshall File, NAACP Papers; Mark V. Tushnet, *The NAACP's Legal Strategy against Segregated Education, 1925–1950* (Chapel Hill, N.C., 1987), esp. 107–9; George B. Tindall, *The Emergence of the New South, 1913–1945* (Baton Rouge, 1967), 565; "NAACP Not Backing Rent Hike Protests," *Baltimore Afro-American,* Oct. 17, 1942; I. A. Newby, *Black Carolinians: A History of Blacks in South Carolina from 1865 to 1968* (Columbia, S.C., 1973), 277–78.

14. Forrester Washington, "A Functional Analysis of the National Urban League and Its Affiliates," November 1943, National Urban League Papers, Library of Congress; Jesse Thomas Moore Jr., *A Search for Equality: The National Urban League, 1910–1961* (University Park, Pa., 1981), 153–54; Michael K. Honey, *Southern Labor and Black Civil Rights: Organizing Memphis Workers* (Urbana, Ill., 1993), 205; "Report on Memphis," Nov. 18, 1943, National Urban League Papers.

15. David M. Tucker, *Lieutenant Lee of Beale Street* (Nashville, 1971), 127–33; Finkle, *Forum for Protest*, 65; *Norfolk Journal and Guide*, July 4, 1942, Feb. 12, 1944; Gunnar Myrdal, *An American Dilemma: The Negro Problem and Modern Democracy* (New York, 1944), 729–32, 768–74, 917–21; Sheldon B. Avery, "Up from Washington: William Pickens and the Negro Struggle for Equality, 1900–1954" (Ph.D. diss., University of Oregon, 1970), 243–46; Julius E. Thompson, *The Black Press in Mississippi, 1865–1985* (Gainesville, Fla., 1993), 23–39, quote at 38.

16. Newby, *Black Carolinians*, 277–80; Stephen O'Neill, "From the Shadow of Slavery: The Civil Rights Years in Charleston" (Ph.D. diss., University of Virginia, 1994), 74; "The Negroes' Role in the War," Surveys Division, Bureau of Special Services, Office of War Information, July 18, 1943, RG 44, National Archives.

17. Kenneth Williams, "Mississippi and Civil Rights, 1945–1954" (Ph.D. diss., Mississippi State University, 1985), 18, 34–36; Chester Himes, "All God's Chillun Got Pride," *Crisis* (June 1944), 188; Haskell Cohen, "Mello Like a Cello," *Negro Digest* 1 (Aug. 1943), 7; Lewis, *In Their Own Interests*, 192; Joseph Burran, "Racial Violence in the South during World War II" (Ph.D. diss., University of Tennessee, 1977), 2, 11–13, 200; O'Neill, "From the Shadow of Slavery," 71–72, 82, 125; Resolution, July 1950, Board of Directors, NAACP Papers. The best analysis of the inhibiting consequences of white domination on black thought and behavior at this time remains Richard Wright, *Black Boy* (New York, 1937), esp. 65–71, 150–57, 160–61. Also see Hortense Powdermaker, "The Channeling of Negro Aggression by the Cultural Process," *American Journal of Sociology* 48 (May 1943), 750–58.

18. Jessie Daniel Ames to Gordon Hancock, April 7, July 24, 1942, and Virginius Dabney to Alfred Dasheill, Aug. 4, 1942, Virginius Dabney Papers, University of Virginia; Jacquelyn Dowd Hall, *Revolt against Chivalry: Jessie Daniel Ames and the Women's Campaign against Lynching* (New York, 1979), 256–60; *Southern Frontier* 4 (Aug. 1943), 3; Raymond Gavins, *The Perils and Prospects of Southern Black Leadership: Gordon Blaine Hancock, 1884–1970* (Durham, N.C., 1977), 117–19; Benjamin Mays, *Born to Rebel* (New York, 1971), 218.

19. Morton Sosna, *In Search of the Silent South: Southern Liberals and the Race Issue* (New York, 1977), 7–9, 105–20, 166; Myrdal, *An American Dilemma*, 466–73; Virginius Dabney, "Nearer and Nearer the Precipice," *Atlantic Monthly* 171 (Jan. 1943), 94–100, and "The South Marches On," *Survey Graphic* 32 (Nov. 1943), 441–43; John Temple Graves, *The Fighting South* (New York, 1943), 120; Johnson, *To Stem This Tide*, 140–42. Also see Walter White, "Decline of Southern Liberals," *Negro Digest* 1 (Jan. 1943), 43; and Lillian E. Smith, "Buying a New World with Old Confederate Bills," *South Today* 7 (Autumn–Winter 1942–1943), 7–30.

20. *Southern Frontier* 4 (Aug. 1943), 3; "Southern Regional Council," *Monthly Summary of Events and Trends in Race Relations* 1 (Aug. 1943), 38–39; Charles S. Johnson et al., *Into the Mainstream* (Chapel Hill, N.C., 1947), 5–11; Virginius Dabney to Guy B. Johnson, April 28, 1945, and Guy B. Johnson to Virginius Dabney, May 8, 1945, Southern Regional Council Papers, Atlanta University; Lillian Smith, "Southern Defensive-II," *Common*

Ground 4 (Spring 1944), 43–45; Guy B. Johnson, "Southern Offensive," ibid. (Summer 1944), 87–93.

21. Randall L. Patton, "The Popular Front Alternative: Clark H. Foreman and the Southern Conference for Human Welfare, 1938–1948," in John C. Inscoe, ed., *Georgia in Black and White: Explorations in the Race Relations of a Southern State, 1865–1950* (Athens, Ga., 1994), 230–35; Lillian Smith to James Dombrowski, May 19, 1942, and Tarleton Collier to Clark Foreman, June 12, 1942, Southern Conference for Human Welfare Papers, Atlanta University; Sosna, *In Search of the Silent South*, 93, 103.

22. Lucy Randolph Mason to Frank Dorsey, July 16, 1943, Lucy Randolph Mason to Philip Murray, Oct. 30, 1944, and E. L. Sandefur to Lucy Randolph Mason, May 29, 1945, CIO Organizing Committee Papers (New York, 1981), series 5–1; Clark Foreman to Philip Murray, Nov. 16, 1944, and James Dombrowski to Durward McDaniel, March 21, 1945, SCHW Papers; Clark Foreman Oral History, Southern Historical Collection, University of North Carolina–Chapel Hill, 55; Honey, *Southern Labor and Black Civil Rights*, 212, 219; Michael Honey, "Black Workers Remember, Industrial Unionism in the Era of Jim Crow," in Gary M. Fink and Merl E. Reed, eds., *Race, Class, and Community in Southern Labor History* (Tuscaloosa, 1994), 134; Michael Honey, "Industrial Unionism and Racial Justice in Memphis," Rick Halpern, "Interracial Unionism in the Southwest: Fort Worth's Packinghouse Workers, 1937–1954," and Judith Stein, "Southern Workers in National Unions: Birmingham Steelworkers, 1936–1951," in Robert H. Zieger, ed., *Organized Labor in the Twentieth-Century South* (Knoxville, 1991), 144–52, 168–69, 198–99, 208; Jack Stieber, *Governing the UAW* (New York, 1962), 124–25; Robert J. Norrell, "Caste in Steel: Jim Crow Careers in Birmingham, Alabama," *Journal of American History* 73 (Dec. 1986), 669–94; Stetson Kennedy, "Total Equality and How to Get It," *Common Ground* 6 (Winter 1946), 63; John Glen, *Highlander: No Ordinary School, 1932–1962* (Lexington, 1988); Robert F. Martin, *Howard Kester and the Struggle for Social Justice in the South* (Charlottesville, 1991), 104–77, 124–28. The extent to which the CIO fought for racial equality during the war is now a matter of significant historical dispute; for the more positive view see Bruce Nelson, *Workers on the Waterfront: Seamen, Longshoremen, and Unionism in the 1930s* (Urbana, Ill., 1988), esp. 259, and "Organized Labor and the Struggle for Black Equality in Mobile during World War II," *Journal of American History* 80 (Dec. 1993), 952–88; Robert R. Korstad, "Daybreak of Freedom, Tobacco Workers and the CIO, Winston-Salem, North Carolina, 1943–1950" (Ph.D. diss., University of North Carolina–Chapel Hill, 1987); and Robert Korstad and Nelson Lichtenstein, "Opportunities Found

and Lost: Labor, Radicals, and the Early Civil Rights Movement," *Journal of American History* 75 (Dec. 1988), 786–811.

23. Columns by J. A. Rogers and Horace Cayton, *Pittsburgh Courier*, April 11, 25, 1942; *Daily Worker*, June 8, 14, 16, 18, 1942, April 12, May 22, July 18, 1943, June 27, 1944; Ben Davis, *The Negro People and the Communist Party* (New York, 1943); Ben Davis, "The Army Tackles Jim Crow," *New Masses* 55 (April 1945), 15–16; Gerald Horne, *Black Liberation/Red Scare: Ben Davis and the Communist Party* (Newark, Del., 1994), 143; Mark Naison, *Communists in Harlem during the Depression* (Urbana, Ill., 1983), 313–14; John Williamson, *Dangerous Scot: The Life and Work of an American "Undesirable"* (New York, 1969), 147.

24. *Negro Quarterly, A Review of Negro Life and Culture* 1 (Spring 1942), 21–32, (Fall 1942), 197–206, (Winter 1943), 295–302; Earl Browder in *Sunday Worker*, March 4, 1945; James W. Ford, *The War and the Negro People* (New York, 1942); Pettis Perry, *The Negro Stake in This War* (San Francisco, 1942); Maurice Isserman, *Which Side Were You On? The American Communist Party during the Second World War* (Middleton, 1982), 141–43; Kelley, *Hammer and Hoe*, 220–22; Art Preis column, *Militant*, Oct. 3, 1942; *Daily Worker*, June 22, 1943; "Have the Communists Quit Fighting for Negro Rights?" *Negro Digest* 2 (Dec. 1944); *People's Voice*, March 17, 1945.

25. Rumors and incidents of racial violence are reported in "Racial Tension Files," Fair Employment Practices Committee, RG 228, and "Reports on Recent Factors Increasing Negro-White Tension," Special Services Division, Bureau of Intelligence, Office of War Information, RG 44, National Archives; Howard Odum, *Race and Rumors of Race* (Chapel Hill, N.C., 1943), esp. 96–101, 113–28; "Cities, North and South: A Reconnaissance Survey of Race Relations," *Monthly Summary of Events and Trends in Race Relations* 1 (Oct. 1943), 11–12; Gloria Brown-Melton, "Blacks in Memphis, Tennessee, 1920–1955: A Historical Study" (Ph.D. diss., Washington State University, 1982), 201–17; Dolores Janiewski, *Sisterhood Denied: Race, Gender, and Class in a New South Community* (Philadelphia, 1985), 141; Clifford M. Kuhn, Harlon B. Joye, and E. Bernard West, *Living Atlanta: An Oral History of the City, 1914–1948* (Athens, Ga., 1990), 77–82. The most sophisticated argument interpreting black violence or antisocial behavior as direct black challenges to racist practices is Robin D. G. Kelley, *Race Rebels: Culture, Politics, and the Black Working Class* (New York, 1994), 35–75.

26. Burran, "Racial Violence in the South during World War II," 129–60; Ulysses Lee, *The Employment of Negro Troops* (Washington, D.C., 1966), 348–79; "Negroes in the Armed Forces," *New Republic* 109 (Oct. 18, 1943), 542–44; "The Pattern of Race Riots Involving Negro Soldiers," *Monthly Summary of Events and Trends in Race Relations* 1 (Aug. 1943),

8–9, 2 (Aug.–Sept. 1944), 1–2; Florence Murray, *Negro Handbook, 1946–1947* (New York, 1947), 347–56; "Violence against Negro Military Personnel" and "Reports—Racial Tension," Civilian Aide to the Secretary of War, Records of the Office of the Secretary of War, RG 107, National Archives; "What the Soldier Thinks," No. 2, Aug. 1943, 14–15, 58–59, War Department, Special Services Division, Research Branch, RG 330, National Archives; Samuel A. Stouffer et al., *The American Soldier, I, Adjustment during Army Life* (Princeton, N.J., 1949), 502–6, 525–26, 587–89. The range of responses to discrimination in the military, and their causes, is portrayed in Charles Fuller, *A Soldier's Play* (New York, 1982), later made into the film *A Soldier's Story*.

27. *Monthly Summary of Events and Trends in Race Relations* 1 (Nov. 1943), 22, and (Jan. 1944), 22; Adam Clayton Powell Jr., "A Big Stride Forward," *Spotlight* 2 (April 1944), 3; William Hastie, "Negro Officers in Two World Wars," *Journal of Negro Education* 12 (Summer 1943), 316–22; *Chicago Defender*, Dec. 2, 1944; *Norfolk Journal and Guide*, Oct. 21, 1944; *Pittsburgh Courier*, March 10, 1945; *Baltimore Afro-American*, March 31, 1945; P. L. Prattis column, *Pittsburgh Courier*, March 31, 1945; *People's Voice*, March 31, 1945.

28. Meier and Rudwick, *Along the Color Line*, 224–37; "Summary of a Report on the Race Riots in the Alabama Dry Dock Shipbuilding Company Yards in Mobile, Alabama," June 25, 1943, National Urban League Papers; *Chicago Defender* and *Pittsburgh Courier*, June, 5, 26, July 17, Aug. 14, 21, 1943; *Crisis* 50 (July 1943), 199.

29. Dominic J. Capeci Jr., *The Harlem Riot of 1943* (Philadelphia, 1977); *New York Age* and *New York Amsterdam News*, Aug. 7, 1943; *Pittsburgh Courier*, Aug. 14, 1943; Adam Clayton Powell Sr., *Riots and Ruins* (New York, 1945), 45–46; Charles V. Hamilton, *Adam Clayton Powell, Jr.: The Political Biography of an American Dilemma* (New York, 1991), 105, 148, 153; *People's Voice*, Aug. 7, 14, 1943; Powell, *Marching Blacks*, 171–72; *New York PM*, Aug. 3, 1943.

30. Stuart Cosgrove, "The Zoot-Suit and Style Warfare," *History Workshop Journal* 18 (Autumn 1984), 78–80; Bruce Tyler, "Black Jive and White Repression," *Journal of Ethnic Studies* 16, no. 4 (1989), 32–38; Langston Hughes and S. I. Hayakawa columns and editorial, *Chicago Defender*, June 19, 1943; Powell, *Riots and Ruins*, 36, 87; Albert Libby, "The Vanguarders," *Common Ground* 6 (Summer 1946), 83–87.

31. William J. Norton, "The Detroit Riots—and After," *Survey Graphic* 32 (Aug. 1943), 317–18; *Pittsburgh Courier*, Oct. 9, 1943; "Federal, State, and City Action" and "Programs of Action on the Democratic Front," *Monthly Summary of Events and Trends in Race Relations* 1 (Aug. 1943), 15, 34, and

2 (Aug. 1944), 1–2; Robert C. Weaver, "Whither Northern Race Relations Committees?" *Phylon* 5 (Third Quarter, 1944), 205–18.

32. Alfred B. Lewis, "Reducing Racial Tensions," *Opportunity* 21 (Oct. 1943), 157; Edwin R. Embree, "Balance Sheet in Race Relations," *Atlantic Monthly* 175 (May 1945), 87–91; "To Minimize Racial Conflicts: Committees to Work on Human Relationships," *American Century* 60 (Jan. 1945), 80; Winifred Raushenbush, "How to Prevent Race Riots," *American Mercury* 57 (Sept. 1943), 302–9.

33. James Boyd, "Strategy for Negroes," *Nation* 156 (June 26, 1943), 884–87; Harvard Sitkoff, *A New Deal for Blacks: The Emergence of Civil Rights as a National Issue: The Depression Decade* (New York, 1978); Meier and Rudwick, *Along the Color Line*, 307–404, esp. 313–62.

34. Minutes of the NAACP Board of Directors, Dec. 14, 1943, Dec. 9, 1944, Roy Wilkins to Rev. E. S. Hardge, Dec. 19, 1944, and Wilkins to Walter White, Dec. 29, 1944, NAACP Papers; *Baltimore Afro-American*, Nov. 17, 1944. From 1948 to 1953 the American Jewish Congress and NAACP collaborated on a joint annual report, *Civil Rights in the United States: A Balance Sheet of Group Relations.*

35. Myrdal, *An American Dilemma*, esp. 520, 625–27, 771, 834–53.

36. Jones, *Blues People*, 180; *Baltimore Afro-American*, Jan. 22, 1944; *Chicago Defender* and *Pittsburgh Courier*, Jan. 29, 1944; David W. Southern, *Gunnar Myrdal and Black-White Relations: The Use and Abuse of An American Dilemma, 1944–1969* (Baton Rouge, 1987), esp. chaps. 3, 4, and 9; Walter A. Jackson, *Gunnar Myrdal and America's Conscience, Social Engineering and Racial Liberalism, 1938–1987* (Chapel Hill, N.C., 1990), 245–52, 272–94.

37. Logan, ed., *What the Negro Wants*, 330, 65, 92, 193, 116, 129, 124, 28, 11, 336–38, 341–42, 151, 242–43, 274.

38. Ibid., 197, 210, 77, 340, 9, 249, 151–52, 187, 15–17, 129, 162, 148, 210–11, 61–62, 106, 344, 304–5, 256, 185–87.

39. Ibid., 233–37, 242, 273–74, 280, 76–77, 334, 305. Although even the Logan and Myrdal books proved too much for southern whites like W. T. Couch, a founder of the SCHW, this does not in and of itself make them examples of racial militancy.

Willkie as Liberal

Civil Liberties and Civil Rights

*In 1991 I accepted an invitation from Indiana University to partic-
ipate in a celebration of the one hundredth anniversary of Wendell
Willkie's birth. My earlier work on the 1930s and 1940s had left me
intrigued by this midwestern Republican's involvement in civil rights
matters. Now I had a reason to do further research on how and why he
became a fighter for, and symbol of, racial justice and brotherhood two
decades ahead of most of his contemporaries. Willkie linked the black
freedom struggle at home to the struggles against colonialism and imperialism abroad, prodded Hollywood filmmakers to present less biased
portrayals of African Americans, and worked closely with the National
Association for the Advancement of Colored People in trying to secure
civil rights legislation. After Willkie's death, the NAACP renamed the
building in which it was headquartered the Wendell Willkie Memorial Building. I include this essay in the collection because the histo-
riographic pendulum, these days, has swung all the way to the doings
of ordinary people at the local level. It should come as no surprise that
after generations of historians have dwelled so extensively on leaders
that a new revisionist cohort would overcompensate and tip the balance
too far. I keep hoping that, whenever germane, we study both the powerless and those who have wielded power, and the consequences they
have wrought. "Willkie as Liberal: Civil Liberties & Civil Rights" first
appeared in* Wendell Willkie, Hoosier Internationalist, *ed. James H.
Madison (Bloomington: Indiana University Press, 1992), 71–87, and
is reprinted by permission.*

There is little agreement among historians and biographers of Wendell Willkie as to why he became one of the most ardent, outspoken

champions of civil rights and civil liberties of his era. Some attribute his concern for the underdog to the influence of his mother, Henrietta Trisch Willkie, the first woman admitted to the Indiana bar and a fiercely independent battler for her beliefs. Some stress the importance of his father, Herman, Elwood's legal defender of the controversial and unorthodox, a lover of justice and pro-Bryan Democrat who had once joined the Socialist Party. And some see the roots of his later beliefs in the youthful experiences of a second-generation American acutely aware of the difficulties faced by minorities in a conformist society. Others see the genesis of the mature Willkie's views in his early idolization of Robert M. La Follette Sr. or enthusiasm for Wilsonian liberalism. Still others explain his highly unconventional defense of unpopular causes as a manifestation of Willkie's guilt over his extraordinary financial success as a corporate attorney or as an indication of a maverick, volatile personality courting political suicide. Contrarily, some describe his tireless promotion of racial equality during the Second World War as political expediency, a deliberate bid to woo African American voters. What some term intellectual growth, the emerging conviction that the defeat of the Axis and the creation of a just and lasting peace required ending racial imperialism at home as well as abroad, others see as psychological need, a gadfly desperate to irritate the complacent, to sting the conservatives of both major political parties.

Whatever the cause, however, none doubt that Wendell Willkie became a passionate exponent of freedom, justice, and democracy. More than any other presidential contender in his time, the rumpled Hoosier dramatically decried prejudice and intolerance. In an unmistakable Indiana twang, Willkie eloquently restated the American creed, sounding the call of equal rights and equal opportunities for all. Some two decades ahead of most of the American people and their political representatives, Willkie openly sided with African Americans in their struggle against discrimination.

Growing up in Elwood, Indiana, a town that had no African American residents but might well have had a sign proclaiming "Nigger, don't let the sun go down on you here," the young Willkie had little opportunity to exhibit signs of racial liberalism. Later, as a student at Indiana University, Willkie devoted most of his political energies to espousing Wilsonian ideals of international cooperation.

The first indication of his pronounced opposition to bigotry did not come until he was a successful lawyer in his early thirties. In 1924 he attended the Democratic National Convention as a delegate from Akron, Ohio, in order, he claimed, "to put the Democratic party on record against the Ku Klux Klan." The following year he played a prominent role in opposing the KKK in Akron politics.[1] As an ambitious business attorney, however, Willkie never sought to represent minorities or unpopular causes, and when he gained fame and fortune as the head of Commonwealth and Southern during the 1930s, Willkie never decried the widespread discrimination against African Americans in the public utilities industry.[2]

Similarly, the hero of Wall Street, the frequent critic of President Franklin D. Roosevelt for the New Deal's excessive spending and concentration of too much power in Washington, only belatedly and gradually became a vocal defender of civil liberties. Following Commonwealth and Southern's victory over the Tennessee Valley Authority and Willkie's first cover story in *Time* as the kind of liberal nonpolitician that the nation needed, he lashed out against the House Un-American Activities Committee (HUAC) in an address to the alumni of Columbia University in November 1939. Known as the Dies committee after its chair, Martin Dies of Texas, HUAC had been established in 1938; its sensationalized public hearings quickly became a forum for wild allegations of communist influence and control, particularly against liberals in the labor movement and in New Deal agencies. Willkie was especially disturbed by the abuses of due process and of the First Amendment in congressional investigations, by their scapegoating tactics and casual charges of conspiracy, and by their use of exposure simply for the sake of exposure. He specifically attacked legislative investigations in which witnesses were without the protection of counsel and denied the right to rebut charges or cross-examine their accusers. Willkie concluded his speech with a sharp critique of the Dies committee's employment of innuendo and inference in publicity to destroy reputations.[3]

Willkie repeated these charges in a March 1940 article in the *New Republic*. Entitled "Fair Trial," the article called for "equal treatment for all under law." It condemned punishing people for their political opinions, asserting that Eugene Debs had been indicted under the Espionage Act and Huey Long had been hounded by the Internal Revenue Service because political authorities wanted them out of the way. In like manner, Willkie wrote, the German-American Bund leader Fritz Kuhn and the communist Earl Browder were now being denied due process because of their political beliefs. "Equal treatment under the law means exactly what it says," Willkie asserted, "whether the man before the tribunal is a crook, a Democrat, a Republican, a Communist, or a businessman; whether he is rich or poor, white or black, good or bad. You cannot have a democracy on any other basis. Those who truly believe in the protection of civil liberties," he continued, "will wonder whether Browder was sentenced to four years in jail and a $2,000 fine because he made a false statement on a passport application or because he was a Communist party member." Articulating a theme he would frequently repeat in the next four years, Willkie proclaimed: "It is well to remember that any man who denies justice to someone he hates prepares the way for a denial of justice to someone he loves."[4]

Following his nomination for the presidency by the Republican Party in 1940, the former utility tycoon exhibited more passion in his defense of civil liberties and the rights of African Americans. Stung by the label affixed to him by Harold Ickes—"the simple, barefoot Wall Street lawyer"—and by Alice Roosevelt Longworth's taunt that his nomination "comes right from the grass roots of every country club in America," Willkie courted the support of prominent civil libertarians and civil rights leaders. With much fanfare he rejected the support of Father Charles Coughlin and the endorsement "of anybody else who stands for any form of prejudice as to anybody's race or religion. I don't have to be President of the United States," he added, "but I do have to live with myself." Still, wanting very much to be president, Willkie made a major effort to recapture the votes of the many African Americans who had deserted the GOP and switched to the Democratic Party with the coming of the New Deal. He understood that he would have to work especially hard to win the support of African Americans who had been directly assisted by the New Deal's relief programs and had come to admire, even love, the president and first lady.[5]

"There is no man more opposed to racial discrimination," Willkie told a group of African American reporters at the Republican nominating convention in Philadelphia. "If I am elected president I will seek to remove all kinds of discrimination from all kinds of groups." He claimed proudly that the Republicans had invited a larger number of African American delegates to the convention than ever before and that they had written into the party platform the strongest civil rights plank in the nation's history, vigorously endorsing federal anti-lynching legislation and protection of the African American's right to vote and pledging that "discrimination in the civil service, army, navy, and all other branches of the government must cease." Going even further, Willkie also promised to end racial discrimination in the nation's capital.[6] Willkie's appeals to African Americans during the campaign earned him the support of the two largest Negro newspapers, the *Pittsburgh Courier* and *Baltimore Afro-American*, and forced President Roosevelt to reassure civil rights leaders of his concern in order to stop a mass defection of black voters to the GOP. In a series of announcements shortly before the election the president promoted an African American colonel to the rank of brigadier general, appointed a prominent NAACP attorney as a special aide to the secretary of war, created the new post of Negro adviser to the director of selective service, and vowed that African Americans would be fully included in the armed forces and in defense employment. These moves enabled Roosevelt to retain the lion's share of the African American vote in 1940 and convinced Willkie of the necessity to continue fighting for civil rights. The combination of political expediency and conviction led him to announce after his defeat that he would continue his battle for racial equality, civil rights, and the brotherhood of man.[7]

In 1941 Willkie plunged into the role of constructive critic of the Roosevelt administration and titular leader of the Republicans, especially those GOP liberals struggling to wrest the party away from its reactionaries. Despite denunciations from those such as conservative Republican congressman Dewey Short of Missouri, who labeled him "Wee Windy War Willkie," a "bellowing, blatant, bellicose, belligerent, bombastic, bombinating, blowhard," the burly Hoosier railed against the forces of isolationism and intolerance. When a special subcommittee of the Senate Committee on Interstate Commerce launched an investigation of "war propaganda disseminated by the motion picture industry," Willkie agreed to serve as counsel for the Hollywood studio heads. With the same flair for dramatizing an issue and for gaining favorable publicity that he had shown in the fight against the TVA, Willkie went on the offensive, insisting on the movie industry's right of free speech. He demolished the charges of Democratic isolationist Bennett Champ Clark and Republican firebrands Gerald Nye and Burton Wheeler that Hollywood was "warmongering" and campaigning for aid to Great Britain, and converted the issue from propaganda for war to freedom from federal censorship. Following the collapse of the hearings, Willkie became chairman of the board of Twentieth-Century Fox and used that office to plead that the film industry "break the accepted Hollywood stereotype of the Negro as a buffoon, a servant, or a minstrel."[8]

As the United States drew closer to war, moreover, Willkie stepped up his attacks on the bigots in the Republican Party. He accused Charles Lindbergh and his followers of anti-Semitism, insisting in September 1941 that if "the American people permit race prejudice to arise at this crucial moment, they little deserve to preserve democracy."[9] In November he became a member of the American Bar Association's Committee on the Bill of Rights, and shortly after, in a speech to the National Conference of Christians and Jews, he pledged to lead the fight against intolerance: "In the courtroom and from the public rostrum, I will fight for the preservation of civil liberties, no matter how unpopular the cause may be in any given instance."[10]

True to his vow but against the urgings of his closest political advisers, who feared adverse consequences, Willkie agreed to act as counsel for a Communist Party official in California, William Schneiderman, who was fighting the revocation of his naturalized citizenship. Two lower federal courts had already concurred with the 1939 decision of the Immigration and Naturalization Service of the Department of Labor that Schneiderman's citizenship should be revoked, and the announcement that Willkie would handle the communist's appeal to the Supreme Court was front-page news and an affront to many Republicans. Nevertheless, in a letter to his friend Bartley Crum, Willkie wrote, "I am sure I am right in representing Schneiderman. Of all the times when civil liberties should be defended, it is now."[11] He later recalled:

I saw myself as the man involved in the case. . . . While I did not agree with his views, he was entitled to them and to a fair trial under our system, and to the safeguards of our constitution. He had arrived in this predicament by a series of accidents of life. I had started as he had from pretty much the same point of thinking. My series of personal accidents had taken me down an opposite road. They might well have been different, and if they had I might now be in his predicament and in such event I would have wanted the type of representation and advocacy that satisfied me.[12]

Willkie pleaded Schneiderman's case before the Supreme Court in November 1942, shortly after returning from his trip around the world, and at a rehearing the following March. The government contended that the Russian-born Schneiderman had concealed his membership in the Communist Party when he applied for citizenship in 1927 and that because the party then "believed in, advocated, and taught the overthrow of this government by force and violence," Schneiderman had failed to meet the requirement of the Naturalization Act passed by Congress in 1906 that an applicant for citizenship must believe in "the principles of the Constitution." Willkie countered that the individual liberty of an American citizen, and not the Communist Party, was on trial, and claimed that the lower court decisions constituted "a drastic abridgement of freedom of political belief and thought." He asked the justices, "Am I to be held responsible for everything Ham Fish says?" emphasizing that the principles of a political party were not fully accepted by all of its members. In addition, quoting Jefferson and Lincoln, Willkie stated that these founders of the Democratic and Republican parties had been more forceful than even Karl Marx in advocating the use of violence when other methods failed. Five justices accepted Willkie's argument. Ruling in Schneiderman's favor, the Supreme Court repudiated the idea of guilt by association. The burden of proof, it affirmed, must be on the government to show that an individual personally advocated illegal doctrines. "Under our traditions," Justice Frank Murphy wrote for the Court majority, "beliefs are personal and not a matter of mere association. Men in adhering to a political party or other organization notoriously do not subscribe to all of its platforms or asserted principles." In addition, Murphy opined, "There is a material difference between agitation and exhortation calling for present violent action which creates a clear and present danger of public disorder . . . and mere doctrinal justification or prediction of the use of force under hypothetical conditions at some indefinite future time." The Schneiderman decision would later be used to stop the government's efforts to deport various radicals and communists, including Harry Bridges, the Australian-born head of the West Coast leftist longshoremen's union. A grateful Bridges told reporters that "Wendell Willkie was the only man in America who has proved that he would rather be right than be President." Conversely, Republican Paul Shafer of Michigan castigated Willkie on the floor of the House of Representatives for doing more to aid the communists than he did for the GOP.[13]

Indeed, conservatives in both major parties considered Willkie's activities and pronouncements in 1942 anathema. His blunt assaults on bigotry and slashing attacks on colonialism at home and abroad provoked their mounting enmity. Yet Willkie stuck to his principles. He defended all Americans of alien descent, asserting that the nation's strength came from its myriad "races, colors and creeds" and that "no American has the right to impugn the patriotism of any other American because of the accident of his birth or race or religion." Alluding to the forced removal of Japanese Americans from the West Coast, Willkie announced: "I have no trust and faith in any extra-judicial proceedings under which any group will be deprived of their rights, under guise of war emergency." "It is the right of every citizen in America," he frequently told reporters, "to be treated by other citizens as an equal. Our liberties are the equal rights of every citizen."[14] Again and again he urged his followers to guard against, and to act against, prejudice. "We cannot allow whispers about Jews, or Catholics, or Negroes, or any other groups, to spread through our ranks. We cannot, above all, allow whispers, rumors, slanders and the like, to cause us to ACT against our fellow citizens."[15] To rebut a *Saturday Evening Post* article by Milton Mayer that Willkie considered a "flagellation of the Jews," he wrote "The Case for the Minorities" for the same magazine. He decried the revival "of age-old racial and religious distrusts" and the demagogic scapegoating of minorities. He denounced discrimination in industry and labor and described being "appalled at the callous indifference of high officers of the Navy to the obvious and undemocratic discrimination against Negroes." And movingly he warned of the dangers of a wartime "period that is psychologically susceptible to witch-hanging and mob-baiting. And each of us, if not alert, may find himself the unconscious carrier of the germ that will destroy our freedom. For each of us has within himself the inheritance of age-long hatreds, of racial and religious differences, and everyone has a tendency to find the cause for his own failures in some conspiracy of evil."[16]

For his "unstinting devotion to the cause of democracy, freedom, oppressed minorities, tolerance and better understanding in America," Willkie received the American Hebrew Medal for 1942. He used the occasion to proselytize for democratic equality rather than "tolerance." "No man has the right in America to treat any other man 'tolerantly,' for 'tolerance' is the assumption of superiority. Our liberties are the equal rights of every citizen." As never before, moreover, Willkie in 1942 wholly identified himself with the African American struggle against racial discrimination and for equal opportunities. Particularly incensed by the "discrimination and the mistreatment" African Americans suffered in the armed forces, Willkie enlisted in their "fight for the right to fight." "They should have the right of every citizen to fight for his country," Willkie forthrightly declared, "in any branch of her armed forces without discrimination."[17] In an address to Freedom House in March he recalled the heroism of Dorrie Miller, a black mess attendant, during the attack on Pearl Harbor and lamented that Miller "cannot enlist in the United States Navy, and only for the reason that he was born with a black skin." Angrily, Willkie called upon his audience to "correct this injustice . . . which makes a mockery of all our fine words."[18] In part because of his pronounced support for the African American "Double V" campaign—victory over the Axis abroad and over Jim Crow at home—some of the barriers against blacks in the military were breached during the Second World War.

Willkie and his African American allies would have less success, although not for want of trying, in diminishing Hollywood's stereotyping of blacks as superstitious buffoons or primitive barbarians, as docile slaves or ignorant servants incapable of anything but the most menial tasks. Willkie's concern that the motion picture industry exhibit greater racial sensitivity deepened as his relationship with Walter White blossomed. Favoring Roosevelt in 1940, the executive secretary of the National Association for the Advancement of Colored People (NAACP) had spurned Willkie's entreaties for a meeting during the campaign. Shortly after the defeat, however, the two accidentally met at a dinner at New York's Waldorf-Astoria and quickly began what White would later describe as one of "the closest and richest friendships of my life." They visited one another frequently, talked incessantly about the varieties of racial oppression, and, usually over their double scotches, mapped strategies to upgrade the status of African Americans. Appointed a special counsel to the NAACP, Willkie joined White in Hollywood in 1941 to discuss with studio executives their derogatory treatment of African Americans in movies. Gaining little but vague promises, the two returned to Hollywood the following year. They pleaded with industry leaders to depict "the Negro as a normal human being and an integral part of human life and activity," and pointed out the offensiveness of racial stereotyping and the harm it did to the war effort. In a fiery, uncompromising speech to a largely Jewish group of film directors and producers, Willkie reminded them "that they should be the last to be guilty of doing to another minority what has been done to them." The two continued their campaign for better screen roles for blacks at the Writers' Congress in Los Angeles in 1943. That year, such films as *Casablanca* and *The Ox-Bow Incident* included a more favorable depiction of blacks than before. "But with the tragedy of Willkie's death in 1944," White recorded in his memoirs, "most of those responsible in Hollywood for changing the pattern appeared to feel that the pressure upon them had been removed." The "new concept of the Negro" that Willkie and White had pressed for did not materialize.[19]

The Hollywood campaign was but one of the many battles for civil rights that Willkie fought during the war. For him, racism had become a national dilemma, a hindrance to U.S. foreign and military policies. "It is becoming apparent to thoughtful Americans that we cannot fight the forces of imperialism abroad and maintain a form of imperialism at home," he thundered to an audience at the NAACP's annual conference in 1942. Nevertheless, he continued, we practice "race imperialism" every day. "The attitude of white citizens toward the Negroes has undeniably had some of the unlovely and tragic characteristics of an alien imperialism—a smug racial superiority, a willingness to exploit an unprotected people. Our very proclamations of what we are fighting for have rendered our own inequities self-evident. When we talk of freedom and opportunity for all nations, the increasing paradoxes in our own society become so clear they can no longer be ignored."[20]

Willkie reiterated this call to end the internal colonization of African Americans in greater detail in "Our Imperialism at Home," a chapter in his best-selling and widely condensed and digested *One World* (1943). Relating how often Arabs and Asians asked him about race relations in the United States, Willkie warned of the adverse consequences that result from mistreatment of African Americans. "We cannot be on one side abroad and the other at home," he wrote; if we are to demand the British liberation of India we must "make all who live in America free." Challenging Americans to end their racism, Willkie insisted that hundreds of millions of nonwhites around the globe will be judging us on the basis of our racial practices and that the future peace and security of the nation require a cessation of "race imperialism" within the United States.[21]

Legitimized by such expressions, and by similar ones from such prominent whites as Eleanor Roosevelt and Vice President Henry Wallace, civil rights leaders and their organizations forcefully demanded equality on the battlefront and on the home front. Unlike their counterparts during World War I, few African American leaders in the Second World War asked blacks to close ranks and ignore their grievances until the war ended. Rather, the very dependency of the government on the loyalty and cooperation of African Americans intensified their insistence on "Democracy in Our Time!" And the more African Americans saw racial barriers begin to be toppled, the more militantly they pressed for the total and speedy dismantling of the entire Jim Crow system. The explosive combination of accelerating African American expectations of change and the slow pace of actual racial progress clashed head-on in 1943 with the equally explosive fear and anger of whites throughout the United States to "keep the niggers in their place." An epidemic of racial conflict resulted: hate strikes against the hiring of black workers, pitched battles between young gangs of whites and blacks, interracial violence at military bases and training camps, and some 200 battles between the races in forty-seven cities.

Willkie responded by redoubling his public pronouncements against racial discrimination. Ever more outspokenly he chastised both Republicans and Democrats for their equivocation on civil rights issues. He lambasted Roosevelt for kowtowing to white supremacists in the Democratic Party, and he excoriated his fellow Republicans for reneging their heritage. Urging the GOP to reclaim the legacy of Lincoln, Willkie explicitly advocated that the Republicans endorse broadened federal powers to ensure equal voting, equal employment, and equal educational rights for African Americans. Nothing less, he added, would bring blacks back to the Republican fold. "The very fact that the Republican party was the instrumentality through which the Negroes were given freedom," Willkie asserted, "makes them more resentful that it should join in acts which prevent them from obtaining the substance of freedom."[22]

Whatever his political calculations, Willkie agreed almost instantly to Walter White's request that he appear on a special coast-to-coast radio program opposing racial violence. Like most other Americans, Willkie had been shocked by the race riot in Detroit in June 1943, the worst such bloodletting in the nation's history. Detroit's riot toll included 34 persons killed, more than 700 injured, over $2 million in property losses, and 100 million man-hours lost in war production. For Willkie, a new day had dawned in racial affairs and the nation could not just return to business as usual. On July 21 he broadcast "An Open Letter to the American People." He had said much of it before, but never with such conviction or to so many millions of bewildered Americans.

Willkie began by surveying the scope of nationwide racial violence, emphasizing that the many instances should not be viewed as singular cases but as a profoundly dangerous national phenomenon, and an even greater threat to America's security in the world. "Two-thirds of the people who are our Allies do not have white skins. And they do have long, hurtful memories of the white man's superior attitude in his dealings with them. Today, the white man is professing friendship and a desire to cooperate and is promising opportunity in the world to come when the war is over. . . . Race riots in Detroit do not reassure them." He enumerated the civil rights to which the African American is entitled—equal protection of, and under, the law; equal opportunity of education; equal opportunity to work and the same pay for the same job; no poll tax; the right "to fight for his country in any branch of her armed services"—and insisted that "we must see to it that he gets them." Willkie again criticized both political parties for failing to secure civil rights legislation: "One party cannot go on fooling itself that it has no further obligation to the Negro citizen because Lincoln freed the slave, and the other is not entitled to power if it sanctions and practices one set of principles in Atlanta and another in Harlem." Willkie ended by relating fascism to racial prejudice: "Such an attitude within our own borders is as serious a threat to freedom as is the attack without. The desire to deprive some of our citizens of their rights . . . has the same basic motivation as actuates the Fascist mind when it seeks to dominate whole peoples and nations. It is essential that we eliminate it at home as well as abroad."[23]

In *Look* magazine several months later, Willkie termed civil rights the most important issue facing the United States. He reminded readers that "while democratic government rests on majority rule, the essence of freedom is the protection of minorities. . . . Now, above all times, we must make these principles a reality, because the whole world is watching us. Only if we can make individual liberty a reality among Americans, can we hope to gain adherents to our cause among other peoples." And, with an eye on the political campaigns to come in 1944, Willkie concluded: "We must not protect these rights fitfully, inconsistently and with political purposes, as has the present administration."[24]

Whether Willkie gained political advantage from his pronouncements on civil rights is problematic. Walter White, both to encourage Willkie to continue advocating a platform almost identical to the NAACP's and to put pressure on the Democrats to do more for civil rights, kept insisting that Willkie was cutting into FDR's popularity with African Americans and would garner a lion's share of the African American vote against Roosevelt. At the same time an autumn poll in the *Pittsburgh Courier* indicated that nearly 85 percent of black voters favored Willkie as the next year's Republican candidate for the presidency. A quite different political message came from the pollster Elmo Roper, however, who warned that Willkie's handling of the race issue was political dynamite and that voters would reject him for being too aggressively concerned about the plight of African Americans.[25]

Shunned by congressional Republicans and most of the GOP's local leadership, Willkie ran a distant fourth in the Wisconsin primary, the first test of his political popularity in 1944, and withdrew from the nominating race. Adding insult to injury, the Republicans then declined to invite the shaggy-haired Hoosier to address the convention, to testify before the platform committee, even to be seated as a delegate. Freed from whatever confines political ambition or party leadership had imposed, Willkie continued to espouse advanced positions on racial equality, on the need to save the Jewish people of Europe, and on the importance of safeguarding the civil liberties of all Americans.

His last political will and testament came in a series of five articles written in June to affect the party platforms, his own model platform, and two postmortems on the inadequacies of the platforms adopted by the Democrats and the Republicans, published as *An American Program* the day before he died in October. No memorial could have been more fitting. The boy from Elwood, which had a reputation among African Americans as "the home of racial prejudice," the onetime symbol of big business conservatism, ended as a political prophet clamoring that racism was the crisis of American democracy. "I write," Willkie proclaimed in the first of the articles devoted wholly to the issue of civil rights, "with the deliberate intent of helping to arouse a public opinion that will require these candidates to put aside generalities, evasions and pious platitudes and deal in concise, concrete terms with this human, this national, this world problem." Like nothing before, alleged Willkie, the war has spotlighted the injustice in America's racial attitudes and actions and "has made us conscious of the contradictions between our treatment of our Negro minority and the ideals for which we are fighting." If blacks are dying to protect liberty they must have the right to live and enjoy liberty. They "have learned that there is nothing more democratic than a bullet or a splinter of steel. They want now to see some political democracy as well." They deserve, and are entitled to, the same rights as other Americans. "The Constitution does not provide for first and second class citizens." African Americans should have an equal chance for economic advancement, an equal share of public services and funds, an equal opportunity to acquire an education of equal quality as given to other citizens, and an equal right to fight for their country in any branch of the armed services, as well as federal protection against mob violence, lynching, and state requirements that effectively disfranchise blacks.[26]

Accordingly, Willkie judged both party platforms in 1944 "tragically inadequate." He blamed the Democrats for surrendering to "the old-line 'white supremacy' bloc of Southern Democrats" and accused the liberal Dr. Jekylls of political expediency in yielding to the reactionary Mr. Hydes on the key political issue of our time. "To call the section on the Negro a plank is a misnomer," he quoted an NAACP declaration. "It is best characterized as a splinter . . . a mouse of evasion." The Republican platform was just a bit better. It specified such problems as lynching, discrimination in the armed forces, and poll taxes that prevent African Americans from voting, but instead of pledging to enact federal remedies—"which constitute the only practical method by which the Negro's rights can be assured him"—the GOP repeated "the old states rights argument and a narrow interpretation of federal power." It had "a magnificent chance to state in modern terms a code of practice that would make real the very principle of freedom upon which the party was founded." Instead, it proposed a grab bag of congressional inquiry, inadequate state law, and a time-consuming, difficult, and unnecessary constitutional amendment that combined still failed to ensure justice to blacks.[27]

In the blunt, muscular phrases so characteristic of the hearty Willkie, he asserted, in the final words penned before he suffered a coronary thrombosis, that the "Negro lives in our midst under discriminations which differ from the racial discrimination practiced by our enemies, the Nazis, only in that ours are illegal and that we are free— if we wish—to fight against them." Restating the major theme of his racial pronouncements since the start of the war, Willkie emphasized the "repercussions all around the world that result from our treatment at home of our colored citizens. . . . We cannot be on one side abroad and the other at home." Making real the promise of democracy for African Americans "will be the test of our sincerity and of our moral leadership in the eyes of hundreds of millions all over the world."[28]

The black press mourned him as the "nation's number one patriot," the African American's "foremost champion."[29] The NAACP and several other civil rights and civil liberties organizations that had received most of the proceeds from *One World* jointly moved into better quarters in Manhattan after the war, naming it the Wendell Willkie Memorial Building. And at his grave site in Rushville, Indiana, the granite open tablet quoting Willkie's words concludes: "We must establish beyond any doubt the equality of men."

Notes

1. Joseph Barnes, *Wendell Willkie* (New York, 1952), 37–38; Ellsworth Barnard, *Wendell Willkie: Fighter for Freedom* (Marquette, Mich., 1966), 66–67.

2. Bishop R. R. Wright Jr., "No Hope for the Race in Willkie Candidacy," *Norfolk Journal and Guide*, October 26, 1940.

3. Barnes, *Wendell Willkie*, 164; Barnard, *Wendell Willkie*, 147.

4. Wendell Willkie, "Fair Trial," *New Republic*, March 18, 1940, 370–72.

5. *New York Times*, August 28, 1940.

6. *Pittsburgh Courier*, July 4 and October 12, 1940.

7. *New York Times*, November 12, 1940.

8. Clayton R. Koppes and Gregory D. Black, *Hollywood Goes to War* (New York, 1987), 18, 42–45, 86–87.

9. *New York Times*, September 14, 1941.

10. Samuel Walker, *In Defense of American Liberties* (New York, 1990), 136.

11. Barnes, *Wendell Willkie*, 321.

12. Carol King, "The Willkie I Knew," *New Masses*, October 24, 1944, 10–11.

13. Barnes, *Wendell Willkie*, 323–24; *United States v. Schneiderman*, 320 U.S. 118 (1943).

14. *New York Times*, January 29 and June 14, 1942.

15. Wendell Willkie, "Address to National Conference of Christians and Jews," February 7, 1942, Speeches Material, Wendell Willkie Papers, Library of Congress, Washington, D.C.

16. Wendell Willkie, "The Case for the Minorities," *Saturday Evening Post*, June 27, 1942, 14 ff.

17. Steve Neal, *Dark Horse: A Biography of Wendell Willkie* (Garden City, N.Y., 1984), 272; Barnes, *Wendell Willkie*, 326–27; *Baltimore Afro-American*, April 15, 1942.

18. Wendell Willkie, "Address at Freedom House," March 19, 1942, Speeches Material, Willkie Papers, Library of Congress.

19. Walter White, *A Man Called White* (New York, 1948), 199–202; *Pittsburgh Courier*, August 8, 1942; Barnard, *Wendell Willkie*, 338.

20. Wendell Willkie, "Address to National Association for the Advancement of Colored People," July 19, 1942, Speeches Material, Willkie Papers, Library of Congress.

21. Wendell Willkie, *One World* (New York, 1943), esp. 14–19, 91, 181–82.

22. Neal, *Dark Horse*, 274.

23. Wendell Willkie, "An Open Letter to the American People," July 21, 1943, Speeches Material, Willkie Papers, Library of Congress.

24. Interview in *Look*, October 5, 1943. Also see Wendell Willkie, "Address to National Association for the Advancement of Colored People," May 26, 1944, Speeches Material, Willkie Papers, Library of Congress.

25. Neal, *Dark Horse*, 276.

26. Wendell Willkie, *An American Program* (New York, 1944), 7–8, 48–49, 58. Also see Wendell Willkie, "Citizens of Negro Blood," *Collier's*, October 7, 1944, 11 ff.

27. Willkie, *An American Program*, 5–8, 33, 39, 58.

28. Ibid., 48–49.

29. *Chicago Defender*, October 14, 1944; *Pittsburgh Courier*, October 14, 1944.

African Americans, American Jews, and the Holocaust

One of several essays written by historians for a volume to honor our mentor William Leuchtenburg, "African Americans, American Jews, and the Holocaust" is my last published essay on the Second World War. Stimulated by the rancor surrounding the debate on most everything about the black-Jewish coalition, I sought to explicate how leaders shaped by different historical and personal experiences could make common cause. I aimed to explain how diverse groups could work together in an organizational alliance, despite the prejudice of their followers. We are, at least in part, what we experience. Hence this essay may very well reflect the failures I encountered as a white man in the late 1960s seeking a job teaching black history, the denunciations I received from black writers for daring to support William Styron's right to interpret slave life as he saw fit, the extent to which I have abandoned the Judaism of my father, the shame occasioned by outbreaks of Jewish racism, the hurt I experienced as a Jew when anti-Semitism became rife among some elements in the civil rights movement, and other phenomena I'm just dimly aware of. Writing this also gave me the opportunity to add further variations on the themes of what stimulated hopefulness, how civil rights emerged as a national issue, the relationship between national organizations and the grassroots struggle, and what brought African American and Jewish American groups together to make a struggle for racial equality possible and, eventually, successful. Yet the past is not our favorite tense. However much historians claim we need to know it to avoid repeating its mistakes, as James Baldwin reminds us, "if people did learn from history, history would be very different." Civil rights history overall, and the relationship of Jews and African Ameri-

cans in the movement in particular, remains contested terrain. I hope this essay continues to stir the pot and maybe even helps prevent another mistake. "African Americans, American Jews, and the Holocaust" originally appeared in The Achievement of American Liberalism: The New Deal and Its Legacies, *ed.* William Chafe *(New York: Columbia University Press, 2003), 181–203, and is reprinted by permission.*

African Americans and Jewish Americans have together journeyed a long, twisted path of enmities and empathies. Jews who currently oppose black goals as well as those who bemoan the dissolution of the civil rights alliance each have their antecedents to emulate, much as anti-Semitic African Americans and blacks who decry such prejudice each have their precedents to employ. Their joint, disjointed history points in no single direction. Today the media trumpet the views of African Americans praising Adolf Hitler or those claiming for themselves a greater victimization than that suffered by Jews during what we now call the Holocaust.[*] Today Jews loudly condemn blacks for trivializing the Holocaust, for not recognizing its uniqueness. Little is heard of the 1930s and 1940s, a time when there was more black anti-Semitism and more Jewish racism among the mass of blacks and Jews than there is now, yet when leaders of both communities, despite being shaped by different historical and personal experiences, sought to make common cause against the common enemy of intolerance and hatred. Both saw themselves as objects of persecution and each other as means to ends. As opportunistic as they were dissimilar, they developed an organizational alliance to achieve acceptance and equality of opportunity in American society.[1]

Nazi and fascist anti-Semitism in the 1930s, and especially the horrors of the Holocaust, proved central to that development and the coming-of-age of the modern civil rights movement. Jews became more sensitive to cries of injustice, more ready for alliances with other underdogs. News of the Holocaust also made some other Amer-

---

[*]I use the term *Holocaust* to signify the systematic extermination of some 6 million European Jews by the Nazi regime. The use of the term by some to refer to other examples of genocide, to other tragedies, to ecological disasters, even to personal psychological pain, has led numerous Jews, and others, to prefer the Hebrew word *Shoah*. I do too, but since most readers are more familiar with *Holocaust*, that is the term used in this essay for the specific Nazi effort to annihilate European Jewry.

icans uneasy or guilty about their own racist beliefs and practices. And all the condemnations of Hitlerism by American government officials and shapers of public opinion, all the Allied talk of fighting a war against doctrines of racial superiority, fueled the righteous insistence of African Americans to end racism in the United States. African American leaders, particularly in the National Association for the Advancement of Colored People (NAACP), used Hitlerism and the Holocaust to generate concern for the plight of blacks and support for the cause of civil rights. They repeatedly pointed to what was happening to European Jewry as a means of advancing their own domestic agenda. They established an analogy between racial practices in Nazi Germany and those in the Jim Crow South to clarify and dramatize the nature of American racism to their fellow Americans. By linking the odious Nazism with Jim Crowism, these African Americans sought to make racial discrimination and segregation similarly anathema and to convince the white majority of the justness of their cause.[2]

Benito Mussolini helped them considerably. Regarding Africans as "inferior beings" and seeing himself as defending "western civilization against the colored races," Il Duce's forces attacked Ethiopia in October 1935, slaughtering defenseless children and women in the country many African Americans regarded as the "Black Zion." Mussolini then issued a Manifesto of Fascist Racism declaring theories of racial equality "absolutely inadmissible," branding the so-called Semitic and Hamitic (i.e., black) races as inherently inferior, and insisting that the purity of the blood of the superior white race not be polluted by miscegenation with blacks or Jews. The Italian Ministry for Africa claimed proudly: "Italy is the first European nation to uphold the universal principle of the superiority of the white race."[3]

If not quite first, Hitler and the Nazis went even further to avoid "racial contamination" by inferiors. Coming to power in 1933, they used the power of the state and their own paramilitary organizations to assault German Jews, boycott their businesses, and discriminate against them. The Law for the Protection of German Blood and Honor and the Third Reich Citizenship Law (the Nuremberg Laws of September 1935) defined Jews by ancestry rather than religion, outlawed marriage and sexual intercourse between Jews and non-Jews, stripped Jews of most rights of German citizenship, and increased earlier restrictions on Jews in all spheres of German educational, social, and economic life. The Nazi government also established an Office for Racial Policy to see that the master race of Aryans was not contaminated by racial inferiors and, on November 9–10, 1938, unleashed *Kristallnacht* (Night of the Broken Glass), a pogrom of arson, destruction, and looting against Jews.

Still worse followed. On the heels of the invasion of the Soviet Union in 1941, Hitler authorized the creation of *Einsatzgruppen* (special mobile units) to accompany the German army and execute Jews. By year's end, they had systematically murdered more than half a million "racial inferiors" in occupied Russia. By then, as well, the Nazis had begun to experiment at Chelmno in Poland with mass executions carried out by means of gas. In January 1942 Nazi officials met at Lake Wannsee, near Berlin, to coordinate the *Endlosung*, the "Final Solution of the Jewish Question." The gassing of prisoners at Auschwitz-Birkenau, Belzec, Majdanek, Sobibor, and Treblinka now became a round-the-clock phenomenon, murdering more than 3 million people, mostly Jews. Not till the approach of the Soviet armies from the east did the Nazis abandon their Polish "death camps" and march the surviving Jewish, Gypsy, Jehovah's Witness, Serb, homosexual, and other "antisocial" prisoners to concentration camps in Germany, where millions more died of disease, exposure, and starvation en route to and in Bergen-Belsen, Buchenwald, Dachau, Mauthausen, Nordhausen, and Sachsenhausen. It was the ultimate triumph of racism in practice.[4]

African American newspapers had begun highlighting the similarities of discrimination and oppression in the United States and in Germany as soon as Hitler and the Nazis began their harassment of German Jewry. Most of their editorials prior to 1936, however, were not at all sympathetic to the plight of German Jewry. The Great Depression engendered enormous anti-Semitism in the United States—by whites and blacks. Well over a hundred new anti-Semitic organizations were established in the second half of the 1930s alone, compared to just fourteen between 1915 and 1933. Indeed, throughout the 1930s and the Second World War, most Americans were neither deeply touched nor troubled by the news about Jews coming out of Europe. A majority believed Nazi persecution of the German Jews was either partly or entirely the Jews' own fault—their being too powerful, their running the economy, their being too radical. Few considered the plight of European Jewry their plight too. Until May 1945 many remained unaware, did not care, or thought the killing of European Jews a Jewish problem for Jews to solve.

Most African Americans, accepting the dominant culture's values and prejudices concerning Jews, followed suit. An amalgam of religious folk beliefs and economic woes compounded their antipathy. Like many Germans and white Christian Americans, many blacks viewed Jews as infidels, usurers, Christ killers. Moreover, to the average African American tenant the Jew was the landlord; to the black worker he was the boss; to the black customer the Jew was the shopkeeper; and to the black domestic the Jew was the stingy woman whose house she cleaned. Still others condemned Jewish organizations in the United States for being blind to American racism, resented the attention paid to German Jewry while the plight of African Americans went ignored, and feared that a focus on anti-Semitism drew energy away from the struggle against Jim Crow. Anti-Semitism also allowed African Americans to give vent to pent-up hostilities and indulge a sense of imaginary superiority.

Given such widespread sentiments, most African American newspapers initially expressed little sympathy for German Jewry. Typically, the *Philadelphia Tribune* warned its readers that "most of what is told about Jewish treatment in Germany is propaganda since the Jews control to a great extent the international press" and opined that to "be a Jew in Germany is hell," but "to be a Negro in America is twice as bad." The *New York Age* added: "If the Jewish merchants in Germany treated German workers as Blumsteins treat the people of Harlem, then Hitler is right." In September 1933, W. E. B. DuBois responded with what he called "unholy glee" to the treatment of Jews by his beloved Germans: "When the only 'inferior' peoples were 'niggers' it was hard to get the attention of *The New York Times* for little matters of race, lynching and mobs. But now that the damned included the owner of the *Times*, moral indignation is perking up."[5]

The Black Nationalist "don't buy where you can't work" campaigns, popular in the early 1930s, were most often explicitly anti-Semitic. Marcus Garvey and Carlos Cooks, the leaders of the Neo-Garveyite African Nationalist Pioneer Movement, blamed the Jews, as lovers of money, for their own persecution. Sufi Abdul Hamid (labeled "a black

Hitler" by Adam Clayton Powell Jr.) became a regular fixture on Har-lem street corners in the 1930s, fulminating against Jewish merchants and employers while sporting a Nazi-like uniform. The Negro tabloid *Dynamite* declared: "What America needs is a Hitler and what the Chicago Black Belt needs is a purge of the exploiting Jew." In Balti-more, at an African American forum on Germany's treatment of the Jews, the audience burst into applause when a speaker praised Hitler's actions. And when Harlemites rioted in 1935 and then again in 1943, Jewish merchants were the chief target of their wrath.[6]

Indeed, much of the black press initially put the onus of Nazism on the Jews themselves, claimed that German Jewry suffered less than African Americans, argued against aiding Hitler's victims since Jews did not assist blacks, and, most emphatically, emphasized the hypoc-risy of those denouncing Germany's treatment of Jews but not the oppression of blacks in the United States. Because Jews would not hire Negroes in their stores, opined the *Baltimore Afro-American*, in those stores "you will find Hitlerism in its most blatant form exer-cised by those who are being Hitlerized in Germany." American Jews, wrote the *St. Louis Argus*, use "the same tactics and methods to persecute and discriminate against Negroes" that Hitler uses against German Jews. "Why shed crocodile tears over the fate of the Jews in Berlin when here in America we treat black folk in the same manner every day?" the *Oklahoma City Black Dispatch* asked. "Why the com-parison is so definite and clear," it added, "we are almost wont to feel Germans secured the pattern of Nazi violence visited upon the Jews from white America."

The *Cincinnati Union* had no doubt that in segregating Jews Ger-many was "taking a leaf from the book of many American cities." Complaining that African Americans had to endure greater persecu-tion "under American Hitlers," the *Amsterdam News* sneered at those rallying to save Europe's Jews "while Negroes were lynched, beaten and burned." "Just how we can charge and snort about Fascism abroad and practice it here" disgusted the *Des Moines, Iowa, Bystander*. The *Louisiana Weekly* insisted that, given the racism in the United States, Germany had "a right to look askance at any criticism leveled at its persecution of unfavored people." "We're tired of reading our favorite dailies and their editorials about Hitler and his Nazis," the *New York Age* chimed in: "It's about time that the papers stayed out of the inter-

nal affairs of other nations and that they help the United States first
sweep its own doors clean." All too commonly in the 1930s, Chandler
Owen summed up, Negroes could be heard saying, "well, Hitler did
one good thing: he put these Jews in their place."[7]

Commonly, African American writers and public figures, like the
Black Nationalist J. A. Rogers and the scholarly Kelly Miller, reiterated these views in newspaper column after column. So did conservative George Schuyler. Traveling in Mississippi in 1935, Schuyler
found "that Negroes of all classes from peons to planters are quite
unconcerned about either the spread of fascism or the fate of the Jews.
Indeed I am not at all exaggerating when I state that a surprising number of articulate Negroes seem to derive a sort of grim satisfaction
from the Nazi persecution of the Jews. They contend that their local
Jews have been indistinguishable from the 'crackers' in their attitude
toward Negroes. . . . They cannot see why, they contend, that under
the circumstances they should get excited about the fate of German
Jews."

Neither did Schuyler. He remained indignant that the American
press paid more attention to the persecution of German Jews than to
the lynchings of Negroes and wrote in the *Courier*: "I would be able
to wail a lot louder and deeper if American Jews would give more
concrete evidence of being touched by the plight of Negroes. . . . If
my Hebrew friends were only as quick to employ capable Negroes as
they are other people and did not get so excited when a decent family moves in their districts, I could pray even harder for Hitler to let
up on them."

Adam Clayton Powell Jr. concurred. He termed Jewish merchants
"the criminals of Harlem" and challenged "Jews to stop crying over
German Jews and get an anti-lynch law passed." In response to an
appeal from the Central Conference of American Rabbis for a "recon-
ciliation of the proverbial friendship of our two peoples," he retorted
that Negro anti-Semitism was regrettable, "but the Jew himself was
its author." And criticizing President Franklin Roosevelt's decision to
admit some additional Jewish refugees in 1938, Powell complained
that as soon as they "were off the boat most of them would settle in the
Bronx Alps" and take the jobs that Negroes deserved to have.[8]

Officials of the NAACP echoed such sentiments. Roy Wilkins
thought that Jews were paying too much attention to "exaggerated

charges of Nazi persecution and not enough to persecuted Negroes" and that the government was doing too much to help European Jews instead of African Americans. "Our sometimes friends," Wilkins said of Jews, "ask us to fight Nazism." But too many Jews, he continued, "never gave a dollar bill to fight lynching or break down prejudice in employment." Walter White, the NAACP's executive secretary, privately considered African American anti-Semitism "legitimate," a justified response to Jewish exploitation of and discrimination against blacks. He chided Jews for "doing to Negroes what they object to others doing to them." He denied the notion that the increasingly prosperous and prominent Jews were "in the same boat" as the poor, isolated Negroes. And he scorned those who protested against Hitlerism but failed to demand that the United States first end its own persecution of minorities.

As late as December 1948, in a letter to a friend, White reiterated that Jewish merchants cheat blacks, that Jewish-owned theaters segregate them, that Jews in Hollywood stereotype African Americans, and that Jews contribute charitably only to atone for their anti-Negro prejudices. White ended the letter with a reminder that he had been candid because the correspondence was private: "I would not want to say such things publicly."[9]

In all these views, a compound of ignorance and indifference sparked with anti-Semitism, African Americans mirrored the ruling sentiments dominant at the time. But, pointedly and publicly, White and other NAACP leaders expressed dramatically different views than those they held privately. Almost from the very start of Hitler's persecution of German Jews, when the association was virtually alone in the black community in supporting campaigns to boycott German goods and the 1936 Olympics in Berlin, the NAACP focused on the plight of the Jews as a way of drawing attention to racial practices in the American South. The "unholy glee" of DuBois lost out to the strategy enunciated in 1933 by William Pickens that the NAACP use a condemnation of Hitlerism to condemn Jim Crow, draw an analogy between the Ku Klux Klan and the Nazi Party, and demand of the American people whether or not they favor maintaining racial practices in the South just like Hitler's racist practices in Germany. Official NAACP resolutions and editorials in the NAACP's *Crisis* as early as mid-1933 denounced the vicious prejudice directed against

Jews by Hitler and equated Nazism with American racism, intending that those who abhorred the former would detest the latter. Pickens hoped that Americans would not favor maintaining racial practices at home that were just like Nazism. Thus, the strategy of the NAACP, according to Walter White, would be "to utilize the present and wise concern over anti-Semitism to call attention more vigorously than ever before to bigotry against the Negro here."[10]

Following this strategy, which most African American organizations and other minority groups did not find congenial, White trumpeted his "wholehearted contempt for, and condemnation of, the unspeakable terror now being inflicted upon the Jewish people in Germany by the sadistic Nazi government." Time and again he pointed to developments in Germany to fortify his case for abolishing racial discrimination in the United States. To arouse opposition to Jim Crow he emphasized the fundamental similarity between racial practices in both countries. He scorned the "counterpart of Hitlerism existing in the United States" and called upon all Americans, especially minorities, to fight fascism abroad and atrocities at home. "We Negroes know what this means since it has happened to us," White said of *Kristallnacht*, "what happens to one minority can happen to others—a lesson which Jews, Negroes, and all minorities must learn."

While frequently associating himself and the NAACP with those protesting Hitler's treatment of the Jews, White never ceased equating Nazi anti-Semitism with American racism, with demands that Americans "clean up our own backyard." When New York City Mayor LaGuardia called for a protest rally at Carnegie Hall to denounce Hitler's persecution of Jews, White telegraphed him about the upsurge of lynchings against blacks, expressing his hope that "you and other speakers will stress the need of simultaneous American action to wipe out bigotry or racial hatred no matter who are the victims nor where such bigotry and oppression exist, including our own country." He publicly mocked Senator William King of Utah for failing to support antilynching legislation while wanting the United States to sever relations with Germany to protest Nazi atrocities. And concerning the admission of Jewish refugees, White wrote to Secretary of State Cordell Hull that the NAACP shared the president's "reported indignation at the outrages being perpetrated upon minorities by the Nazi government. But we would be even more enthusiastic if our government could be equally indignant at the lynching, burning alive, and torture with blowtorches of American citizens by American mobs on American soil which have shamed America before the world for a much longer time than persecution under Adolf Hitler."[11]

Resolutions adopted at the NAACP annual conferences throughout the decade mirrored White's efforts to equate the oppression of Jews and African Americans. The association clearly sought to use events in Europe to change public attitudes in the United States. Nowhere was this more evident than in the articles and editorials of its monthly magazine *The Crisis*. Far more than most non-Jewish publications, *The Crisis* forthrightly expressed "profound and poignant sympathy" for the plight of European Jewry. It claimed that blacks felt that way more than most Americans because "they have known the same type of persecution ever since the beginning of America," because "Negroes are persecuted here in much the same manner that 'non-Aryans' are persecuted in Central Europe." Both are "segregated, humiliated, and terrorized." African American "feelings go out to the Jews. They know what Hitler means because they have known slave overseers, plantation riding bosses, high sheriffs."

To highlight the harms done by American racism, *The Crisis* spotlighted Nazi terrorism. "The only essential difference between a Nazi mob hunting down Jews in Central Europe and an American mob burning black men at the stake in Mississippi is that one is actually encouraged by its national government and the other is merely tolerated." It focused on the Nazi treatment of Jews to draw attention to racial discrimination in the United States. "Maybe some day we will see that until a Negro can freely study medicine at, say, the University of Michigan, we cannot make a convincing argument as to why Jews should be permitted to study at Heidelberg; or that until we stamp out the rope and the faggot as amusements for sections of our population, we cannot make a good case against the cruelties of Storm Troopers." And it emphasized the shared oppression of Jews and African Americans. "The tales of humiliation, terror and cruelty have a familiar ring to us. We know all about being driven off the streets, having our women kicked and beaten, being barred from public places, being at the mercy of hoodlums and bloodthirsty mobs, having 'scientists' prove us something less than human, being restricted in employment and residence, having separate schools set up for us, having our youth put on a quota basis in colleges and universities, and hearing and reading violent tirades against our race."[12]

To underscore the NAACP's strategy that minorities must "unite to fight the spread of Hitlerism," *The Crisis* published numerous articles in the 1930s by prominent American Jews. Most, like Rabbi Stephen S. Wise's reprinted address to the 1934 NAACP annual meeting, centered on the common plight of the two minorities. A series by Jacob J. Weinstein spelled out the need for the two to work together against discrimination and prejudice in the United States. And to illustrate that they had done just that in the past, another series featured rabbis who had championed the cause of freedom and citizenship for black slaves, Jewish abolitionists, and Jews who fought alongside John Brown in Kansas. It concluded: "Jews and Negroes, because they often face identical problems and because they embrace a common destiny as victims of prejudice and bigotry," should therefore stand together—"the struggle for racial equality is indivisible."

The Crisis also made the argument for an African American–Jewish American alliance by reprinting editorials from the Jewish press that called upon Jews to shed their racist prejudices and to fight with blacks for their common goals. In "We Must Stand Together," the *Jewish Frontier* acknowledged the need for African Americans to give voice to their own grievances while condemning German anti-Semitism and emphasized that Jews and blacks should struggle together against racial discrimination and bigotry. Likewise, *The Reconstructionist* proclaimed that now was the time for blacks to insist that the United States put its "own house in order and wipe out every last vestige of anti-Negro discrimination" and that "if the injustices inflicted upon Jews in Germany will arouse the conscience of America to do justice to the Negro racial minority, it will be some consolation to us Jews." *The Reconstructionist* editorial concluded: "Both self-interest and our holiest traditions demand our making common cause with the Negro in his fight for equality."[13]

Despite the widespread prejudices among the masses of both African Americans and American Jews toward one another, the Nazi persecution of German Jews forged, hesitantly, haltingly, a commonality of purpose between American black and Jewish leaders and opinion shapers. Each, to help their own cause, expressed condemnations of both German and American racism. Especially in New York City, which had large communities of blacks and Jews and was home to most of the major betterment and rights organizations of both groups, a common agenda began to emerge. The *American Hebrew* newspaper asked, "If Mussolini's fascism and Hitler's Nazism can join forces, why shouldn't their joint victims, Negroes and Jews ally to fight them?" And no less than the NAACP, National Urban League (NUL) director Lester Granger, and the league's journal *Opportunity* answered affirmatively for such an alliance to "erase the shadow of the Swastika from our land." Utilizing the same analogies and arguments as the NAACP, the NUL condemned Nazi actions against German Jews while emphasizing the similarity of oppression of Jews and African Americans. Never failing to remind its readers that racial prejudice was just as sordid and cruel when directed against Mississippi blacks as against German Jews, the league also condemned black anti-Semitism, urging African Americans to combat it wherever it appeared.[14]

So, gradually, did numerous other African American community leaders. Adam Clayton Powell Jr. was among those who shed earlier prejudices to associate his cause with those fighting anti-Semitism. He announced that the same psychology underlay prejudice against blacks and Jews and that Hitler's persecution of Jewry and the plight of African Americans were inextricably intertwined. And he called, often and loudly, for a black-Jewish alliance "to stop Fascism." Ralph Bunche similarly assailed black anti-Semitism while stressing that the problems of both Jews and African Americans, "their grievances and their fears are cut to a common pattern." Many followed in linking Hitler's actions with the need for Jews and blacks to, in William Pickens' phrase, "stand with unbroken ranks side by side."[15]

To underscore its necessity, as well as the similarity of persecutions, African Americans took to designating racism in the United States as just a variant of Hitlerism. The *Baltimore Afro-American* termed the white South and Nazi Germany as "mental brothers," the oppression of blacks as "American Nazism," and the exclusion of African Americans from a college as "Nazis at Williams." "From the way Hitler talks," it editorialized, "one would think he is a member of the Ku Klux Klan and a native of Alabama." Indeed, the *Afro-American* christened Hitler as the Imperial Wizard of the German Ku Klux

Klan, and columnist Kelly Miller termed him "the master Ku Kluxer of Germany."

Numerous editorial cartoons depicted Hitler as a Klansman and Klansmen as wearing swastikas. Nazis were transformed into "crackers," and southern racists into Nazis (different names, said the *Afro-American*, but the "same result"). In like manner, the *Amsterdam News* labeled the exclusion of blacks from the major leagues "Nazism in Baseball," racial segregation as "Nazism in America," and the refusal of the Daughters of the American Revolution to permit Marian Anderson to sing in Constitution Hall as "Nazism in Washington." Lynch mobs, added *The Crisis*, were storm troopers; terrorist attacks on Negroes who sought to vote in Brownsville, Tennessee, were the "work of Himmler's Gestapo"; and such terms as "Gestapo in Memphis," "the Himmler of the U.S.A.," and "Fuehrer Crump" were the way a *Crisis* writer referred to the police of Memphis, its police chief, and mayor.

Despite the continued estrangement between the mass of African Americans and the mass of American Jews, despite the disparity of their progress into the American mainstream, their mutual identification as victims of discrimination and oppression now began to hold sway. As Scottsboro lawyer Samuel Leibowitz exclaimed to a Harlem Elks' convention, in urging them to reject anti-Semitism: "Both of us, Negroes and Jews are in the same boat together."[10]

Once the war in Europe began, censorship in Germany and the lands it occupied, as well as its desire to keep its mass murder of Jews secret, brought a diminution in news of Nazi persecution in both the Negro press and the mainstream American press. But what was known, however fragmentary, piecemeal, caused some African American organizations and periodicals to increase their efforts to place the black struggle for justice and equality in an international context and to solidify the emerging leadership alliance of Jews and African Americans. *The Crisis*, especially, continued to employ the imagery of Nazism to call attention to American racism, to convince the white majority of the justness of the NAACP's reform cause. Segregation in the armed forces was "America's *Mein Kampf*," violence against black servicemen was Hitlerism or the work of "cracker Fascists," antiblack rioters in Detroit were referred to as "Nazi-minded mobsters," and almost without fail, Mississippi's white supremacist senators Bilbo and Eastland were labeled "America's Hitler and Goebbels." Similarly, the Urban League's *Opportunity* entitled an article on Governor Eugene Talmadge "A Georgia Hitler." More than a year after the war ended, *The Crisis* continued to describe the KKK as Nazis and to accuse it of trying to build "an American *Volkstaat*." The monthly kept labeling white supremacists as fascists or Nazis and described violence against African Americans as "Southern *Schrecklichkeit*."[17]

Knowing well the claim of the *Amsterdam News* in 1942 that "there never has been such general anti-Semitic sentiment in Harlem as exists right now," and the 1943 warning of the *Pittsburgh Courier* of "the dangerous and disastrous spread of anti-Semitism among Negroes," those African American leaders engaged in the wartime crusade for civil rights nevertheless sought to exorcise the prejudice of blacks against Jews. Describing anti-Semitism in the United States as "doing Hitler's work here at home," *The Crisis* observed that anti-Semitic actions in Boston and New York seemed "like something out of Berlin and Warsaw." The cause of each minority is the cause of all minorities, it continued, and "every beating of a Jewish child is an invitation to the lyncher of Negroes." At its 1944 annual conference, the NAACP adopted a resolution to combat anti-Semitism among Negroes.

Langston Hughes, Paul Robeson, and Adam Clayton Powell Jr. played leading roles in publicly allying African Americans and American Jews. Like Walter White, they asserted that anti-Semitism and racism are the same kinds of bigotry and that blacks indulging in anti-Semitism were playing Hitler's game. So too did the Urban League, which established volunteer Service Councils to better relations between blacks and Jews. "No Negro is secure from intolerance and race prejudice," summed up A. Philip Randolph at a Madison Square Garden rally of the March-on-Washington Movement, "as long as one Jew is a victim of anti-Semitism."[18]

Shortly after the United States entered the war, the NAACP Board of Directors pledged "its unqualified and unlimited effort on behalf of the persecuted Jews of the world, which includes anti-Semitism in the United States as well as slaughter in Poland." Little more was said or done for almost a year, until December 1942, when a delegation of representatives from major Jewish organizations submitted a memorandum to President Franklin Roosevelt on the deliberate, systematic annihilation of European Jewry. Using the information supplied by the World Jewish Congress, the American Jewish Congress (AJC) publicized news of the Holocaust and communicated hurriedly with the NAACP concerning it. As Rabbi Stephen Wise wrote to Walter White in mid-December, there will be no Jews left in Europe at the end of the war unless the NAACP "associate[s] itself with the action to prevent Hitler from accomplishing his purposes."

At its next meeting, the NAACP board adopted a resolution that it stood "appalled at the cold-blooded campaign of extermination of the Jews" and would do whatever it could to end this slaughter. White and other prominent African Americans joined with major labor, religious, and liberal spokesmen at various emergency conferences to save the Jews of Europe and associated themselves with appeals for action to stop the extermination of the Jews. They pledged "to do whatever we can to help rescue Jews from the clutches," knowing, as White wrote to the AJC, that "if Jews can be slaughtered today," Negroes will be tomorrow. And they contributed financially toward the relief of Jews overseas, knowing, in Lester Granger's words, its importance "as another means of building goodwill between American Negroes and their fellow-citizens of Jewish faith."[19]

As the Holocaust intensified the insecurity felt by African American and American Jewish leaders, both reached out to the other. Jewish publications featured articles by and about African Americans. Editorials in the Jewish press, like "Defend the Negro," sent by the Independent Jewish Press Service to all its subscriber newspapers, made the case for the civil rights of blacks. Numerous essayists stressed the commonality of African American and Jewish needs and goals, as did editorial cartoons, such as the *Jewish Survey*'s "Help Wanted—No Negroes, No Jews." That magazine similarly featured a picture of a Negro and a Jewish soldier, arms intertwined, in the battle against Nazism. In 1942, as well, the Central Conference of American Rabbis began to adopt annual resolutions deploring discrimination against blacks and promising support in the struggle for black equality. It issued a "Justice for Negroes" message calling upon Jews, "who ourselves have been victims of injustice," to combat African American inequities. American rabbis then inaugurated an annual "Race Relations Sabbath."

In the same spirit, the Bronx Rabbinic Council joined with the

National Council of Jewish Women to campaign for the fair treatment of Negro domestics. American Jewish Congress youth groups sponsored interracial forums and prepared petitions protesting racial discrimination. Numerous Jewish and black organizations featured speakers from the other race. Interracial Committees, Councils Against Intolerance in America, and Committees for Racial and Religious Understanding, largely composed of Jews and African Americans, became ubiquitous.[20]

For the first time, both black and Jewish leaders forthrightly endorsed what Louis Reddick called "the establishment of an all out alliance." W. H. Jernigan, national chairman of the Fraternal Council of Negro Churches, urged African Americans and Jews "to unite in a common cause against Hitlerism," striking hard and quickly against racial and religious discrimination. So did the editors of the *Jewish Forward* and the *Jewish Survey*, arguing that "both their fates were becoming inextricably intertwined," and they needed to overcome their mutual oppressors. Jointly discussing the mutual value of such an alliance, Rabbi Lou Silberman and Walter White agreed on the necessity of blacks and Jews pooling "our intelligence and idealism not only to defeat the Hitlers and the Rankins of the world, but to root out the prejudices from our own hearts." And in addresses to the NAACP, an American Jewish Congress officer described how the fate of Jews and African Americans "dovetailed," requiring that they work together to challenge their common oppressors.[21]

In 1944 the American Jewish Congress established a Commission on Community Interrelations, under social psychologist Kurt Lewin, to eliminate conflict between minority groups. It worked with the NAACP, as did the AJC's Commission on Law and Legislation (changed to Commission on Law and Social Action in November 1945). Headed by Will Maslow, the Commission on Law and Social Action combated discrimination in employment, education, and housing against blacks as well as Jews. By so doing, by seeking to promote civil rights for all minorities, Rabbi Wise wrote to the NAACP's Thurgood Marshall, the fight against anti-Semitism is bound up "with the fight for the status and rights of all minority groups in this country." The 1945 platform of the AJC, "Full Equality in a Free Society," promised Negroes "that in all the causes for which they struggle they can count upon finding the Jews and the American Jewish Congress on the side of justice." Morality and self-interest had intersected. A marriage of convenience, Will Maslow termed it: "It was in our interest to help them. We had the staff, the money and the political muscle to do it."[22]

Convinced that they had a common enemy in Nazism, both at home and abroad, the NAACP also forged bonds with the more conservative American Jewish Committee and Anti-Defamation League of B'nai B'rith. Previously concerned solely with anti-Semitism and the threat to Jews, such groups now redefined their mission to creating a more pluralistic and egalitarian society for all and reached out to work with the National Association of Colored Women, the National Council of Negro Women, the Urban League, and others. Together they promoted a liberal, reformist creed of equality. Believing that justice and social acceptance would come shortly after the war's end, they concentrated on appeals to conscience and on the political process, abjuring mass pressure tactics.

Leaders of both African American and Jewish institutions joined in testifying before legislative committees for antidiscrimination and anti-KKK laws, as well as for higher quotas for Jewish refugees. Along with other Jewish and black organizations they collaborated on celebrating diversity and inclusion, urging Hollywood to end degrading stereotypes, seeking to analyze and cure prejudice, mobilizing public opinion against intolerance, lobbying in favor of the creation of a Jewish state in Palestine, campaigning for civil rights legislation, especially a permanent Fair Employment Practices Committee, and challenging discrimination in the law. Well before the Supreme Court's *Brown* decision in 1954, every single major Jewish civic organization had filed friends of the court briefs in behalf of the NAACP's suit to end segregation in public education. This was the "democracy, liberalism, and freedom" that A. Philip Randolph lauded as the enemies of anti-Semitism and "the hopes of the Negro."[23]

The Holocaust had both frightened Jews and blacks into a defensive alliance and emboldened them to capitalize on the revulsion and guilt engendered by Nazism's horrors. The descriptions by Private John Stribling Jr. in the *Chicago Defender*, among many others, of the "horrible odor of burned human flesh," of "naked human bodies piled on top of each other," of "bodies dissected for human experimentation," of prisoners "blind, crippled, and half-insane, they could barely walk," brought increased sympathy for Jews and decreased "respectability" for racism. The shocking photographs and newsreels of corpses stacked like cordwood, of boxcars heaped with the bones of dead prisoners, of bulldozers shoving emaciated bodies into hastily dug ditches, of the barely alive liberated, living skeletons lying in their own filth, their vacant, sunken eyes staring through barbed wire, proved a turning point in racial attitudes.

The horror of what has occurred in its name demolishes the doctrine of racial superiority, wrote Ralph McGill in an *Atlanta Constitution* editorial; and the editor of the *Detroit Free Press*, after visiting the concentration camps, stated, "I found in the hell that once was Germany an indictment of my own beloved America." This view was elaborated upon by African American columnists throughout the year. Moreover, the theme of a common oppression made its way into the songs of African American composer William Grant Still, the fiction of Chester Himes, the scholarship of Oliver Cox. W. E. B. DuBois, whose *Souls of Black Folk* had contained numerous references to Jews as sly, dishonest, unscrupulous, omitted them in a postwar edition, admitting that he "did not realize until the horrible massacre of German Jews, how even unconscious repetition of current folklore such as the concept of Jews as more guilty of exploitation than others, had helped the Hitlers of the world."

The Holocaust, and all the depravity associated with it, had revealed the logical conclusion of prejudice, and many Jewish and African American commentators now made the "we're in the same boat" argument as justification for a civil rights alliance. "The barbaric excesses of Nazism have made it impossible to escape the full implications of racial and religious prejudice, no matter what its form" wrote Kenneth Clark: enlightened African Americans and Jews must pool their efforts to overcome prejudice and discrimination. Much as a letter to the editor of the *Norfolk Journal and Guide* had prophesied, or hoped, in 1934: "When history is written a hundred years from now, Adolf Hitler of Germany will be given credit for showing the world the absurdity of race prejudice." The "Final Solution" would ultimately lead to the demise of racism being socially acceptable, intellectually justified, or legally permissible.[24]

The magnitude of the Holocaust gave racial reformers a powerful weapon, one that became yet stronger as nonwhite nations raised the issue of race in international relations and the Soviet Union sought to exploit American racism for its own ends. Momentum for racial changes in the United States flowed from all the official condemnations of the Holocaust and official declarations in favor of nondiscrimination accompanying the creation of the United Nations and the United Nations Educational, Scientific, and Cultural Organization (UNESCO), from the establishment of the Commission on Human Rights and its special Subcommission on the Prevention of Discrimination and Protection of Minorities, and from the UN's adoption in 1948 of the Universal Declaration of Human Rights and the Convention on the Prevention and Punishment of the Crime of Genocide. The racial awareness catalyzed by the Holocaust along with the necessity of keeping the two-thirds of the world's peoples who were nonwhite out of the Soviet orbit pushed liberal cold warriors into openly condemning racial discrimination and segregation in the United States—a process that would eventually result in the legal ending of those practices.[25]

Eventually, but not quickly, not automatically. The course of civil rights in the United States was not all onward and upward, not an unbroken line of progress from barbarism and indifference to compassion and liberality. Bursts of reform and of reaction alternated. And in the end, the walls of segregation and disfranchisement would tumble only after African Americans mobilized massively for their own freedom. Much would be achieved, but hardly all that was required, before the black-Jewish civil rights coalition collapsed at the end of the 1960s. While benign neglect, in the main, characterized relations between African Americans and Jews thereafter, particularized instances of conflict often made headlines. Prominent Jews bade farewell to their former allies and embraced neoconservative policies on affirmative action, voting rights, and the welfare state; and a new generation of African American scholars and demagogues employed anti-Semitism as a weapon in the battle for who would speak for black America. Each often referred to the Holocaust, in one way or another, to make its case for victimization, as both anti-Semitism and racial prejudice proved more resilient and pervasive than liberal reformers had presumed.[26]

The only thing we learn from history, some like to say, is that we don't learn from history. Certainly the lessons once learned, the impulses generated, the notion that justice and self-interest need not be opposites, become easier to forget as the Holocaust recedes into the historical past. Who remembers Leon Bass? An African American in the 183rd Combat Engineer Battalion who helped bury the dead at Buchenwald, Bass consequently dedicated his remaining years to speaking out against anti-Semitism and racism. Or who remembers Paul Parks? A black draftee ordered to go into Dachau as part of a burial squad, a stunned Parks wandered by the still-warm ovens and emaciated bodies until he encountered a Jewish prisoner who spoke English. Why? Why the Jews? What did they do? Nothing, said the prisoner, nothing, they were killed just because they were Jews. "I understand that," Parks slowly responded, "I understand that because I've seen people lynched just because they were black." He returned from Europe determined to make his own country a better country, becoming one of Martin Luther King's negotiators in the struggle to end racial discrimination in the South and a key leader in the effort to desegregate the public schools of Boston. Who recalls Paul Cowan's remembrance? One of the Jews who accounted for nearly two-thirds of the white volunteers who went south in 1964 for the Freedom Summer, Cowan would later write that "there was no doubt in any of our minds that we were risking our lives to achieve the very American goal of integration because our kinsmen had been slaughtered in Lithuania, Poland, and Germany."

Alas, as James Baldwin reminds us in *Nobody Knows My Name*, too few Jews actually thought that way: "One can be disappointed in the Jew—if one is romantic enough—for not having learned from his history, but if people did learn from history, history would be very different." And that would prove true for African Americans as well. Leaders and organizations of both groups after the 1960s became increasingly particularist, less universalist. Each turned inward, stressing distinctiveness, separateness. Each used the Holocaust, not as a call for unity, not as a reason for alliance, not as a common warning against the perils of prejudice and discrimination, but as an ideological weapon in the contest for special treatment, as proof of their claim for greater victimization. The unlearned and the forgotten keep African Americans and Jews today as separate and apart organizationally as they were before the Holocaust.[27]

Notes

1. Hugh Pearson, "Blacks and Jews View the Holocaust," *Wall Street Journal*, April 19, 1996; Hasia Diner, *In the Almost Promised Land: American Jews and Blacks 1915–1935* (Westport, Conn., 1977), 241–43.

2. Lunabelle Wedlock, *The Reaction of Negro Publications and Organizations to German Anti-Semitism* (Washington, D.C., 1942), 91, 189; Lenora Berson, *The Negroes and the Jews* (New York, 1971), 175.

3. Dennis Mack Smith, *Mussolini* (New York, 1982), 182; Paul Gordon Lauren, *Power and Prejudice, The Politics and Diplomacy of Racial Discrimination*, 2nd ed. (New York, 1996), 129–30. Various Jewish organizations associated with the Popular Front joined with black groups to support Ethiopia. See William R. Scott, *The Sons of Sheba's Race: African-Americans and the Italo-Ethiopian War, 1935–1941* (Bloomington, Ill., 1993); Joseph E. Harris, *African-American Reactions to War in Ethiopia, 1936–1941* (Baton Rouge, 1994).

4. George Mosse, *Toward the Final Solution: A History of European Racism* (New York, 1978), 191; A. Jamer Gregor, *The Ideology of Fascism* (New York, 1969), 241–82; Leni Yahil, *The Holocaust: The Fate of European Jewry, 1932–1945* (New York, 1990). Also see Lucy Dawidowicz, *The War against the Jews* (New York, 1975).

5. Charles H. Stember et al., *Jews in the Mind of America* (New York, 1966), 53–62, 138; Leonard Dinnerstein, *Antisemitism in America* (New York, 1994), 203–7; David S. Wyman, *The Abandonment of the Jews: America and the Holocaust, 1941–1945* (New York, 1984), x–xi; Kenneth B. Clark, "Candor about Negro-Jewish Relations," *Commentary* 1 (February 1946), 8–14; Richard Wright, *Black Boy* (New York, 1945), 70; James Baldwin, *Notes of a Native Son* (Boston, 1962), 28, and "The Harlem Ghetto: Winter 1948," *Commentary* 5 (February 1948), 165–70; Rabbi Robert Gordis, "Negroes Are Anti-Semitic Because They Want a Scapegoat," in Leonard Dinnerstein, ed., *Antisemitism in the United States* (New York, 1971), 132–37; Brenda Gayle Plummer, *Rising Wind: Black Americans and U.S. Foreign Affairs, 1935–1960* (Chapel Hill, N.C., 1996), 67–68; editorials, *Philadelphia Tribune*, April 6, October 12, 1933, July 5, 1934; Isabel B. Price, "Black Responses to Anti-Semitism: Negroes and Jews in New York, 1880 to World War II" (Ph.D. diss., University of New Mexico, 1973), 230; W. E. B. DuBois, "As the Crow Flies," *Crisis* 40 (September 1933), 197. American Jewish Committee, *The Jews in Nazi Germany: The Factual Record of Their Persecution by the National Socialists* (New York, 1933), is an early, largely ignored effort to alert Americans to what was happening in Germany.

6. *The Black Man* 1 (July 1935), 9; Roi Ottley, *New World A'Coming* (New York, 1943), 118–19, 129, 334; Adam Clayton Powell Jr., *Marching*

Blacks (New York, 1945), 75, 81; Wedlock, *Reaction of Negro Publications and Organizations to German Anti-Semitism,* 72–73, 171–73; "What the Black Belt Needs Is a Hitler to Fight for Our Race and Purge Us of the Exploiting Jew," *Dynamite,* May 28, October 22, 1938; Edward L. Israel, "Jew Hatred among Negroes," *Crisis* 43 (February 1936), 39, 50. Also see S. A. Haynes, "Jews and Negroes," *Philadelphia Tribune,* July 26, 1934; Harold L. Sheppard, "The Negro Merchant: A Study of Negro Anti-Semitism," *American Journal of Sociology* 53 (September 1947), esp. 96–99; Ella Baker and Marvel Cooke, "The Bronx Slave Market," *Crisis* 42 (November 1935), 330; Lawrence D. Reddick, "Anti-Semitism among Negroes," *Negro Quarterly* 1 (Summer 1942), 113; George Britt, "Poison in the Melting Pot," *Nation* 148 (April 1, 1939), 374–76; Oscar R. Williams Jr., "Historical Impressions of Black-Jewish Relations Prior to World War II," *Negro History Bulletin* 40 (July–August 1977), 728–31; and Box C-208, NAACP Papers, Library of Congress, Washington, D.C., for more on black anti-Semitism.

7. *Baltimore Afro-American,* June 17, 1933, August 24, 1935, February 22, 1936; *St. Louis Argus,* July 15, 1938; "From the Press," *Crisis* 46 (January 1939), 19, (March 1939), 83, and 45 (September 1938), 300; *Amsterdam News,* December 7, 1935, March 14, 28, 1936, June 12, 1937; Chandler Owen, "Should the Negro Hate the Jew," *Chicago Defender,* November 8, 1941.

8. J. A. Rogers columns in *Philadelphia Tribune,* September 21, 1933, July 26, 1934; Kelly Miller, "Race Prejudice in Georgia and in Germany," *Washington Tribune,* June 23, 1933, "Race Prejudice in Germany," *Opportunity* 14 (April 1936), 102–5, columns in *Norfolk Journal and Guide,* April 1, 1933, December 17, 1938, January 21, 1939, and "Hitler Hits Back," *Chicago Defender,* December 10, 1938; George Schuyler to Walter White, December 22, 1935, NAACP Papers, II, L-7, article in *New York World Telegram,* November 21, 1938, and columns in *Pittsburgh Courier,* January 23, February 20, 1937, November 26, December 3, 1938; Powell in *Amsterdam News,* March 7, 1936, January 23, February 20, 1937, April 9, 16, July 16, 23, 1938; *Norfolk Journal and Guide,* December 17, 1938.

9. Wilkins in *Amsterdam News,* March 20, December 11, 1937, and *Philadelphia Tribune,* December 22, 1937; White to William Hastie, July 20, 1939, White to Dr. Ames, November 18, 1938, White to Claude McKay, December 23, 1938, White to Hubert Delany, September 15, 1939, and White to George Mintzer, December 2, 1948, NAACP Papers, II, A-325. Also see Cleophus Charles, "Roy Wilkins, the NAACP and the Early Struggle for Civil Rights" (Ph.D. diss., Cornell University, 1981).

10. Pickens to DuBois, July 25, 1933, DuBois Papers, University of Massachusetts, reel 39; Pickens, "Why the Negro Must Be Anti-Fascist," *New*

Masses, May 30, 1939, 29–30; Pickens, "Nine Hundred Jews on a Ship," *Norfolk Journal and Guide,* June 24, 1939; "Stay Out of Nazi Olympics," *Crisis* 42 (September 1935), 273; White to Max Yergan, November 30, 1938, NAACP Papers, C-208. Also see Pickens, "The Jewish People and Prejudice," *Norfolk Journal and Guide,* August 19, 1939. There are many examples in the Negro press of using the plight of German Jewry to call attention to the evils of racism in the United States. See, for example, the following editorials in the *Baltimore Afro-American:* "Jim Crow for Jews Now," October 14, 1933, "The German Cracker," December 21, 1935, and "The Nazis and Dixie," February 22, 1936.

11. Press release, "N.A.A.C.P. Secretary Denounces Nazi Pogroms: Says All Must Unite to Protect Minority Rights Here and Save Democracy," November 18, 1938; White address to NAACP annual meeting, January 5, 1936; "Nazism and the Negro," a series of 1936 WMCA radio addresses by White; and White address, "The Nazi Terror — My Reaction," November 27, 1938, all in NAACP Papers, Box 208, "Anti-Semitism 1935–1938"; *Amsterdam News,* November 15, 1938; "Walter White Scores Persecution of Jews," *Crisis* 45 (December 1938), 399–400; Roy Wilkins to Walter White, March 25, 1938, and White to Cordell Hull, March 25, 1938, NAACP Papers, I, C-208; also see *Crisis* 45 (September 1938), 339.

12. Conference resolutions appear annually in the September *Crisis.* "Walter White Scores Persecution of Jews," 399–400; editorials, *Crisis* 45 (September 1938), 301, (December 1938), 393, ibid. 42 (September 1935), 273, ibid. 47 (July 1940), 209, and ibid. 42 (September 1935), 273. Also see ibid. 43 (September 1936), 273, and 45 (April 1938), 113. Earlier efforts by African Americans to use the plight of the Jews to draw attention to racial abuses in the United States are mentioned in Arnold Shankman, "Brothers across the Sea: Afro-Americans on the Persecution of Russian Jews, 1881–1917," *Jewish Social Studies* 37 (Spring 1975), 114–21.

13. Rabbi Stephen S. Wise, "Parallel between Hitlerism and the Persecution of Negroes in America," *Crisis* 41 (May 1934), 127–29; Jacob J. Weinstein, "The Jew and the Negro" and "The Negro and the Jew," ibid. (June 1934), 178–79, and (July 1934), 197–98; Harry Essrig, "Einhorn: Champion of Racial Equality," ibid. 47 (October 1940), 314–15, "John Brown's Jewish Associates," ibid. (December 1940), 380–81, and "Jewish Friends of Negro Emancipation," ibid. 48 (January 1941), 16; ibid. 46 (January 1939), 29, and (October 1939), 308. Also see "Anti-Semitism among Negroes," ibid. 45 (June 1938), 177.

14. Norton Belth, "Problems of Anti-Semitism in the United States," *Contemporary Jewish Record* 2 (July 1939), 43–57; "Americans All," *National Jewish Monthly* 53 (April 1939), 298; *American Hebrew,* December 13, 1936;

Joseph Roucek, "The Forgotten Man in Europe and America," *Opportunity* 11 (March 1933), 73–74; Verna Arvey, "Tolerance," ibid. 18 (August 1940), 244; Elmer Carter, "The Way of Madness," ibid. 16 (October 1938), 292; Lawrence Reddick, "What Hitler Says about the Negro," ibid. 17 (April 1939), 108–10; editorials, ibid. (January 1939), 2, (June 1939), 164, (November 1939), 324; "The Negro and Nazism," ibid. 18 (July 1940), 194–95.

15. Adam Clayton Powell Jr., "Soap Box," *Amsterdam News,* February 19, March 18, April 16, 1938; Ralph Bunche, "Foreword," in Wedlock, *Reaction of Negro Publications and Organizations to German Anti-Semitism,* 3, 10; William Pickens, "German Fascists and Free Speech in America," *Norfolk Journal and Guide,* March 11, 1939; editorial, "Fascism Spreads," *Amsterdam News,* March 19, 1938; Owen, "Should the Negro Hate the Jew?"; "Danger Is Seen in Anti-Jewish Onset as Probe Is Begun," *Atlanta Daily World,* August 15, 1938; M. Beaunorus Tolson, "Keep That Chin Up, My Jewish Brother!" *Philadelphia Tribune,* March 11, 1939; Robert Bagnall, "Taken in Stride," ibid., August 4, 1938.

16. Editorials in *Baltimore Afro-American,* February 22, 1936, August 24, October 5, 1935, April 1, 1933, April 11, May 2, 1936; Miller in *Washington Tribune,* June 23, 1933; editorials in *Amsterdam News,* February 11, April 8, 15, 1939; *Crisis* 45 (September 1938), 301, (December 1938), 393, ibid. 47 (August 1940), 232; Thomas F. Doyle, "Gestapo in Memphis," ibid. 48 (May 1941), 152–54, 172–73; *New York Times,* August 22, 1939.

17. Editorials, *Crisis* 48 (May 1941), 151, (July 1941), 215; "A Georgia Hitler," *Opportunity* 19 (August 1941), 226–27; Harold Preece, "The Klan's 'Revolution of the Right,'" and "Klan 'Murder, Inc.' in Dixie," *Crisis* 53 (July 1946), 202, 220, (October 1946), 299–301; editorial, ibid. (September 1946), 276. The sole African American in Congress, Arthur W. Mitchell, wrote to Roosevelt urging the United States government to take greater measures to protect European Jews. "October 12" in Janus Adams, *Freedom Days: 365 Inspirational Moments in Civil Rights History* (New York, 1998).

18. *Amsterdam News,* February 14, 1942; *Pittsburgh Courier,* October 23, 1943; Marie Syrkin, "Anti-Semitic Drive in Harlem," *Congress Weekly* 8 (October 31, 1941), 6–8; *Crisis* 51 (February 1944); Adam Clayton Powell Jr., "What Negroes Think of Jews," *New Currents* 1 (September 1943), 15–16; Langston Hughes column, *Chicago Defender,* March 10, 1945; Walter White and Rabbi Lou H. Silberman, "The Minority Problem from the Inside Looking Out," *Hebrew Union College Monthly* 30 (April 1943), 6–7; *Pittsburgh Courier,* August 4, 1945; Randolph quote in Gunnar Myrdal, *An American Dilemma* (New York, 1944), 852. See also editorial, "The Dangers of Anti-Semitism," *Chicago Defender,* March 17, 1945. More examples of

African American wartime efforts to combat anti-Semitism are found in the NAACP Papers, II, A-325.

19. Minutes of the NAACP Board of Directors, February 1942, NAACP Papers, II, A-134; *Congress Weekly*, December 4, 1942; Stephen Wise to Walter White, December 17, 1942, and Edwin C. Johnson to Walter White, June 23, 1943, NAACP Papers, II, A-374; Walter White to American Jewish Congress, August 30, 1943, NAACP Papers, II, A-325; Lester Granger to Walter White, June 21, 1943, NAACP Papers, II, A-446. On what was known and what was reported, see Deborah Lipstadt, *Beyond Belief: The American Press and the Coming of the Holocaust, 1933–1945* (New York, 1986). The *New York Times* began printing stories on the slaughter of millions of Jews in June 1942, although the Allied governments did not publicly acknowledge it until December.

20. See articles and editorials from Jewish publications in NAACP Papers, II, A-325, A-361, A-380, L-7; "Defend the Negro" and "Help Wanted—No Negroes, No Jews," in NAACP Papers, II, A-325; *Jewish Survey* 2 (June 1942); *Year Book, Central Conference of American Rabbis* (New York, 1942). On the activities of the American Jewish Congress, see NAACP Papers, II, C-300; Lucille B. Morton, "On the Civil-Liberty Front," *New Republic*, June 26, 1944, 839–40; Clark, "Candor about Negro-Jewish Relations," 9. Also see columns by Roy Wilkins, *Amsterdam News*, February 28, 1942, April 17, 1943.

21. Reddick, "Anti-Semitism among Negroes," 105; W. H. Jernigan, "Tolerance Is Indivisible," *Jewish Survey* 2 (August 1942); *New York Jewish Forward*, March 3, 1942; Louis Harap, "Anti-Negroism among Jews," *Negro Quarterly* (Summer 1942), 107; White and Silberman, "Minority Problem from the Inside Looking Out," 6–7; Jacob X. Cohen, "Fighting Together for Equality" and "The Negro and Anti-Semitism," in NAACP Papers, II, C-300. Also see Marshall F. Stevenson Jr., "Points of Departure, Acts of Resolve: Black-Jewish Relations in Detroit, 1937–1962" (Ph.D. diss., University of Michigan, 1988).

22. Milton R. Konvitz, "Jews and Civil Rights," in Peter I. Rose, ed., *The Ghetto and Beyond: Essays on Jewish Life in America* (New York, 1969), 274–80; American Jewish Congress pamphlet, "Accent on Action, A New Approach to Minority Group Problems in America," Bernard Gittelson to Walter White, June 14, 1945, Alexander H. Pekelis to Thurgood Marshall, June 15, 1945, and Rabbi Stephen Wise to Thurgood Marshall, April 11, 1946, NAACP Papers, II, C-300; Maslow in Berson, *The Negroes and the Jews*, 96. Also see Jonathan Kaufman, *Broken Alliance: The Turbulent Times between Blacks and Jews in America* (New York, 1988); Edward S. Shapiro, "Black-Jewish Relations Revisited," *Judaism* 44 (Summer 1995), 379.

23. Cheryl Greenberg, "Liberation and Liberalism: The Politics of Black-Jewish Relations in the 1960s" (paper presented at the Organization of American Historians' 1996 annual meeting), is an indispensable account of the emerging alliance, as is Stuart Svonkin, *Jews against Prejudice: American Jews and the Fight for Civil Liberties* (New York, 1997). Files "Negro Race Problems" and "Negro-Jewish Relations," and *ADL Bulletin*, Anti-Defamation League Papers, Anti-Defamation Library, New York City; "Negro Jewish Relations File," American Jewish Congress Papers, American Jewish Congress Library, New York City; 1945 platform of the Central Conference of American Rabbis, *Pittsburgh Courier*, February 3, 1945; Myron Harshhaw to George Schuyler, June 30, 1943, George Schuyler Papers, Schomburg Archives, New York Public Library; Kaufman, *Broken Alliance*, 97–100; Walter White column and story on Randolph, *Chicago Defender*, January 27, 1945.

24. "Chicago GI Tells Horrors of Nazi 'Murder Factory' Prison Camp," *Chicago Defender*, May 12, 1945; *Atlanta Constitution*, August 8, 1945; "Editor Sees Parallel of Nazi Germany in America," *Pittsburgh Courier*, May 26, 1945; Joseph Bibb column, ibid., March 31, 1945; Marjorie McKenzie column, ibid., May 12, 1945; Horace R. Cayton column, ibid., December 8, 1945; letter to the editor, *Norfolk Journal and Guide*, July 21, 1934; Lauren, *Power and Prejudice*, 144. The overall impact of the news of the Holocaust is best covered in Robert H. Abzug, *Inside the Vicious Heart: Americans and the Liberation of Nazi Concentration Camps* (New York, 1985). See also William Grant Still's "Wailing Woman" (1946); Chester Himes, *If He Hollers Let Him Go* (New York, 1945); Oliver Cox, *Race, Caste and Class* (New York, 1948); W. E. B. DuBois, *The Souls of Black Folk* (Milkwood, N.Y., 1973), 42–43; Clark, "Candor about Negro-Jewish Relations"; and references to the Holocaust later made by Martin Luther King Jr., *A Testament of Hope: The Essential Writings and Speeches of Martin Luther King, Jr.* (San Francisco, 1991), 50, 356.

25. Alphonse Heningburg, "What the Urban League Expects for All Races as a Result of the San Francisco Conference," *Opportunity* 23 (Summer 1945), 123; editorial, "The Jews Look Ahead," *Atlanta Daily World*, May 6, 1945; Plummer, *Rising Wind*, 164–65; Jonathan Seth Rosenberg, "How Far the Promised Land? World Affairs and the American Civil Rights Movement from the First World War to Vietnam" (Ph.D. diss., Harvard University, 1997). Also see Carol Anderson, "Eyes Off the Prize: African Americans, the United Nations, and the Struggle for Human Rights, 1944–1952" (Ph.D. diss., Ohio State University, 1995).

26. Roy Wilkins, "Jewish-Negro Relations: An Evaluation," *American Judaism* 12 (Spring 1963), 4–5; Eugene I. Bender, "Reflections on Negro-

Jewish Relationships: The Historical Dimension," *Phylon* 30 (Spring 1969), 59–65; Marguerite Cartwright, "Do I Like Jews?" *Negro History Bulletin* 21 (November 1957), 38–39; Murray Friedman, *What Went Wrong? The Creation and Collapse of the Black-Jewish Alliance* (New York, 1995).

27. Kaufman, *Broken Alliance*, 5–6, 52–53; Paul Cowan, *An Orphan in History* (New York, 1983), 6; Baldwin quoted in Dinnerstein, ed., *Antisemitism in the United States*, 131.

Harry Truman and the Election of 1948

The Coming of Age of Civil Rights in American Politics

Yet another essay written in the late 1960s, when I proudly considered myself a New Leftist, "Harry Truman and the Election of 1948" began as a bill of indictment, a categorical denunciation of liberals for doing too little, too late. It then became a critique of Truman as, at best, a reluctant champion of civil rights, pressured by forces beyond his control. It concluded, nevertheless, with civil rights benefiting from being identified with the president of the United States and with the Democratic Party. All motives aside, that sparked ever-rising expectations of African Americans and ever-increasing pressures on the political system to respond to those expectations. Indicative of the then swelling tide of revisionism, characterized by a strong animosity toward American liberalism, "Harry Truman and the Election of 1948" was awarded the Fletcher M. Green Award for best essay submitted by a graduate student to the Journal of Southern History, *1970–1972. Written in the same period, but a more radical statement of the revisionist case against liberalism in general and against the significance of Truman's civil rights program in particular, is my "Years of the Locust: Interpretations of Truman's Presidency since 1965," in* The Truman Period as a Research Field: A Reappraisal, 1972, *ed. Richard Kirkendall (Columbia: University of Missouri Press, 1974), 75–112. "Harry Truman and the Election of 1948: The Coming of Age of Civil Rights in American Politics" was originally published in* Journal of Southern History 37 *(November 1971), 597–616.*

175

A year before the national election of 1948 Clark M. Clifford, an administrative assistant and special counsel to the president, presented a forty-three-page confidential memorandum to Harry S. Truman. The memo, referred to as "The Politics of 1948," suggested the electoral strategy for Truman in the upcoming election. Clifford particularly emphasized the importance of the Negro vote, warning that because of Henry A. Wallace's growing identification with the civil rights issue and Thomas E. Dewey's presumed popularity with Negro leaders, as well as the Republican policy of embarrassing the Democrats by publicly favoring anti–poll tax and antilynching legislation, Truman would lose the Negro vote unless he acted decisively. "Unless there are new and real efforts," wrote Clifford, "(as distinguished from mere political gestures which are today thoroughly understood and strongly resented by sophisticated Negro leaders), the Negro bloc . . . will go Republican." In order to outbid the Republicans and steal Henry Wallace's thunder, the president must "go as far as he feels he possibly could go in recommending measures to protect the rights of minority groups." Administration strategy must be premised on the assumption that "it will get no major part of its program approved. Its tactics must, therefore, be entirely different than if there were any real point to bargaining and compromise. Its recommendations . . . must be tailored for the voter, not the Congressman; they must display a label which reads 'no compromises.'" Clifford confidently predicted that Truman's espousal of civil rights would not lose him southern support. "As always, the South can be considered safely Democratic," he concluded, "and in formulating national policy, it can be safely ignored."[1]

Clifford's political advice harmonized with Truman's need to do *something* for civil rights. Suddenly assuming the presidency in 1945, Truman found himself in the middle of a stream of events heralding a Second Reconstruction. Although President Franklin D. Roosevelt had never supported civil rights legislation, the accelerating northward migration of Negroes and the endorsement of racial equality by leading New Dealers built up pressure on the government to act on behalf of the Negro. Wendell L. Willkie's appeal to the Negro voter in 1940 and the strong civil rights plank in the Republican Party platform in 1944 increased that pressure. The Second World War itself spurred the forces for civil rights, quickening the expectations of those insisting that the national government do more and emboldening Negro organizations to demand and threaten more.[2]

Events in the postwar years speeded up the stream of the new Reconstruction. While Congress would not act and the executive branch hesitated, the Supreme Court began to roll back the permissible areas of legal discrimination. Militant leftists and communists effectively prodded established civil rights leaders to be more aggressive and made American racism the prime target of their propaganda machines. The Cold War, the struggle for independence of the nonwhite nations of Africa and Asia, and the establishment of the United Nations with its promise of human rights for all tied the success of American foreign policy to the progress of civil rights. And the emergence of a new Negro middle class and a new generation of college-educated, war-tempered Negro spokesmen eager to collect on the promises of a hundred years all converged to push civil rights to the fore as a national issue.[3]

Truman at first hesitated to do anything that would offend the southern whites in his party. It appears he hoped liberal gestures would compensate for the lack of liberal action. He publicly supported a permanent Fair Employment Practices Committee in 1945 when it had little chance of passage, but he failed to battle for appropriations for the temporary committee created by Roosevelt. The president publicly urged the abolition of the poll tax but did nothing to enforce the Supreme Court's "white primary" ruling or to aid the FEPC's fight to end discrimination in the hiring of bus company personnel in Washington, D.C. Similarly, Truman refused to take a strong stand on the move to unseat Mississippi senator Theodore G. Bilbo or the refusal by the Daughters of the American Revolution to rent Constitution Hall to Hazel Scott, the wife of Negro congressman Adam Clayton Powell Jr.[4]

Only after a succession of horrible racial murders in the South in 1946 had aroused the national conscience and provided much grist for the communist propaganda mill did Truman condemn racist violence. Genuinely shocked by the incidents, yet fearful of splitting the Democratic Party by a vigorous assertion of national will, Truman temporized by appointing a Committee on Civil Rights to investigate law enforcement procedures and recommend measures to safeguard the civil rights of minorities.[5]

While the president's committee deliberated, the pressures on Truman to act continued to build. Still hoping to avoid a break with the South, Truman cautiously stepped up his rhetoric while avoiding overt acts. He addressed a mass rally of the National Association for the Advancement of Colored People (NAACP) in front of the Lincoln Memorial in June 1947, proclaiming the need for new federal legislation but omitting any specific recommendations. Not satisfied, the NAACP and other civil rights organizations joined to petition the United Nations to aid the Negro's struggle against discrimination. Then in October the Committee on Civil Rights presented its report, *To Secure These Rights*, to the president. Ranging far beyond its initial instructions to suggest new safeguards against racial violence, the committee pointed out the inequities of life in Jim Crow America and the need to protect the rights of citizenship and personal security; spelled out the moral, economic, and international reasons why the government must act; and recommended the end of discrimination and segregation in public education, employment, housing, the military, public accommodations, and interstate transportation.[6]

Truman heralded the report as "an American charter of human freedom" but avoided any commitment to implement it. While administration insiders debated the course the president should follow, Truman clung to the belief that, like FDR, he could keep urban liberals and Negroes in the party's ranks by public gestures without precipitating an open revolt by the South. Like Clifford, he hoped he could do right—politically, internationally, morally, and according to his own sense of history—without overly alienating the white South. In his 1948 State of the Union address Truman promised Congress a special civil rights message.[7]

Truman sent his civil rights message to Capitol Hill on February 2, 1948. The president proposed closing the gap between American ideals and practices pointed out by his Civil Rights Committee by asking Congress to abolish the poll tax, make lynching a federal crime, curtail discrimination in employment, and prohibit segregation in interstate commerce. Following the recommendations of his committee, Truman also advocated establishing a full civil rights division in the Justice Department and a Joint Congressional Committee on Civil Rights to report regularly to the president. The president wanted southern Democrats to realize that all this required congressional approval and that the executive branch sought no crusade of its own. Moreover, Truman refused to submit his committee's proposal to withdraw federal grants from states that practiced discrimination, and he sidestepped the recommendation to outlaw segregation in the nation's capital in favor of a more innocuous request for "home rule" in the District. Despite such limitations, most Negro leaders and columnists hailed the president's program as "Lincolnesque," the greatest freedom document since the Emancipation Proclamation.[8]

Southern segregationists immediately and violently denounced the message as both a cheap political trick and an attempt to tyrannize the nation. Clifford and Truman had anticipated southern criticism but not the determined, prolonged, and vituperative barrage which followed. Congressional and editorial attacks upon the president bristled with accusations of "a stab in the back," ingratitude to the South, which had put him in the White House, and crassly "out-Wallacing Henry Wallace." To Representative Ed Lee Gossett of Texas, the president's program proved that urban liberals had captured the Democratic Party and that they intended to crawl on their bellies through the dirt to kiss the feet of minorities. To Senator James O. Eastland of Mississippi it proved that organized mongrel minorities plotting to "Harlemize" the nation now controlled the government. Louisiana's Senator John H. Overton ominously asked southern Democrats to vote Republican or to boycott the national Democratic ticket. Other warnings to the president by Senators Harry F. Byrd of Virginia and Richard B. Russell of Georgia quickly led to talk of an administration retreat, and Alben W. Barkley of Kentucky, the Democratic leader in the Senate, flatly refused to sponsor the president's omnibus civil rights bill.[9]

Five days after the presidential message the Southern Governors Conference, meeting in Wakulla Springs, Florida, dropped its regular agenda to consider the civil rights program. While avoiding a call for an outright bolt from the party, the governors unanimously passed a resolution authored by South Carolina's J. Strom Thurmond scoring the national leaders for insulting the people of the South and establishing a special committee of governors to convince the administration to change its course. Two weeks later fifty-two southerners in the House formally condemned the civil rights message and endorsed the governors' resolution. In the Senate twenty-one southerners under Russell's leadership pledged to "stand guard" and prevent any civil rights measure from becoming law. A Gallup poll showed Truman dropping thirteen points in February as the favored presidential candidate in the South.[10]

To put teeth into the verbal threats, southern donors canceled an estimated half million dollars in contributions for the Democratic National Committee. The talk of a southern bolt could no longer be dismissed as the usual secessionist rhetoric of fire-eaters. George Gallup reported the president's support in the South dropped from 59 percent in October 1947 to 35 percent in late March 1948. In that same period the number of southerners disapproving Truman's policies leaped from 18 to 57 percent. Another Gallup poll indicated southern voters to be nine-to-one against the civil rights program.[11]

The administration quietly backtracked to conciliate the southerners in the party. Even if Clifford's analysis remained correct as a strategy against Dewey and Wallace in November, Truman first had to make sure of his renomination. With many urban liberals flirting with the idea of nominating General Dwight D. Eisenhower, Truman could not afford to lose much southern support at the convention. At the same time he had to avoid any appearance of capitulating to the South for fear of losing the crucial northern city and labor delegations. In order to avoid alienating either major wing of the party, Truman attempted to defuse the civil rights issue by remaining silent. After his civil rights message to Congress he neither repeated nor repudiated it. At a meeting in late February with a special delegation of southern governors, J. Howard McGrath, chairman of the Democratic National Committee, refused to condemn the president's civil rights recommendations but praised the party loyalty of the South and promised to support adoption of the weak civil rights plank of 1944 in the 1948 platform. Not satisfied, the southern governors publicly would accept nothing less than a total denunciation of the civil rights program by the president. When Truman refused, a reconvened Conference of Southern Governors in Washington resolved on March 13 that their states should send delegates to the convention opposed to Truman and that their presidential electors should not vote in November for any candidate favoring civil rights. Governors Thurmond, Fielding L. Wright of Mississippi, and Ben T. Laney of Arkansas, going still further, urged all opponents of civil rights to assemble in Jackson, Mississippi, in May. The Jackson conference supported the governors' resolution and agreed to convene afterward in Birmingham if the Democratic convention did not repudiate civil rights.[12]

These extraordinary measures against a program that had little chance of passage convinced many liberals that southern conservatives were using the civil rights issue as a cover for taking over the party. Conservatives had often used the Negro question in the South to bludgeon their liberal opponents, and it now appeared that Truman was the target of a similar strategy. Behind the cries of "nigger domination," basic ideological and political considerations were readying segments of the South for revolt. Since 1936 growing numbers of southerners had come to fear that the Democratic Party was becoming an instrument of urban liberalism. Although racial questions were secondary in conservative southern opposition to the New Deal, the activities on behalf of the Negro by those close to Roosevelt increased southern antagonism. Moreover, Roosevelt's landslide victory in 1936 had decreased the relative numerical significance of the Solid South in both Congress and the Electoral College, and the abolition of the two-thirds convention rule had ended the South's ability to veto distasteful policies and candidates. The handwriting on the wall materialized in 1940 when the Democratic convention nominated FDR for a third term, dumped Vice President John Nance Garner of Texas for an ardent New Dealer, Henry A. Wallace, and included a civil rights plank in the platform. Although the Deep South still refused to consider the Republican Party an honorable alternative, important defections in the border states occurred during wartime elections, and in 1944 Mississippi and the Texas Regulars defied the national party by placing a slate of uninstructed electors on the ballot.[13]

The respite offered the South by the replacement of Dr. New Deal with Dr. Win-the-War and by the substitution of Truman for Wallace in 1944 proved illusory. The South's initial delight in the "safe" Truman turned to disappointment and then disgust. All the trends furthering civil rights and isolating the South accelerated, increasing the southern image of itself as a beleaguered minority. Southerners eyed suspiciously a liberal-dominated Supreme Court, a labor drive to unionize Dixie, and a Republican-controlled Congress that could not safely be counted on to thwart civil rights legislation. The senator they had helped coerce Roosevelt to accept as his running mate had turned on them. The Missourian whom they had expected to submit tamely to southern congressional influence had chosen to pursue an independent course. The border state politician they had thought "right" on the race issue had met cordially with Negro leaders, personally addressed the NAACP, established the first President's Committee on Civil Rights, and proposed the most sweeping civil rights bill since Reconstruction.[14]

In addition, the South saw itself losing the battle of the census. The wartime migration had doubled the number of Negroes in the north-central states and increased by half those in the northeastern and western states. Every Negro going to the North meant another potential voter pressuring both parties for civil rights legislation. Every Negro leaving the South helped decrease southern representation in Congress and southern electoral votes, further minimizing the South's bargaining power in the Democratic Party. Not to act immediately meant the sure demise of southern political power and the southern way of life. Southerners believed "their" party had been stolen by the bosses, the union officials, and the organized minorities of urban slums. It had to be reclaimed.[15]

Primarily, the southern conservatives sought to dictate, or at least be able to veto, the candidates and policies of the Democratic Party in order to protect southern industrialists and cotton planters, to contain the expansion of federal economic controls, and to maintain the racial status quo. To accomplish this they planned to restore the two-thirds convention rule and prevent the party from strengthening the 1944 civil rights plank. Failing this, they intended to run their own national candidates, hoping to throw the election into the House of Representatives. There they planned to bargain their votes to ensure election of a president beholden to the South. Even if this did not succeed, they believed a divided Democratic Party *surely* would be smashed by the Republicans everywhere but in the South. Holding the key congressional posts, the southern Democrats would then pick up the pieces and rule the party again, thwarting the liberal plan to "knife the South."[16]

Concurrently with the southern revolt, urban liberals, long stymied by the dominance of the South in Congress and obsessed with the Wallace specter on their left, plotted a civil rights revolt of their own. Although the revolt did not formally take shape until 1948, it had its roots in the battles between anticommunist liberals and those clinging to a faith in the Popular Front immediately after the war. The Americans for Democratic Action (ADA) recognized civil rights as an important vote-getting issue in northern cities, as a means to counter communist appeals to the urban Negro, as a handy lever against southern Democrats, and as a needed moral justification for their own anticommunist liberalism. Aided by established Negro leaders searching for "responsible" allies, the ADA spearheaded the revolt in the northern Democratic Party. While rooted in a deep human concern for racial justice, the civil rights issue also seemed the perfect means to shift the center of the Democratic Party leftward. The first ADA convention in 1947 had endorsed a general proposal for civil rights, but at its second annual meeting, after the southern rebellion surfaced, the ADAers incorporated all the recommendations of the President's Committee on Civil Rights into their platform. Throughout the spring of 1948 ADA rallies and publications highlighted the civil rights issue, and ADA officials prominently supported the drive to end Jim Crow practices in the armed forces.[17]

ADA leaders decided in March to make a public fight over the civil rights plank in the Democratic platform. In a letter to McGrath, ADA national chairman Leon Henderson threatened to desert the party if it dared compromise with the South. Like the southern governors, the ADAers quietly garnered support to impress the administration with the seriousness of its threat to get its way or bolt. A letter signed by Minneapolis mayor Hubert H. Humphrey and James Roosevelt of California in late March requested all Democratic leaders to promise to battle for an uncompromising civil rights plank. By the time of the convention some fifty party and labor union officials had agreed to join with the ADA and civil rights organizations to write the president's whole civil rights program into the platform.[18]

The liberal ideologues might have been voices braying in the wilderness of Democratic politics had it not been for the twin growth of the northern Negro vote and the Progressive Party threat. Civil rights publicists confidently predicted that the Negro vote in 1948, *the* balance of power, would swing at least 228 electoral votes in twelve states. Northern Democrats pondered the prospect of electoral ruin if forced to run with an unpopular incumbent at the head of the ticket and with a watered-down stand on civil rights.[19]

The Republicans had taken a stronger position than the Democrats on civil rights in both 1940 and 1944 and seemed eager to do so again. Moreover, Truman, unlike Roosevelt, lacked the personal magnetism to overcome a weak platform, and most Negro newspapers strongly preferred Dewey and Earl Warren to the "Missouri Compromise." Governor Warren had accented civil rights in his bid for the Republican nomination, and Dewey, as governor of New York, took credit for securing the first state fair employment practices act, for establishing a State Commission Against Discrimination, and for appointing influential Negroes to highly visible state posts.[20]

Henry Wallace and his Progressive Party, liberals feared, would be even more likely to woo Negro votes away from the Democrats. Even before Truman's civil rights message to Congress in February, the Progressive nominee had called for sweeping civil rights legislation, and while Truman temporized, Wallace stormed through the South attacking white supremacy. Because of his calculated insistence on addressing only nonsegregated audiences, Wallace's southern tour consistently made headlines in the Negro press. Everywhere he spoke he asserted: "Discrimination and segregation must go!" His future running mate, Senator Glen H. Taylor of Idaho, endeared himself to Negro voters by introducing a Senate bill to outlaw segregation in the District of Columbia and by getting arrested by Birmingham police commissioner Eugene "Bull" Connor for defying the city's segregation ordinance. Numerous Negro intellectuals joined the Progressive bandwagon, and heavyweight boxing champion Joe Louis, then the most celebrated Negro in America, publicly contributed to Wallace's campaign fund. Negro political strategists admitted Wallace could not win but argued that a Negro vote for Wallace would force the two national parties to do more for civil rights after the election.[21] The practical politicians awoke to the Wallace threat when Leo Isacson, a Progressive candidate aided by the Negro vote, defeated the regular Democratic nominee for Congress by a near two-to-one margin in a widely followed election in Bronx boss Edward J. Flynn's home district.[22]

As both the southern conservatives and the ADAers used the civil rights issue to increase their leverage in the party, both sought to "dump Truman" before forcing their racial views on the rest of the party. Throughout the spring Democrats of all sections and persuasions joined in a campaign to draft General Dwight D. Eisenhower. Since everyone had some reason to dislike Truman and knew *certainly* he could not win in November, it did not matter that no one really knew what "Ike" stood for. The general, at least, would have a fighting chance against the Republicans and could salvage their local tickets. Although Eisenhower had publicly testified in favor of continuing segregation in the armed forces before a congressional committee in March, most of the same ADAers who demanded a showdown on civil rights at the convention joined a bizarre coalition of southern conservatives and big-city bosses to woo the war hero. Not until the general fired three emphatic rebuffs from Morningside Heights did the despondent Democrats surrender. However mild about Harry they might be, the Democrats had no one else to turn to.[23]

While the extreme wings of the party continued to fire up the civil rights issue, Truman worked diligently to dampen it and ensure his nomination. He refused all attempts to get him to comment publicly on the race question. Privately he tried to placate all but the most bitter extremists within the party; publicly he tried to enlarge the Democratic middle by concentrating on New Deal pocketbook issues. He dropped his plans to send the omnibus civil rights bill drafted in the White House to Congress, telling reporters that as a former senator he knew that Congress did not like to have a ready-made bill handed to it for adoption. In addition, despite the recommendation by the president to create a civil rights division in the Justice Department, the Bureau of the Budget reduced the appropriations requested for the understaffed Civil Rights Section.[24]

Truman's handling of the issue of segregation in the National Guard clearly illustrated his preconvention policy of compromise and moderation. Steering carefully between the Scylla and Charybdis of the urban liberals' demand to desegregate all Guard units and the southern insistence on maintaining total segregation, Truman pushed for an agreement which would allow each state to decide its own racial policy. It also appears that the need to pacify the southern-dominated military administration, which strongly opposed his stand on the National Guard, and to avoid reheating the civil rights controversy led Truman to delay issuing his promised presidential nondiscrimination orders in the armed forces and federal employment. Against the urgings of the NAACP and Negro press Truman delivered an address in May at Girard College in Philadelphia, then receiving national publicity for its policy against admitting Negroes. To underscore his removal from the civil rights issue, the president made seventy three speeches on his "nonpolitical" tour of eighteen states in June, mentioning civil rights just once.[25]

By the time the Democratic convention opened in July the battle lines had clearly emerged. The administration, fearing a major party split more than the extremist threats of the Dixiecrat and the Wallace wings, wanted a compromise on civil rights. Those most alienated from the president and most passionately committed to a fixed position on racial issues were determined to play "rule or ruin" politics. And the power brokers both North and South, the party leaders still retaining close ties to the White House, watched and waited, determined to follow whatever course would best enable them to save their local tickets and control the party after the expected November defeat. Each new poll predicting Dewey's victory diminished the administration's control over the party and the chances for a civil rights compromise.[26]

Truman won the first round at the convention when the platform committee, after a bitter wrangle between ADAers, southern conservatives, and administration stalwarts, endorsed a compromise pushed by cabinet members and White House aides to readopt the vague 1944 civil rights plank. On the convention floor the Truman cadres also appeared in control as they beat back efforts to unseat the contested Mississippi delegation and to restore the two-thirds rule. But beneath the appearance of administration power, the ADA, the NAACP, and an assortment of labor and Negro delegates busily plotted to press a confrontation over the platform. Threatening a roll call of the states and, if need be, of every delegate to make them vote publicly for or against the civil rights plank, the liberals forced the big-city bosses and union officials to desert the administration and join their crusade. On the final vote the industrial states of the North and West defeated the South and the Truman loyalists by 651½ to 582½, thereby pledging the Democratic Party to support the president's stated civil rights program.[27]

What had seemed impossible in the spring had happened. A civil rights revolt engineered by a small group of urban liberals and Negroes had defied the incumbent president and the national party leadership. According to *Time*, "The South had been kicked in the pants, turned around and kicked in the stomach." But Truman too had been handled unceremoniously. To pacify southern regulars, the president had been forced to support the seating of a state delegation which had already announced its intention to oppose him and to walk out of the convention, and though he had remained publicly noncommittal on the platform, his aides worked throughout the convention against the ADA plank. All of Truman's convention officers opposed the strong civil rights plank, and on the vote to praise and support the president's own program, his home state of Missouri and McGrath's Rhode Island both voted no. But this was not enough to stop the northern delegates, who for their own needs forced an unenthusiastic president into the role of civil rights tribune. After being encouraged for more than a year by Truman's own acts and words, the partisans of civil rights could not now be stopped easily.[28]

But Truman had an election to win, and he hesitated to commit the party to an all-out civil rights campaign. Unwilling to give up southern support, he carefully soft-pedaled civil rights both in his acceptance speech and in his message to the special session of Congress. Not until the States' Rights Democratic Party convention in Birmingham in July failed to attract many leading southern Democrats did Truman finally issue his long-delayed executive orders establishing a fair employment board within the Civil Service Commission and a President's Committee on Equality of Treatment and Opportunity in the Armed Services. The Dixiecrats expectedly cried foul, but most southern Democrats, as Clifford had predicted, discounted the effect of the orders and stayed safely in the Democratic fold. While Negro leaders privately grumbled at the limitations of the executive orders, all publicly praised Truman for issuing them. For better or worse, events had made Truman the candidate of civil rights, and the Negroes could not desert him.[29]

Still Truman temporized, turning his attention again to the white South. For two months he avoided speaking out on civil rights, personally preaching party unity in the South while deputizing friendly Negro and liberal Democrats to praise his civil rights record in the North. In a studied attempt to isolate the Dixiecrats, Truman would not fight to break the southern filibuster on the anti–poll tax bill, avoided Thurmond's demand to debate civil rights, and ignored Wallace's taunt that he was all talk and no action. In mid-August Clifford presented another confidential memorandum on the campaign to the president. He stressed again the crucial importance of winning as large a plurality of Negro votes as possible and specifically urged Truman to deliver a major campaign address in Harlem. The Negro vote, wrote Clifford, "will more than cancel out any votes the President may lose in the South."[30]

A week before the election, when the polls showed most of the South could be expected to vote Democratic and when the need to reduce Dewey's lead in the North was urgent, Truman became the first American president to speak in Harlem. More than 65,000 Negroes turned out on October 29 to hear the president warmly praise his Civil Rights Committee's report on its first anniversary and, for the first time since his February message, unequivocally back the program charted by the committee. Contrasting his record with the vague generalities of the Dewey campaign, Truman pointed with pride to the civil rights report, to his antidiscrimination executive orders, and to his Justice Department for getting the Supreme Court to outlaw racially restrictive housing covenants. And continuing to give the do-nothing Eightieth Congress hell, Truman blamed it for not passing his civil rights proposals. The flood of publicity on this speech drowned out all the earlier presidential silence on civil rights and, together with his appointment of the Civil Rights Committee, the February message to Congress, the amended Democratic plank on civil rights, and the antidiscrimination orders, established Truman more firmly as the leader of the Second Reconstruction.[31]

Election day, November 2, despite the pollsters and pundits, Truman became "the first President to lose in a Gallup and win in a walk." Although the closeness of the election enabled each element of the Democratic coalition to claim it had contributed the critical "swing" votes, many political analysts credited the Negro vote with being the decisive factor. Dewey would have won if Truman had not polled a higher percentage of the Negro vote than Roosevelt had done in any of his four presidential victories. Truman's plurality of Negro votes in California, Illinois, and Ohio provided the margin of victory. The election statistics buoyed the optimism of Negro leaders, who looked for a greater Negro role in political affairs and the speedy enactment of the president's civil rights program.[32]

Although the euphoric hopes of Negroes proved premature in Truman's second administration, the campaign of 1948 is a milestone in the coming-of-age of the civil rights issue. For the first time since Reconstruction, civil rights occupied a central place on the political stage. Never before had so many written and said so much about the Negro's right to equality. Going beyond the usual promises of patronage and lucrative advertising contracts, both national parties and the Progressives competed for the Negro vote by stressing their concern for civil rights. Each of the three parties had a Negro division in its national committee, special newspapers and pamphlets, and Negro leaders and celebrities who praised the party and emphasized how it would do more for civil rights than its opponents. Special appeals for the Negro vote were not new, but the accent on civil rights was. The Democrats, for example, had been attracting Negro voters since 1934 by publicizing the economic benefits they received from the New Deal. In 1948 Democratic campaign literature centered on Truman's civil rights record and speeches. All three parties underlined the national character of the race problem and the need for the federal government to do more.[33]

Moreover, Negroes participated in the 1948 campaign in greater numbers than ever before. Some thirty Negro delegates and alternates attended the Democratic convention, and George Vaughan of Missouri, Esther Murray of California, Willard Townsend of the United Transport Employees, and George L. P. Weaver, director of the CIO Committee to Abolish Discrimination, played leading roles in the fight for a strong civil rights plank. Congressman William L. Dawson's appointment as secretary of the Democratic Congressional Committee and assistant chairman of the Democratic National Committee symbolized the increasing stature of Negroes within the party. The Progressive Party made an even greater effort to give Negroes positions of prominence. Lankin Marshall Howard, a Negro attorney, gave the keynote address at the convention, and the Progressives consistently spotlighted the support of W. E. B. DuBois, Canada Lee, and Paul Robeson. Although Dewey's expectations of a comfortable victory led to a campaign which did not stress issues, the Republicans did establish a National Council of Negro Republicans and hired Val Washington of the *Chicago Defender* to publicize their civil rights record as John P. Davis did for the Democratic National Committee.[34]

Finally, the election of 1948 legitimized the issue of civil rights. Once the almost private domain of Negro protest groups, leftist clergymen, and communist-dominated unions and front organizations, civil rights became part of the agenda of respectable urban liberalism in 1948 and was identified with both national parties and the president of the United States. If Truman was a reluctant champion often pressured by forces beyond his control and if his account of the convention fight in his memoirs is at best disingenuous, the identification, nevertheless, was made. This itself, along with the countless words preached on the issue, began to educate Americans about the righteousness of the crusade for equality. Gallup polls after the election consistently showed a higher percentage of voters in favor of civil rights than did the preelection polls. Most important, Truman's identification with the civil rights movement in 1948 sparked a whole new set of expectations. It increased the pressure on the future presidents, especially Democrats, to support civil rights. It made it easier for liberals of both parties to speak out for civil rights, for the Supreme Court to revitalize the Fourteenth Amendment and reverse a century of law unfavorable to the Negro, for civil rights partisans to receive a respectful hearing at the White House, and for Negroes to believe that they would soon share the American Dream.[35]

Notes

1. Confidential memorandum to president, November 19, 1947, Clark M. Clifford Papers (Harry S. Truman Library, Independence, Mo.). For the importance of the Negro vote in Truman's early career see Franklin D. Mitchell, *Embattled Democracy: Missouri Democratic Politics, 1919–1932* (Columbia, Mo., 1968), 124–38, 162, and David L. Jones, "Senator Harry S. Truman: The First Term" (unpublished M.A. thesis, University of Kansas, 1964), 96–99. During World War II the switch of Negro voters accounted for Republican victories in St. Louis and Missouri. Harlem, which had voted four-to-one Democratic in 1938, switched overwhelmingly to Dewey in 1942 and 1946. See editorial in *Baltimore Afro-American*, April 24, 1948, for Negro reasons to support Dewey.

2. Roy Wilkins, Oral History Memoir, 98–100 (Nicholas Murray Butler Library, Columbia University, New York City); Eleanor Roosevelt, *This I Remember* (New York, 1949), 162. Also see Richard M. Dalfiume, "The 'Forgotten Years' of the Negro Revolution," *Journal of American History* 55

(June 1968), 90–106, and Robert E. Park, "Racial Ideologies," in William F. Ogburn, ed., *American Society in Wartime* (Chicago, 1943), 165–84.

3. Jack Greenberg, *Race Relations and American Law* (New York, 1959), chaps. 1–2, and Wilson Record, *Race and Radicalism: The NAACP and the Communist Party in Conflict* (Ithaca, N.Y., 1964), chaps. 3–5. Also see Lee Nichols, *Breakthrough on the Color Front* (New York, 1954), and Harold R. Isaacs, *The New World of Negro Americans* (New York, 1963), pt. 1.

4. William C. Berman, "The Politics of Civil Rights in the Truman Administration" (unpublished Ph.D. dissertation, Ohio State University, 1963), chap. 1, and Barton J. Bernstein, "The Ambiguous Legacy: The Truman Administration and Civil Rights," in Bernstein, ed., *Politics and Policies of the Truman Administration* (Chicago, 1970), 270–74. Unlike Mrs. Eleanor Roosevelt, who resigned from the Daughters of the American Revolution because of the Marian Anderson incident, Mrs. Bess Truman refused to stay away from a DAR tea and carried home a box of party cake for the president. *New York Herald Tribune*, October 13, 1945.

5. Walter F. White, *A Man Called White: The Autobiography of Walter White* (New York, 1948), 322–33. Also see Samuel Lubell, *The Future of American Politics* (New York, 1951), chaps. 1–3.

6. *Public Papers of the Presidents of the United States: Harry S. Truman, Containing the Public Messages, Speeches, and Statements of the President, January 1 to December 31, 1947* (Washington, 1963), 311–13; volumes in this series will hereinafter be cited as *Truman Public Papers* along with the proper year. Also see *Crisis* 54 (August 1947), 233; *To Secure These Rights: The Report of the President's Committee on Civil Rights* (Washington, 1947), especially pt. 4.

7. *Truman's Public Papers*, 1947, 479–80, 482; Berman, "The Politics of Civil Rights," 64–70; Bernstein, "The Ambiguous Legacy," 276–83; personal memorandum of Clark Clifford, December 9, 1947, Clifford Papers; *Truman Public Papers*, 1948 (Washington, 1964), 3–4.

8. Drafts of message in Clifford Papers. For public reactions see Channing Tobias to Truman, February 6, 1948, Files of Philleo Nash, Box 24; David Niles to Truman, February 16, 1948, Files of Philleo Nash, Box 4 (Truman Library; cited hereinafter as Nash Files). Also see *New York Times* and *New York PM*, February 3, 1948, and column by Walter White, *New York Herald Tribune*, February 15, 1948.

9. *Cong. Record*, 80 Cong., 2 Sess., 976–77 (February 3, 1948), 1069–72 (February 4, 1948), 1120–23 (February 5, 1948), 1193 (February 9, 1948), 1321–22 (February 16, 1948). Also see *Baltimore Sun*, February 4, 1948; *Washington Post*, March 8, 1948; President's Personal File 200, February 2, 1948, Truman Papers (cited hereinafter as PPF); Walter White to Leon

Levine, February 26, 1948, National Association for the Advancement of Colored People Records, Box 368 (Manuscript Division, Library of Congress, Washington, D.C.; cited hereinafter as NAACP Records).

10. *Cong. Record*, 80 Cong., 2 Sess., 1198–99 (February 9, 1948); *New York Times*, February 7, 8, 24, 1948; *Washington Post*, February 21, March 7, 1948; articles by Gould Lincoln in *Washington Evening Star*, February 10, 26, 1948; *Nashville Banner*, March 1, 1948; Congressman Frank Boykin to J. Howard McGrath, February 6, 1948, J. Howard McGrath Papers (Truman Library); Walter White memorandum to NAACP branches, February 13, 1948, NAACP Records, Box 367.

11. *Cong. Record*, 80 Cong., 2 Sess., A2056–58 (April 1, 1948), A2176–79 (April 7, 1948); column by Marquis Childs, *Washington Post*, February 13, 1948; column by David Lawrence, *Washington Evening Star*, February 9, 1948; Elmer Davis broadcast, February 19, 1948, Elmer Holmes Davis Papers, Box 16 (Manuscript Division, Library of Congress); *Washington Post*, March 10, April 4, 10, 1948; John M. Fenton, *In Your Opinion* (Boston, 1960), 67–68.

12. Transcript of Conference of Southern Governors with Senator J. Howard McGrath, February 23, 1948, McGrath Papers; Jack M. Redding, *Inside the Democratic Party* (Indianapolis and New York, 1958), 136–37; V. O. Key Jr., *Southern Politics in State and Nation* (New York, 1949), 329–34. Also see columns by Drew Pearson and Joseph and Stewart Alsop, *Washington Post*, February 13, 1948; by Arthur Krock, *New York Times*, May 7, 1948; and by Marjorie McKenzie, *Pittsburgh Courier*, June 19, 1948; *Truman Public Papers, 1948*, 127, 165; *Jackson Daily News*, May 11, 1948.

13. Alexander Heard, *A Two-Party South?* (Chapel Hill, N.C., 1952), 20–33; Emile B. Ader, *The Dixiecrat Movement: Its Role in Third Party Politics* (Washington, 1955). Important articles on the southern revolt include Manning J. Dauer, "Recent Southern Political Thought," *Journal of Politics* 10 (May 1948), 327–53, and Sarah M. Lemmon, "The Ideology of the 'Dixiecrat' Movement," *Social Forces* 30 (December 1951), 162–71. Also see James F. Byrnes, *All in One Lifetime* (New York, 1958), 94–95, and Bascom N. Timmons, *Garner of Texas: A Personal History* (New York, 1948), 214–24, 240–44.

14. Charles W. Collins, *Whither Solid South? A Study in Politics and Race Relations* (New Orleans, 1948), 228–39, 258–64; William M. Tuck, "Improvement and Preservation of State and Local Government," *Vital Speeches* 12 (March 15, 1946), 338–41; Fielding L. Wright, "Give the Government Back to the People," *American Magazine* 146 (July 1948), 36–37, 126–27. Compare with Olin Johnston to Truman, April 18, 1945, PPF 598; and A. Willis Robertson to Truman, October 12, 1945, PPF 1312, Truman Papers.

15. Advertisement of Birmingham County Democratic Campaign Committee, Truman Papers, PPF 200 (February 2, 1948); Elmer Davis broadcast, July 12, 1948, Davis Papers, Box 17. Also see columns by Raymond Brandt in *St. Louis Post-Dispatch*, March 21, 1948, and by Marquis Childs in *Washington Post*, March 30, 1948.

16. *The 80th Congress and the Lobbies*, Civil Rights File, Democratic National Committee Papers, Box 179; memorandum from John Edelman to Textile Workers Union locals, September 20, October 12, 1948, John W. Edelman Collection (Labor History Archives, Wayne State University Libraries, Detroit, Mich.); Tris Coffin, *Missouri Compromise* (Boston, 1947), 61; Elmer Davis broadcast, July 16, 1948, Davis Papers, Box 17. Also see columns by Thomas L. Stokes, *Atlanta Constitution*, October 25, 1948; Edward A. Harris, *St. Louis Post-Dispatch*, August 18, 1948; and James Morgan, *Boston Globe*, September 19, 1948. Many southern politicians were particularly upset by Truman's 1946 veto of the bill vesting ownership of the tidelands offshore oil in the states and his 1947 veto of the Taft-Hartley Bill.

17. *ADA World*, June 18, July 24, November 21, 1947; January 8, February 19, March 2, May 10, 1948. Alonzo L. Hamby, "Harry Truman and American Liberalism, 1945–1948" (unpublished Ph.D. dissertation, University of Missouri, 1965), 12.

18. *ADA World*, March 31, 1948; Clifton Brock, *Americans for Democratic Action: Its Role in National Politics* (Washington, 1962), 96; *New Orleans Times Picayune*, July 5, 1948.

19. Walter F. White, "Will the Negro Elect Our Next President?" *Collier's* 120 (November 22, 1947), 26, 70–71; "Negro Vote Will Hold Whiphand in '48 Election," *Pittsburgh Courier*, February 28, 1948; Henry L. Moon, *Balance of Power: The Negro Vote* (Garden City, N.Y., 1948), which Walter White pointedly sent to the president, Truman Papers, PPF, 393.

20. Helen Gahagan Douglas to David Niles, May 14, 1947, Nash Files, Box 24; Joseph Lawrence to McGrath, May 18, 1948, Colored Folder, McGrath Papers; George S. Schuyler, Oral History Memoir, 606–07 (Columbia University); Lubell, *Future of American Politics*, 100–101. Also see series by George C. Moore for the Associated Negro Press News Service on Official File 93-Misc., Truman Papers (cited hereinafter as OF); and editorials in *Baltimore Afro-American*, October 9, 16, 1948; *Pittsburgh Courier*, October 23, 30, 1948; and *Norfolk Journal and Guide*, October 30, 1948, the first time this Negro newspaper backed a Republican since 1924. The *Chicago Defender* was the only major Negro newspaper to support Truman in 1948.

21. Milton Stewart to McGrath, January 28, 1949, Colored Folder, McGrath Papers; Karl M. Schmidt, *Henry A. Wallace: Quixotic Crusade*,

1948 (Syracuse, N.Y., 1960), 59–156; Wilson Record, *The Negro and the Communist Party* (Chapel Hill, N.C., 1951), 280–81; *Crisis* 55 (February 1948), 41. Also see columns by W. E. B. DuBois, *Chicago Defender*, January 3, February 21, March 20, 1948; by P. L. Prattis, *Pittsburgh Courier*, January 3, May 22, 1948; and by Harry Keelan, *Baltimore Afro-American*, March 27, 1948. Joe Louis later supported Dewey. See *Pittsburgh Courier*, October 30, 1948.

22. *New York Times*, February 16, 22, 1948; Lubell, *Future of American Politics*, 85–87; Schmidt, *Henry A. Wallace*, 67–71.

23. Elmer Davis broadcast, July 8, 1948, Davis Papers, Box 17; *Time* 52 (July 12, 1948), 11–12; NAACP press release, July 9, 1948, NAACP Records, Box 376; Marquis Childs, *Eisenhower: Captive Hero: A Critical Study of the General and the President* (New York, 1958), 112–19; Redding, *Inside the Democratic Party*, 148–49. See also editorials in *Baltimore Afro-American*, April 17, 1948, and *Chicago Defender*, April 24, 1948; and article by Lem Graves Jr., *Pittsburgh Courier*, May 8, 1948.

24. *Truman Public Papers*, 1948, 179, 279, 422; William L. Batt Jr., to Gael Sullivan, April 20, 1948, Clifford Papers; Walter White to Truman, April 7, 1948, OF 413, Truman Papers; letter to editor by Henry Epstein, *New York Times*, May 9, 1948; file on Civil Rights Bill of 1948, Stephen J. Spingarn Papers, Box 41 (Truman Library). On the promise of the administration to introduce a civil rights bill see minutes of the Board of Directors, February 9, 1948, NAACP Records. Also compare Truman's messages to the NAACP of June 19 and October 27, 1948. The earlier one does not even mention civil rights, while the one sent right before the election is a ringing endorsement of civil rights; both in PPF 393, Truman Papers.

25. Philleo Nash to Clifford, April 9, 1948; Clifford to Truman, April 9, 1948, Clifford to Secretary of the Army Kenneth C. Royall, July 19, August 10, 1948, Segregation in the Armed Forces File, Clifford Papers; minutes of the Board of Directors, March 8, 1948, NAACP Records; Walter White to David Niles, April 29, 1948, Nash Files, Box 7. See also editorials in *Baltimore Afro-American*, April 10, 24, May 8, 1948; *Chicago Defender*, February 21, 28, May 8, 1948; and *Pittsburgh Courier*, February 21, March 20, June 12, 1948; and column by J. A. Rogers, ibid, June 5, 1948.

26. Column by Walter Lippmann, *Washington Post*, July 13, 1948; Emanuel Celler, *You Never Leave Brooklyn: The Autobiography of Emanuel Celler* (New York, 1953), 67–71; *Time* 52 (July 19, 1948), 21–22. McGrath so feared igniting the civil rights issue he would not even answer the NAACP's request for his views on the "Declaration of Negro Voters." Fred C. Kilguss to Walter White, June 4, 1948, NAACP Records, Box 376.

27. *Democracy at Work: Being the Official Report of the Democratic*

National Convention . . . (Philadelphia, 1949), especially 102–27, 134–42, 167–210; Robert Bendiner, "Rout of the Bourbons," *Nation* 167 (July 24, 1948), 91–93; Helen Fuller, "The Funeral Is Called Off," *New Republic* 119 (July 26, 1948), 10–14; Irwin Ross, *The Loneliest Campaign: The Truman Victory of 1948* (New York, 1968), 121–26; William L. Batt Jr. to Clifford, July 9, 1948, Clifford Papers.

28. *Time* 52 (July 26, 1948), 13; Elmer Davis broadcast, July 15, 1948, Davis Papers, Box 17; Wilkins, Oral History Memoir, 96. Sam Brightman, Oral History Memoir, 25–27 (Truman Library), claims Truman made no effort to stop the ADA plank. I do not think the facts support this contention. For the Dixiecrat view of the convention see *Birmingham States Rights,* July 26, 1948, and *Alabama* 13 (July 23, 1948); both are in NAACP Records, Box 367. For the president's account see Harry S. Truman, *Memoirs,* 2 vols. (Garden City, N.Y., 1955–1956), 2:180–84.

29. Clarence Mitchell to Roy Wilkins, February 18, 1948; Walter White to David Niles, July 23, 1948, NAACP Records, Box 368; Donald Dawson to Clark Clifford, March 8, 1948, Clifford Papers; materials on the two executive orders, Nash Files, Boxes 6, 28; Leon Henderson to Truman, July 22, 1948, McGrath Papers; Robert Church to Thomas Dewey, July 16, 1948; Roy Wilkins to Robert Church, August 9, 1948, NAACP Records, Box 368.

30. William L. Batt Jr., to Clifford, August 11, 1948; confidential memorandum to president, August 17, 1948, Clifford Papers; *Atlanta Constitution,* October 21, 1948; *New York Times,* September 10, October 20, 1948; column by Arthur Krock, *New York Times,* October 19, 1948. Also see J. Strom Thurmond to Truman, September 25, 1948, OF 200-2-H, Truman Papers.

31. See drafts of speech and newspaper reports in Nash Files, Box 29.

32. Philleo Nash memorandum for the president, November 6, 1948, Clifford Papers; "The Negro Prefers Truman," *New Republic* 119 (November 22, 1948), 8; Henry L. Moon, "What Chance for Civil Rights?" *Crisis* 56 (February 1949), 42–44; Arnold Aronson and Samuel Spiegler, "Does the Republican Party Want the Negro Vote?" ibid. (December 1949), 365–66. Also see Stephen Spingarn to Charles Murphy, May 22, 1950, Box 25; unsigned memorandum, "The Negro Vote in 1952," Box 42, Spingarn Papers; Republican National Precinct Workers, *So, We Lost the Election* (n.p., n.d.), Archibald Carey Papers (Chicago Historical Society, Chicago, Ill.); minutes of the Board of Directors, December 13, 1948, NAACP Records.

33. Kenneth Birkhead, associate director of public relations, Democratic National Committee, Oral History Memoir, 18–22; William L. Batt Jr., director of research division, Democratic National Committee, Oral History Memoir, 16–18, both in Truman Library; campaign material, Nash Files, Box 29. Also see campaign materials of the *Citizen,* published by the

National Wallace for President Committee, and the *Progressive Citizen*, published by Progressive Citizens of America.

34. Sam Brightman, Oral History Memoir, 37–38; *Chicago Defender*, July 24, 1948; *Pittsburgh Courier*, July 3, 24, 1948; and columns by Louis Lautier and Leon Snead in *Baltimore Afro-American*, July 3, 1948. Compare with the Democratic convention of 1924, when a Negro was permitted to attend for the first time but only as an alternate, or the one in 1928, where the few Negro delegates were segregated from whites by chicken wire.

35. Truman, *Memoirs*, 2:182; Gallup polls in *Washington Post*, July 26, 1948; January 16, 1949. Also see messages in OF 596A, Boxes 1510, 1511, Truman Papers; Louis W. Koenig, ed., *The Truman Administration: Its Principles and Practice* (New York, 1956), 94.

Martin Luther King Jr.

Seeing Lazarus, 1967–1968

I had long thought of writing a biography of Martin Luther King Jr. Friends repeatedly dissuaded me. What civil rights historians favored, in the main, were social rather than political studies, books that focused on ordinary folk, not leaders; women, not men; revolutionaries, not reformers; grassroots organizations, not national ones; "Black Power," not the "beloved community" of black and white together; and individual or community empowerment, not legal victories from the federal government. Nevertheless, with the advice and encouragement of my friend and publisher Thomas LeBien, I decided to compose a meaningful and readable account of King's career for this generation. If this meant going against the tide, so be it. I tried to depict the man in all his humanness, not as an icon. I sought, as well, to depict King's core religious beliefs as the key to his politics, to link his greatness to his rhetoric, to indicate the long-standing radicalism of his calling, and, above all, to emphasize his relevance to today's world rather than as a dreamer frozen in time at the 1963 March on Washington. The words describing King's commitment to nonviolence and desegregation just flowed out of me. I had never before written anything so easily or that gave me such pleasure. This essay is excerpted from "Seeing Lazarus, 1967–68," chapter 8 in Harvard Sitkoff, King: Pilgrimage to the Mountaintop *(New York: Hill and Wang, 2008). Reprinted by permission.*

Grief would shadow King's spirit in the last year and a half of his earthly journey. In the fall of 1966, Stokely Carmichael reaped headlines, and political havoc, by increasingly portraying Black Power as a bitter rejection of both white society and King's nonviolence and by depicting the score of ghetto riots that summer as revolutionary violence to overthrow a reactionary society. Meanwhile, capitalizing on the backlash against racial violence and "crime in the streets," Republicans, many of them right-wing conservatives, replaced forty-seven Democratic incumbents in the House and three in the Senate. At the same time, King watched the war in Vietnam expand ominously, multiplying the numbers of Americans shipped home in body bags— 16 percent of them blacks in 1966—and causing appropriations for the War on Poverty to be slashed by a third.

King despaired of a "white society more concerned about tranquility and the status quo than about justice and humanity." As never before, Coretta thought him morose. He smoked constantly and overate heedlessly. His depression, she recalled, was "greater than I had ever seen before." He brooded that "people expect me to have answers and I don't have any answers." Worried that Black Power had made him irrelevant, he feared a looming race war.

Unlike most mainstream civil rights leaders, however, King did not jump on the anti–Black Power bandwagon. Instead, he decried the "white backlash" and insisted that "America's greatest problem and contradiction is that it harbors 35 million poor at a time when its resources are so vast that the existence of poverty is an anachronism." As no other public figure, black or white, he decried the socioeconomic conditions that underlay the urban riots, insisting on a fundamental restructuring of the American system. He called for mass protests until the government provided a guaranteed annual income of $4,000 to every American adult. He proposed that the Southern Christian Leadership Conference (SCLC) organize "the poor in a crusade to reform society in order to realize economic and social justice."

King mused to his aides that the only way to get the nation to address poverty might be to get large numbers of very poor people to march on Washington. "We ought to come in mule carts, in old trucks, any kind of transportation people can get their hands on. People ought to come to Washington, sit down if necessary in the middle of the street and say 'We are here; we are poor; we don't have any money; you have made us this way; you keep us down this way; and we've come to stay until you do something about it.'"

"There are few things more thoroughly sinful than economic injustice," King thundered to a church convention in Texas. Laying bare his troubled soul, he vouched that "Christianity has always insisted that the cross we bear precedes the crown we wear. To be a Christian one must take up his cross, with all its difficulties and agonizing and tension-packed content, and carry it until that very cross leaves its mark upon us and redeems us to that more excellent way which comes only through suffering."

King knew he would suffer. No longer the darling of the liberal media, he knew what he must do. But, not knowing how to do it, King called for a staff retreat at the Penn Center in Frogmore, South Carolina, to mull SCLC's future. He admitted his chagrin that the movement's "legislative and judicial victories did very little to improve the lot of millions of Negroes in the teeming ghettos of the North" and his despair that "the roots of racism are very deep in America." To his seventy-five staff members, King expressed his conviction that "something is wrong with the economic system of our nation." He emphasized the need to pursue "substantive," not "surface," changes that would make "demands that will cost the nation something."

Few of his aides and advisers saw it King's way. Hosea Williams wanted SCLC to concentrate on voter registration in the South; Jesse Jackson thought it should devote its resources to an expanded Operation Breadbasket in northern cities. Stanley Levison warned that whites were not ready for "deep radical change" and to maintain that black equality could be achieved only "with the revolutionary alteration of our society" was "poor tactics." Others feared King's increasing economic radicalism would frighten potential donors and foundations and worsen the serious money problems SCLC already faced. The lack of support for a mass-action campaign focused on economic justice and the incessant clash of executive staff egos further depressed King, as did the constant fund-raising trips to keep the financially sinking SCLC afloat. They left him little time for reflection, or for home and family. Despite his awareness of FBI surveillance, King's need for respite, for solace, increased his quest for sexual liaisons.

Perhaps in atonement, King openly trumpeted his prophetic rage at the military conflict halfway around the world that had replaced civil rights as the nation's most pressing concern. Leaving for Jamaica in mid-January 1967 for a month of solitude to work on his next book, *Where Do We Go from Here*, King happened upon "The Children of Vietnam," an illustrated article in the January *Ramparts* magazine.

Suddenly he stopped, recalled his aide Bernard Lee: "He froze as he looked at the pictures from Vietnam. He saw a picture of a Vietnamese mother holding her dead baby, a baby killed by our military. Then Martin pushed the plate of food away from him. I looked up and said, 'Doesn't it taste any good?' and he answered, 'Nothing will ever taste good for me until I do everything I can to end the war.'" Upon seeing the pictures of children maimed and murdered by the United States, King committed himself to whatever was necessary to oppose the war. He would "no longer remain silent about an issue that was destroying the soul of our nation."

He knew this meant incurring the wrath of the president of the United States. He knew it would deprive the civil rights movement of his precious time and energy. He knew it would cause a drop in contributions to the SCLC—already 40 percent lower than a year earlier. He knew it would mean allying himself with radicals whom most Americans despised and that it would destroy whatever slim chances remained for the kind of massive federal expenditures required by the ghettos. But King had crossed his Rubicon.

Considering himself a "realistic" rather than a "doctrinaire" pacifist, King believed "the potential destructiveness of modern weapons of war totally rules out the possibility of war ever serving again as a negative good." An alternative must be found, he wrote. "The choice today is no longer between violence and nonviolence. It is either nonviolence or nonexistence." Accordingly, he spoke out first against the Vietnam War at Howard University in March 1965, just as President Johnson began his escalation of the conflict. To audiences that year in the Roxbury neighborhood of Boston and in Petersburg, Virginia, King declared that the war must be stopped and called for a negotiated settlement. When it was extremely unpopular to do so, he stated, "We must even negotiate with the Vietcong." Going further yet, he suggested that Americans go to Vietnam to rebuild some of the villages they had destroyed.

However, in August 1965, when King sought the backing of SCLC's board for his idea to send personal letters to all the leaders involved in the war, urging a speedy negotiated settlement, the board demurred. It recognized King's right to speak as an individual but affirmed that SCLC existed for the purpose of securing the civil rights of Negroes. The board said that SCLC's "resources are not sufficient to assume the burdens of two major issues." SCLC would not get involved in foreign affairs.

Despite the rebuke, King called on the president to "seriously consider halting the bombing" of North Vietnam and to state "unequivocally" his willingness to negotiate with the Vietcong. Taking his Nobel Peace Prize to heart, valuing the importance of his reputation as a proponent of nonviolence, resenting the patronizing attitude of the administration that he was "out of his depth" on foreign policy, and foreseeing that the war abroad would be paid for by starving social programs at home, King pressed on with his intention to plead with all the warring parties to settle their differences at the conference table. To those who wanted him to stick to racial matters he repeated, "Injustice anywhere is a threat to justice everywhere," and "Justice is indivisible." He could not be for democracy and humanitarianism and not be against colonialism and imperialism. "I will not stand by when I see an unjust war taking place and fail to take a stand against it."

But Lyndon Johnson had had enough. He gave King the cold shoulder at the Voting Rights Act signing ceremony in August. The following month, he directed UN Ambassador Arthur Goldberg to persuade King that the president sought a peaceful resolution of the conflict, that secret negotiations were under way and peace was quite near, and that any public criticism "would give aid and comfort to the enemy and stiffen" its diplomatic position. At the same time, Johnson had one of his senatorial cronies, Thomas Dodd of Connecticut, publicly blast King for having "absolutely no competence" to speak about foreign affairs and for unpatriotically aligning himself "with the forces of appeasement." The news media seemed to see it all through Johnson's eyes. In an article entitled "Confusing the Cause," *Time* declared that King should stop meddling where he did not belong. King, most columnists echoed one another, had no business speaking about foreign affairs. Public opinion polls indicated that most blacks and whites agreed.

Dismayed by the president's offensive and by the public disapproval of his antiwar activities, a frustrated King decided to call it quits. He could not fight the war while fighting for civil rights. "I'm already over-loaded and almost emotionally fatigued," Martin confided to friends, and "can't battle these forces who are out to defeat my influence . . . to cut me down." He needed to "withdraw temporarily," to "gracefully pull out so I can get on with the civil rights issue." Most of the SCLC staff, following Andy Young in thinking that anti-war activists were "a bunch of crazies," breathed a sigh of relief.

Yet King's conscience churned away. Quietly, he turned to James Lawson, who journeyed to Vietnam in 1965 on a peace-seeking mission for King and then helped form the Southern Coordinating Committee to End the War in Vietnam, and to James Bevel, who preached that the "Lord can't hear our prayers here in America because of all the cries and moans of His children in the Mekong Delta." Constantly urging Martin to take a more radical stand on Vietnam, Bevel claimed that the Lord had appeared to him sitting on the dryer in his Chicago laundry room, "saying my children are dying in Vietnam, my children are suffering. They are your brothers and sisters too. You must help them." Mostly, Martin listened increasingly to his wife on Vietnam. A committed pacifist, Coretta Scott King had joined the Women's International League for Peace and Freedom as a student at Antioch, continued her peace activities later in the National Committee for a Sane Nuclear Policy, and picketed the White House over Vietnam even before Martin first spoke against the war. Her views on the war in Vietnam, more than anyone else's, nurtured his beliefs. "I did not march, I did not demonstrate, I did not rally," he later wrote about the remainder of 1965. "But as the hopeful days became disappointing months, I began the agonizing measurement of government promising words of peace against the baneful, escalating deeds of war. Doubts gnawed at my conscience." Without a doubt, Martin told an aide, "the position of our government is wrong and it is getting wronger every day."

Lashing out at the administration's efforts to muzzle critics of the war, to depict advocates of negotiation "as quasi-traitors, fools, or venal enemies of our soldiers and institutions," King declared to a New York audience that he would not be silenced. He quoted Amos on justice, Isaiah on renouncing violence, and Micah on beating swords into plowshares. As a minister, "I am mandated by this calling above every other duty to seek peace among men and to do it even in the face of hysteria and scorn."

As 1966 began, the Georgia state legislature barred the Student Nonviolent Coordinating Committee's (SNCC's) Julian Bond from taking his elected seat because of SNCC's call for young blacks to take up civil rights work rather than submit to the military draft. King publicly joined the campaign to get Bond seated. "We are in a dangerous period when we seek to silence dissent," King told newsmen, adding that "in my current role as a pacifist I would be a conscientious objector." In his next Sunday sermon, King proclaimed, "Our hands are dirty" in Vietnam, and depicted dissent and nonconformity as the essence of true Christianity.

Later in the spring, King won the approval of the SCLC board for a resolution branding as "immoral" the U.S. support of South Vietnam's military junta, calling on President Johnson to "seriously examine the wisdom of prompt withdrawal" from the war, and condemning the conflict "on the grounds that war is not the way to solve social problems" or ensure America's interests. "The intense expectations and hopes of the neglected poor in the United States must be regarded as a priority more urgent than pursuit of a conflict so rapidly degenerating into a sordid military adventure." The following month, on CBS's *Face the Nation*, King renewed his public demand for a halt to the U.S. bombing of North Vietnam. In August another SCLC board resolution denounced Johnson's "relentless escalation" of the war and demanded he immediately and unilaterally de-escalate the conflict. Late in the year, King sadly told a Senate subcommittee: "The bombs in Vietnam explode at home; they destroy hopes and possibilities for a decent America."

Making his first public appearance in more than two months at an antiwar rally in Los Angeles in late February 1967, King lambasted Johnson's Vietnam War policies for morally isolating the United States. "We are engaged in a war that seeks to turn the clock of history back and perpetuate white colonialism." He decried the American military's atrocities, "our paranoid anti-Communism," and "deadly western arrogance." Unable to bear "the betrayal of my own silences," King thundered that it was time to halt the bombing, negotiate with the Vietcong, and "deal positively and forthrightly with the triple evils of racism, extreme materialism and militarism. . . . We must demonstrate, teach, and preach," King concluded, "until the very foundations of our nation are shaken."

Several days later, at a meeting in New York, Whitney Young berated King. "The Negro is more concerned about the rat at night and the job in the morning than he is about the war in Vietnam," the head of the Urban League declared. "If we are not with him [Johnson] on Vietnam, then he is not going to be with us on civil rights." "Whitney, what you're saying may get you a foundation grant," King shot back, "but it won't get you into the kingdom of truth." Livid, Young pointed to King's ample stomach: "You're eating well." The two former comrades in the movement, now politically far apart, had to be physically separated. King telephoned Young hours later to apologize for the outburst, to no avail. They renewed the argument, neither man backing down or changing the other's mind.

King had little more success with the SCLC board or his closest advisers. He reminded the board of "those little Vietnamese children who have been burned with napalm" and that African Americans were paying the heaviest price for the war, both in battlefield casualties and in cutbacks in social welfare programs. But some preachers thought he was imposing his views like a bishop, and the board refused to adopt King's resolution committing the SCLC to active opposition to the war. Nor could he sway Levison, Rustin, and his closest aides to support his wish to take part in the upcoming April 15 protests against the war. Bevel, alone, advocated that King march. All the rest derided his joining a "squabbling, pacifist, socialist, hippie collection." Warned by Levison that it would cause a severe drop in contributions, King replied, "I don't care if we don't get five cents in the mail. I am going to keep preaching my message." He patiently explained, "At times you do things to satisfy your conscience, and they may be altogether unrealistic or wrong tactically." The war was so evil, he said, that "I can no longer be cautious about this matter. I feel so deep in my heart that we are so wrong in this country and the time has come for a real prophecy and I'm willing to go that road."

He would go alone, if need be. As he told a reporter for the New York Times, "We are merely marking time in the civil rights movement if we do not take a stand against the war." America must realize that international violence is just as immoral as racial segregation. "It is out of this moral commitment to dignity and the worth of human personality that I feel it is necessary to stand up against the war in Vietnam."

In late March, King and Dr. Benjamin Spock led 5,000 demonstrators in downtown Chicago, the first antiwar march of Martin's career. There, he railed at the cruel irony of blacks and whites dying together "for a nation that has been unable to seat them together in the same schools."

A week later, King addressed some 4,000 congregants in New York's stately Riverside Church. "A time comes when silence is betrayal," he began, reading the remarks largely written by Professor Vincent Harding of Spelman College. King declared his opposition to his government a "vocation of agony." But "my conscience leaves me no other choice."

In measured rhetoric that would be reported around the world, King enumerated the many reasons the war in Vietnam must be ended. First, our military intervention in Vietnam had "broken and eviscerated" the War on Poverty "as if it were some idle political plaything of a society gone mad on war." Like "some demonic destructive suction tube," it robbed funds from domestic programs and sent poor black youth to fight and die out of all proportion to their numbers. In addition, "I knew that I could never again raise my voice against the violence of the oppressed in the ghettos without having first spoken clearly to the greatest purveyor of violence in the world today— my own government." His Christian ministerial role and convictions required him to adopt a broad world perspective rather than a narrow American one. Furthermore, a moral obligation "to work harder than I had ever worked before" to end war had been "placed upon me in 1964" by the Nobel Peace Prize.

King harshly condemned America's puppet government in South Vietnam as a vicious dictatorship and questioned the very basis of U.S. foreign policy. Given America's neocolonialism, he thought Vietnam no aberration. He pictured America siding with "the wealthy and the secure while we create a hell for the poor" of Vietnam, and he demanded once again that the United States end all its bombing and negotiate with the Vietcong. King also now insisted on a date by which all foreign troops would be out of Vietnam and asked all young men to declare themselves conscientious objectors if drafted.

This business of burning human beings with napalm, of filling our nation's homes with orphans and widows, of injecting poisonous drugs of hate into the veins of peoples normally humane, of sending men home from dark and bloody battlefields physically handicapped and psychologically deranged, cannot be reconciled with wisdom, justice, and love. A nation that continues year after year to spend more money on military defense than on programs of social uplift is approaching spiritual death. . . . Somehow this madness must cease.

"The war in Vietnam is but a symptom of a far deeper malady within the American spirit," King concluded. It was time, he said, that America lead a world revolution against "poverty, racism, and militarism." If "we are to get on the right side of the world revolution, we as a nation must undergo a radical revolution of values. We must rapidly begin the shift from a 'thing-oriented' society to a 'person-oriented' society." His voice resounding in the immense Gothic cathedral, the preacher declared, "If we do not act, we shall surely be dragged down the long, dark, and shameful corridors of time reserved for those who possess power without compassion, might without morality, and strength without sight." He closed with Amos' "justice will roll down like waters and righteousness like a mighty stream."

Given that 73 percent of Americans in the spring of 1967 supported the war, and only 25 percent of African Americans opposed it, the speech ignited a firestorm of criticism. Virtually every American newspaper and magazine rebuked King. Typically, the *Washington Post* declared the speech "unsupported fantasy," adding that King had gravely injured the civil rights movement and himself. "Many who have listened to him with respect will never again accord him the same confidence. He has diminished his usefulness to his cause, to his country and to his people." Under the title "Dr. King's Error," the *New York Times* belittled King's intelligence and claimed that he had done "a disservice" to both the civil rights and peace movements. Even Negro-owned newspapers like the *Pittsburgh Courier* accused him of "tragically misleading" African Americans, and the NAACP adopted a resolution stating that the effort to join the civil rights and peace movements is "a serious tactical mistake" that serves neither cause.

Newsweek denounced his demagoguery; *Time* complained he had set back the cause of Negro advancement; *U.S. News and World Report* accused him of "lining up with Hanoi"; and *Life* magazine arraigned him for uttering "a demagogic slander that sounded like a script for Radio Hanoi." Baseball legend Jackie Robinson, Negro senator Edward Brooke of Massachusetts, and African American Ralph Bunche, the UN undersecretary-general, added their public criticism of the speech.

"What is that goddamned nigger preacher doing to me?" Johnson raged. "We gave him the Civil Rights Act of 1964, we gave him the Voting Rights Act of 1965, we gave him the War on Poverty. What more does he want?" The preacher would never again be invited to the White House. Henceforth, King would be on the outside, in a picket line, shouting peace chants through the wrought-iron gates.

In July, the black ghettos exploded in the most intense and destructive wave of rioting the nation had ever experienced. Unprecedented numbers of blacks in some three-score cities, North and South, coast to coast, took to the streets, looting and burning, throwing Molotov cocktails, and firing upon police. In the rioting in Newark, New Jersey, the police and National Guard killed 25 blacks and wounded or arrested another 1,300. In Detroit, where nearly 4,000 fires destroyed 1,300 buildings, most of the 43 deaths and many of the 1,000 wounded came at the hands of untrained and jittery National Guardsmen. All told, the long, hot summer of 1967 resulted in at least 90 deaths, more than 4,000 wounded, and nearly 17,000 mostly black arrests. "There were dark days before, but this is the darkest," a dispirited King told Levison as he watched his "dream turn into a nightmare."

King placed the ultimate blame for the riots on white America. "The turmoil of the ghetto is the externalization of the Negro's inner torment and rage. It has turned outward the frustration that formerly was suppressed in agony." He pleaded for an immediate program to end unemployment, beseeching Washington for a New Deal effort to provide a job to everyone who needed work. Unless the government acted at once, he declared, "this tragic destruction of life and property" will spread. Neither Congress nor the president responded. King feared time was running out for America and all he believed in. He had to act.

His preoccupation with Vietnam became a preoccupation with leading a massive crusade of urban civil disobedience. King sought to force the nation to attack the root causes of black nihilism. Despite racial matters having changed more in the previous decade than in any decade since the Civil War, King knew much more was needed. As he had written just after the Watts riot in 1965, the "explosive Negro community in the North has a short fuse and a long train of abuses." He wished to "transmute the deep rage of the ghetto into a constructive and creative force." He had to salvage nonviolence as a strategy for change. King had already called for a "radical redistribution of power." On various occasions during the spring, he insisted that America's "moral sickness," its "repulsive moral disease," necessitated radical measures.

"I didn't get my inspiration from Karl Marx," King liked to say. "I got it from a man named Jesus." Publicly, Martin avoided using the word *socialism*. He feared giving his enemies—whether in the White House, the FBI, or the economically conservative black church—cause to claim he was a communist or a Marxist. But many of his speeches clearly expressed his preference for what Coretta said were his long-held democratic socialist beliefs.

He had already called for a Bill of Rights for the Disadvantaged similar to the GI Bill of Rights. Justified by "the robberies inherent in the institution of slavery," it advocated preferential employment practices and home and business loan subsidies for African Americans. Writing in *Why We Can't Wait* (1964), King insisted that the "relevant question" is how "can we make freedom real and substantial for our colored citizens? What just course will ensure the greatest speed and completeness? And how do we combat opposition and overcome obstacles arising from the defaults of the past?" Harkening back to what Indian prime minister Jawaharlal Nehru had told him about the preferential treatment given to untouchables in applying for jobs and education, King answered: "compensatory consideration for the handicaps he has inherited from the past," preferential treatment that would equip blacks to compete on a just and equal basis now. "Giving a man his due may often mean giving him special treatment."

In *Where Do We Go from Here* (1967), his final book, he pictured "the good and just society" as neither capitalism nor communism but "a socially conscious democracy" that would close the gulf "between superfluous wealth and abject poverty" and end "cut-throat competition and selfish ambition." It "is morally right," King declared, "to insist that every person have a decent house, an adequate education, and enough money to provide basic necessities for one's family."

The year before he had told the SCLC staff, "You can't talk about ending slums without first saying profit must be taken out of slums." King cautioned that "this means we are treading in difficult waters, because it really means that we are saying that something is wrong with capitalism." He had no blueprint but was sure "God never intended for some of his children to live in inordinate superfluous wealth while others live in abject, deadening poverty." Maybe, he concluded, "America must move toward a Democratic Socialism." He often used the example of Sweden as a model that the United States should follow.

On more than one occasion, he told his Ebenezer congregation: "I choose to identify with the underprivileged. I choose to identify with the poor. I choose to give my life for the hungry. I choose to give my life for those who have been left out. . . . This is the way I'm going. If it means suffering a little bit, I'm going that way. . . . If it means dying for them, I'm going that way." Throughout the spring, his sermons at black churches dealt increasingly with poverty and class exploitation. Only by reallocating power, King preached, could we "wipe out the triple interlocking evils of racism, exploitation, and militarism." He called for a "human rights revolution" that placed economic justice at the center. He talked of moving from a reform movement into a "new era, which must be an era of revolution." The time had come to raise new questions, to change the rules. America must be born again. "The whole structure of American life must be changed."

"For years," King told journalist David Halberstam in April 1967, "I labored with the idea of reforming the existing institutions of the society, a little change here, a little change there. Now I feel quite differently. I think you've got to have a reconstruction of the entire society, a revolution of values." By this he meant "the possible nationalization of certain industries, a guaranteed annual income, a vast review of foreign investments, an attempt to bring new life into the cities." Only these, just possibly, might stem the exhortations from those like H. Rap Brown, who had succeeded Stokely Carmichael as head of SNCC, for African Americans to "get your guns" and "kill the honkies."

On ABC's *Issues and Answers* that summer, King again called for a radical reconstruction of society. "Many of the allies who were with us during the first phase of the Movement," he warned, "will not be with us now because it does mean dispersing the ghetto; it does mean living next door to them; and it does mean the government pouring billions of dollars into programs to get rid of slums and poverty and deprivation." Giving no quarter to former allies who now thought him misguided, King emphasized that "this is why the civil rights movement has to restructure itself, in a sense to gear itself for an altogether new phase of struggle."

Speaking to the tenth-anniversary convention of SCLC in Atlanta in mid-August, King made no effort to sugarcoat his militancy. He began by quoting Victor Hugo's *Les Miserables*: "If the soul is left in darkness, sins will be committed. The guilty one is not he who commits the sin, but he who causes the darkness." Whites, he exclaimed, caused the darkness. "They created discrimination. They created slums. They perpetuate unemployment, ignorance, and poverty." To combat those, he called for the creative extremism of civil disobedience. It was time to disrupt business as usual in "earthquake proportions," until "the tragic walls that separate the outer city of wealth and comfort and the inner city of poverty and despair shall be crushed by the battering rams of the forces of justice."

King then asked:

> "Why are there 40 million poor people in America?" When you begin to ask that question, you are raising questions about the economic system, about a broader distribution of wealth. When you ask that question, you begin to question the capitalistic economy. . . . But one day we must come to see that an edifice which produces beggars needs restructuring. . . . You see, my friends, when you deal with this, you begin to ask the question, "Who owns the oil?" You begin to ask the question, "Who owns the iron ore?"

He quoted Jefferson—"I tremble for my country when I reflect that God is just"—and concluded that for America to be born again, it must adopt Christian democratic socialism.

That meant strategies that did not depend on the goodwill and political support of the federal government and tactics that would compel "unwilling authorities to yield to the mandates of justice."

* * *

As King worked to build his Poor People's Campaign, James Lawson, now a minister of a church in Memphis, pleaded with him to assist in a strike by the city's black sanitation workers over the mayor's refusal to recognize their union. Once again his aides objected to King volunteering, as he had done in Albany in 1961, to come in at the last moment to a situation that others had planned and controlled. "We felt like you couldn't take on everything, and if we went into Memphis, we'd get bogged down there and never get back to Washington," added Andy Young. "But Martin said he couldn't turn his back on those garbage workers." Picturing the mainly poor, black, displaced rural migrants "carrying the man's garbage," King claimed, "it is criminal to have people working on a full-time basis and a full-time job getting part-time income."

Late in January, when heavy rains made sewer work impossible in Memphis, twenty-one black workers had been sent home with only two hours of wages while their white coworkers remained "on the clock" and received a full day's pay. Moreover, two black workers had been crushed to death by their compactor because they were not allowed to sit out the rain in the cab like white workers. To make matters worse, the dead men's status as unclassified workers meant that their families received no benefits. To protest the unjust treatment by the city, a "wildcat strike" by the mostly black sanitation workers began on February 12.

Memphis' newly elected segregationist mayor, Henry Loeb, eager to crush black assertiveness and stay black gains, resolved to break the strike. He issued an ultimatum: Return to work or be fired. The next day he began hiring nonunion workers to replace the strikers. Loeb's blue-helmeted riot police then brutally maced and clubbed African Americans walking in a protest march that had been organized by black ministers and union leaders. This galvanized the black community, stimulating almost daily marches and a boycott of the downtown stores. A local labor dispute had become a racial struggle with national implications.

King thought the conflict was a good way to dramatize race-based poverty and to highlight the interplay of class and racial oppression — the very reason for a Poor People's Campaign. He would speak in Memphis the next day, March 18. As Ralph Abernathy told Coretta: "We're going to Washington by way of Memphis."

* * *

On Wednesday, April 3, King returned to Memphis, checking into the black-owned Lorraine Motel, where his room, 306, faced a parking lot below and the back windows of a cheap, run-down rooming house across the street. He learned that afternoon that a U.S. district court judge in Memphis had issued a restraining order against the march. King said he would march anyway. "We are not going to be stopped by Mace or injunctions," he informed reporters. "It is a matter of conscience. We have a moral right and responsibility to march."

A heavy rainstorm buffeted the city that night. Sensing that few people would venture out in the storm to hear him speak at Mason Temple, King sent Abernathy in his place. His phone soon rang. Abernathy pleaded, "They want to hear you, not me. This is your crowd." They had braved tornado warnings, he went on; don't let them down. Wearily, Martin gave in, despite his exhaustion.

King mounted the podium to the accompaniment of blasts of thunder. He began in sorrow, his voice filled with self-pity, his theme one of death. He spoke of his stabbing, of the present being a time of nonviolence or nonexistence. "But only when it's dark enough can you see the stars," he said. King saw God in the masses of people rising up, [Yessir! Yessir!] and whether they were in Johannesburg, South Africa; Nairobi, Kenya; Accra, Ghana; New York City; Atlanta, Georgia; Jackson, Mississippi; or Memphis, Tennessee, [Tell it, doctor.] "the cry is always the same: 'We want to be free.'" [Oh yes!] The applause shook the stained-glass windows. The rain rattled windows and hammered the roof. King warned that "if something isn't done, and in a hurry, [Yes doctor.] to bring the colored peoples of the world out of their long years of poverty, their long years of hurt and neglect, the whole world is doomed."

He spoke of the many threats on his life "from some of our sick white brothers" just as the storm crested. "But it doesn't matter with me now." [Tell it.] He paused. "Because I've been to the mountaintop."

The sounds of sobs alternated with thunder claps. What happened to him, he said, "doesn't matter with me now, because I've been to the mountaintop. [Go ahead.] And I don't mind. Like anybody, I would like to live a long life—longevity has its place." The thousands seated before him hushed. His voice trembled. "But I'm not concerned about that now." He had delivered this peroration before, but never with such fervor. As lightning flashed, King exclaimed, "I just want to do God's will. And He's allowed me to go up to the mountain. And I've looked over, and I've s-e-e-e-e-n the promised land. [Yes, yes, yes.] I may not get there with you. But I want you to know, tonight, [Oh yeah.] that we, as a people, will get to the promised land. [Yes! Go ahead.] And I'm happy tonight. I'm not worried about anything. I'm not fearing any man. Mine eyes have seen the glory of the coming of the Lord. . . ." He did not finish. As the audience cheered wildly, Martin stumbled into Abernathy's embrace.

The assembly's enthusiastic reception elated King. He went off happily for a late dinner and the companionship of one of his special female friends. Many hours later, he returned to the Lorraine Motel, where he joked with his brother and then left with another longtime mistress for her room. Abernathy would not awaken him until noon.

Later that day Young returned from court with the announcement that the judge would allow a restricted march on the following Monday. Although they were set to march anyway, Young's positive news led to a pillow fight and much horseplay between King and his colleagues. He then got ready for dinner, relishing the prospect of his favorite soul-food meal at a preacher-friend's home.

Having a moment to spare, King stepped out on his room's balcony, looked down at the parking lot, and joshed with his driver and jazz musician Ben Branch. "Ben," he said, smiling, "I want you to sing 'Precious Lord' for me tonight like you never sung it before." He added, "I want you to sing it real pretty."

A ringing noise pierced the air. Some thought it a car backfire or a firecracker. Others took cover near the rented limousine. The bullet—shot out of a high-velocity rifle from the rooming house opposite the motel—smashed through King's neck, exploded his right cheek and jaw, and severed his spinal cord.

King flew backward. His body slammed up against the wall, then fell to the balcony floor. Abernathy rushed to his friend and leader. He took him in his arms. Blood gushed from the gaping wounds. "Martin, Martin, this is Ralph. Do you hear me? This is Ralph." No answer. The bullet, fired by one man but aimed by many, stilled King's voice forever—yet his words would never die.

The Second Reconstruction

To commemorate the coming twentieth anniversary of the passage of
the 1964 Civil Rights Act, the editors of The Wilson Quarterly *asked*
me to introduce their special issue assessing black gains and setbacks
with a brief overview of the developments that led Congress to pass that
sweeping legislation. It sums up many of my notions about the 1930s
and 1940s that appear in the previous essays. I underscored what the
movement had accomplished, "to keep hope alive" for students with no
memory of disfranchisement or of separate and unequal public facili-
ties. Yet, in the era of Ronald Reagan, at a time when I could not possi-
bly imagine an African American named Obama in the White House,
I concluded, glumly, with the observation that the Second Reconstruc-
tion was over. It would not be the last time I was wrong; it would be
an error I was happy to have made. "The Second Reconstruction" first
appeared in The Wilson Quarterly 8 *(Spring 1984), 49–59, and is*
reprinted by permission.

"There comes a time," Lyndon Baines Johnson liked to say, quoting
Cactus Jack Garner, "in poker and politics, when a man has to shove
in all his stack."

For LBJ, the moment came on November 22, 1963. President
Kennedy was dead. Few Americans knew what to make of his suc-
cessor. To the press, the Texan was known as a wheeler-dealer with a
cynical disdain for principle. He had stolen (it was rumored) his first
election to the Senate. In Congress, he had frequently thwarted the
aims of the Democratic Left. His dislike of the Kennedy family was
plain. Now, as president, he needed to establish his legitimacy.

Less than twenty-four hours after taking the oath of office in Dallas aboard Air Force One, President Lyndon Johnson decided to "go
for broke" on civil rights.

On November 27, five days after JFK's assassination, Johnson told a joint session of Congress that "no memorial, oration, or eulogy could more eloquently honor President Kennedy's memory than the earliest passage of the civil rights bill for which he fought." In the months that followed, Johnson steered through the House and Senate an omnibus civil rights statute, a bill even stronger than the one that Kennedy had submitted in June 1963. It was no easy task.

The Strength of an Idea

In the Senate, a coalition of southern Democrats and conservative Republicans had stood for decades as an impassable barrier to any significant civil rights legislation. Led by Richard Russell (D-Ga.), the southerners mounted a filibuster to keep the bill from coming up for a vote. They counted on the civil rights forces being unable, as they so often had been in the past, to muster the 67 votes needed to impose cloture. Winter turned to spring as Russell's stalwarts droned on and on. Finally, in May, after several "good long talks" at the White House, Senate minority leader Everett Dirksen (R-Ill.) cast his lot with the president. With the help of Dirksen's moderate Republicans, cloture was invoked. The Senate approved Johnson's civil rights bill, 73 to 27, on June 29.

It was the first major civil rights legislation since the era of Reconstruction, and it represented the beginning of a belated effort by the executive and legislative branches of government to back up what the federal courts had been saying for more than a decade. Among other things, the Civil Rights Act of 1964 prohibited racial discrimination by employers and labor unions and in most places of public accommodation, authorized the government to withhold money from public programs practicing discrimination, created an Equal Employment Opportunity Commission, and gave the attorney general power to file suits against school districts that maintained segregated facilities.

What is did *not* do, as opponents of civil rights legislation had feared that it might, was require employers to hire workers on the basis of race to correct some sort of racial imbalance.

"No army," Everett Dirksen had said when announcing his support of the civil rights bill, "can withstand the strength of an idea whose time has come." Legal equality for blacks had been a long time coming. That it finally arrived was due in part to economic and demographic changes that had brought blacks north and into the Democratic Party. The Kennedy assassination provided moral impetus.

But most important of all was the disciplined, organized pressure—in the form of sit-ins, marches, and boycotts that frightened many whites, hurt others economically, and focused national attention on the Negro's plight—by blacks who had grown tired of waiting. "For years now I have heard the word 'Wait,'" the Reverend Martin Luther King Jr. declared in 1963. "It rings in the ear of every Negro with piercing familiarity. This 'Wait' has always meant 'Never.'"

Forging Alliances

During the final quarter of the nineteenth century, with the gains of Reconstruction beginning to recede, all three branches of the federal government had permitted the white South to reduce blacks to a state of peonage, to segregate them, and to disenfranchise them. Blacks did what they could to protest (to escape) the closed, rigid caste system that was the southern way. Largely bereft of white allies, their successes were few.

For most blacks, life would not change until World War II. There were, nevertheless, a few glimmers of hope. Some stemmed from the mass migration of blacks to the urban North between 1910 and 1920. Few found the promised land, but most experienced some relief from the tenantry, poverty, and ignorance of the Black Belt. Northern blacks, moreover, could vote. Politically, the Negro began to command attention.

The New Deal gave blacks some economic assistance and considerable symbolic consolation, though Franklin Roosevelt made few concrete attempts to end de jure racial discrimination. Responding to the growth of the black vote in the North, and its pronounced shift away from the party of Lincoln after 1932, Roosevelt appointed more than 100 blacks to senior government posts and tripled the number of black federal employees. In the administration of relief programs, Roosevelt also made sure that blacks received a fair share of the pie, even in the segregated South. And the first lady identified herself closely with civil rights leaders and organizations. As *All in the Family*'s Archie Bunker would later complain, "Eleanor Roosevelt discovered the colored . . . We didn't know they were there."

FDR's appointments to the Supreme Court (including Hugo Black, Felix Frankfurter, and William O. Douglas) also made a difference. The high court's favorable decisions in cases involving the exclusion of blacks from juries, the right to picket against racial discrimination in employment, disenfranchisement, discrimination in the pay of black teachers, and the admission of blacks to graduate education all helped make the Afro-American less a *freedman* and more a *free man*.

Inevitably, the rising expectations of American blacks began to exceed Washington's performance. The onset of World War II helped bring matters to a head. The ideological character of the struggle against fascism (and Nazi racism), along with the government's desperate need for men in both overalls and uniform, led many blacks to anticipate a better deal. The result, when this did not occur, was a new militancy in black communities.

In 1941, for example, A. Philip Randolph of the Brotherhood of Sleeping Car Porters threatened to mobilize an all-black march on Washington unless the president opened up jobs in the defense industry to blacks. Roosevelt responded with Executive Order 8802, which created a Fair Employment Practices Commission and prohibited racial discrimination in companies and unions in war-related work. This, combined with a wartime labor shortage, created jobs for 2 million blacks. Another 200,000 entered the federal civil service. The number of black union members doubled, to 1,250,000.

The war created the preconditions for a successful black crusade on behalf of racial justice. By war's end, many blacks in the North held decent blue-collar jobs. They were, as a group, more self-confident than ever before. Membership in the biracial National Association for the Advancement of Colored People (NAACP) had grown sevenfold (to 351,000) during the war years. Several strong alliances had been forged: with the liberal wing of the Democratic Party, for example, and with Big Labor. Meanwhile, the new prominence of the United States as a world power, and its claim to moral leadership in the Cold War, elevated the "race problem" into a national embarrassment.

Harry Truman became the first U.S. president to identify his office with the specific objectives of the civil rights movement. He did so despite intense opposition from within his own party. The coalition of southern Democrats (including freshman Senator Lyndon B.

Johnson of Texas) and conservative Republicans on Capitol Hill stymied Truman's efforts to create a permanent Fair Employment Practices Commission and killed his proposed antilynching and anti–poll
tax laws. When the president endorsed the civil rights plank written
into the 1948 Democratic platform, Strom Thurmond (D-S.C.) and
other southern delegates walked out of the convention and formed
the splinter Dixiecrats, a split that nearly cost Truman the election.

Assault on Jim Crow

Truman rarely got his way in Congress on civil rights issues, but he
issued executive orders in 1948 ending segregation in the military and barring racial discrimination in federal employment and
in work done under government contracts. His Justice Department prepared amicus curiae briefs backing the positions taken
by the NAACP as its lawyers argued major civil rights cases before
the Supreme Court. One such case, involving an eight-year-old in
Topeka, Kansas, named Linda Brown—who had to travel a mile by
bus to reach a black elementary school even though she lived only
three blocks from a white elementary school—began its journey
through the courts in 1951.

No issue in the immediate postwar years meant more to blacks
than school desegregation, and the NAACP's Legal Defense and
Education Fund, led by Thurgood Marshall, coordinated a series
of lawsuits in several states charging that segregated education was
discriminatory per se. Many blacks and liberal whites believed that
a Supreme Court decision ruling "separate but equal" schooling
unconstitutional would promptly spell the end of Jim Crow in every
other area of life.

On May 17, 1954, in the case of *Oliver Brown et al. v. Board of
Education of Topeka*, the Supreme Court, headed by former California governor Earl Warren, ruled that separate educational facilities
"are inherently unequal" and deprived blacks of the equal protection
of the laws guaranteed under the Fourteenth Amendment. The landmark decision was greeted with hosannas by black leaders and hoots
by southern politicians. Senator James Eastland (D-Miss.) asserted
that the South would neither "abide by nor obey this legislative decision by a political court."

Eastland was right, at least for a while.

For a decade after 1954, despite the Supreme Court's decision in *Brown* and its subsequent rulings against other forms of segregation, virtually nothing of consequence changed in the South. In 1960, fewer than 1 percent of southern black children attended school with white children.

"Massive Resistance"

Part of the blame lay with the Supreme Court. A year after *Brown*, the Court issued its so-called *Brown II* decision, rejecting the NAACP's plea to order instant and total school desegregation and adopting instead a "go slow" approach. The Court assigned responsibility for drawing up desegregation plans to (white) local school authorities, requiring only that desegregation proceed with "all deliberate speed," a tempo otherwise undefined.

For his part, President Dwight D. Eisenhower was not disposed to press the matter. He did not like the *Brown* ruling. He stated flatly once that "I do not believe you can change the hearts of men with laws or decisions." No bigot, but blind to the importance of ending racial injustice, Eisenhower had no intention of enforcing compliance with the high court's ruling in the South. He was under no pressure from Congress to do so.

Not surprisingly, Washington's indifference emboldened white supremacists in the South, who pursued a campaign of "massive resistance" to desegregation. State governors felt free to defy the president himself, as Orval Faubus demonstrated at Little Rock, Arkansas, in 1957. When Eisenhower intervened on that occasion with U.S. troops, it was less to ensure that nine black students safely took their seats at Central High School than to uphold the law and assert his authority as chief executive.

Eisenhower's failure to use his office as a "bully pulpit" to persuade whites that racial discrimination ran counter to both law and morality was a lost opportunity. The costs would be high. Denied the fruits of the victories that they had won in court, and without support in Washington, blacks now looked to new tactics, organizations, and leaders. A battle that had been waged indoors, before the bench, now burst into the streets.

It began in Montgomery, Alabama, when Mrs. Rosa Parks, a black woman, said no to a bus driver on December 1, 1955. Her refusal to give up her seat to a white man on a crowded bus, and her subsequent arrest, sparked a bus boycott that would unite the city's 50,000 blacks and demonstrate the effectiveness of nonviolent mass protest. Led by twenty-six-year-old Reverend Martin Luther King Jr., pastor of the Dexter Avenue Baptist Church, 90 percent of Montgomery's blacks shunned the Montgomery City Line beginning on Monday, December 5. Despite lawsuits, arrests, and bombings, they stayed off the buses for 381 days until vindicated by the Supreme Court.

The bus boycott won sympathetic coverage in the northern news media. Blacks across the country took heart. More important, blacks now had a charismatic leader in the person of Martin Luther King Jr. Not only had he fused the precepts of Christ, Gandhi, and Jefferson into a moral demand for racial justice; he had also displayed, in the course of a trying and dangerous year, a genius for organization. Eventually united in King's Southern Christian Leadership Conference, black ministers became a key element in the civil rights struggle. (Today, twenty-five black Protestant denominations claim 17 million members; their churches remain local bulwarks of black social and political life.)

A Stroke of the Pen

Stirred by the example of Montgomery, black student activists began employing the "sit-in" at local restaurants throughout the South to demand the right to equal service. By the end of 1960, despite thousands of arrests, sit-ins had accomplished their purpose in 140 southern towns and cities, and blacks were busily conducting wade-ins at beaches, kneel-ins at churches, sleep-ins at motels, and read-ins at public libraries. In 1961, the Congress of Racial Equality (CORE) stepped up its Freedom Ride campaign. To prod the White House and its new occupant, John F. Kennedy, into enforcing the Supreme Court desegregation orders, interracial groups of CORE members in May began boarding Greyhound and Trailways buses in Washington, D.C., and riding into the Deep South.

The momentum of protest placed the new administration in a difficult position. As a senator, John F. Kennedy had seldom raised his voice in support of racial justice. But needing the black vote (and the white liberal vote) to win the presidency in 1960, he campaigned as a champion of racial equality. However, his narrow margin of victory—roughly 100,000 votes—gave him little room to maneuver. On the Hill, he faced the same coalition of southern Democrats and conservative Republicans that had thwarted Harry Truman.

For most of his thousand days in the White House, Kennedy expediently balanced the conflicting claims of white and black, North and South, conservative and liberal. He appointed more blacks to high federal office than any previous president but deferred to James Eastland, chairman of the Senate Judiciary Committee, on the appointment of several outright segregationists to the federal bench. He intervened to desegregate the University of Mississippi when a crisis forced his hand but did little to push integration in the public schools of the old Confederacy. He procrastinated for two years before fulfilling his campaign pledge to end discrimination in federally financed housing with "a stroke of the presidential pen."

On to Black Power

Unless the pressure became unbearable and relentless, Kennedy would not, or could not, act. Civil rights leaders, tired once more of waiting—worried, too, that lack of progress would strengthen the growing radical fringe of the movement—launched a new series of mass protests in April 1963.

The confrontation that King and his aides had plotted for Birmingham worked to perfection. Birmingham was more than just unyielding on segregation. It was, for Negroes, a dangerous city. Blacks called it "Bombingham" for the eighteen racial bombings and more than fifty cross-burning incidents that had occurred there since 1957. Leading the vanguard of the last-ditch defenders of segregation was police commissioner Eugene ("Bull") Connor. King counted on Connor's vicious response to peaceful black demonstrations to awaken both the nation and the president.

He was not disappointed. The vivid, televised scenes of police dogs lunging at peaceful protesters, of surging nightsticks and electric cattle prods, of high-pressure water hoses ripping the clothes off black women, of thousands of hymn-singing children being hauled off to jail—all of this aroused the conscience of millions of Americans. It went on for two months.

"The sound of the explosion in Birmingham," King observed, "reached all the way to Washington." In June, when Alabama governor George Wallace sought to bar two black students from enrolling in the University of Alabama, the president decided that the time had come.

In an address to the nation on June 11, Kennedy asserted his leadership on what he called "a moral issue . . . as old as the Scriptures and . . . as clear as the American Constitution." He backed up his words with a deed, urging Congress to enact the most comprehensive civil rights law in U.S. history. That August, some 250,000 Americans participated in the March on Washington, massing before the Lincoln Memorial to show their support for the legislation that Kennedy had sent to the Hill.

Yet, in the three months remaining to him, Kennedy had little more to say on civil rights, perhaps heeding opinion polls which indicated that white Americans thought he was moving too fast on integration. Congress took no action on the civil rights bill. President Kennedy traveled to Dallas in November, apparently content to let future events create the sense of urgency necessary to vanquish the southern foes of equal rights in Congress. Ironically, his assassination did just that.

A year after the Civil Rights Act of 1964 was signed into law, in the wake of renewed black protest demonstrations, this time in Selma, Congress passed a Voting Rights Act that President Johnson declared would "strike away the last major shackle" of the Negro's "ancient bonds." The act prohibited literacy tests and other devices long employed to deter black voters in the South. It authorized federal examiners to register qualified black voters directly. Within four years, the number of southern blacks registered to vote would grow from 1 million to 3.1 million. The lock on the ballot box was broken.

But so, in some respects, was the civil rights movement. The summer of 1965 brought an escalation of the war in Vietnam and a bloody race riot in Watts, Los Angeles. The Watts riot inaugurated a succession of "long hot summers" for a troubled nation and spelled the end of the era of nonviolence. Within a year, the civil rights movement was hopelessly divided over strategy and tactics, over Black Power and black separatism. A resentful Lyndon Johnson, who believed himself betrayed by those he had sought to help, devoted only forty-five words to civil rights in his 1967 State of the Union address. The Second Reconstruction had set much in motion, but it was over.

Index

Abernathy, Ralph, 211–13
Africa, 15, 177
African American history, 5–7, 11
Agricultural Adjustment
    Administration (AAA), 24
Alexander, Will, 28, 31, 59
Alexandria, La., 72
American Civil Liberties Union
    (ACLU), 98
American Council on Race
    Relations, 114
American Dilemma, An (Myrdal),
    16, 41, 68, 116, 119
American Federation of Labor, 107
American Jewish Congress, 114,
    116, 161–62
Americans for Democratic Action
    (ADA), 183, 186–87
American Youth Congress, 35
Ames, Jessie Daniel, 104
Amsterdam-Star News, 67, 159
Anderson, Marian, 35–36
antilynching bills, 17, 35–38, 102,
    116, 178, 219
anti–poll tax bills, 17, 35–37, 54,
    80, 102, 106, 116, 177–78, 187,
    219
anti-Semitism, 147–50, 160, 163
    and blacks, 151–54, 157–58, 165
Asia, 15, 139, 177
Association of Southern Women
    Against Lynching, 7, 105
Atlanta, Ga., 105–6, 210

Atlanta Constitution, 164
Aurand, Henry, 49–52

Baker, Ella, 102
Baldwin, James, 147, 166
Baltimore Afro-American, 44, 99,
    133, 152, 158
Barkley, Alben W., 179
Bass, Leon, 166
Beaumont, Texas, 46, 72, 74, 111
Belle Isle park, 47–48, 56, 76
Bethune, Mary McLeod, 32
Bevel, James, 202, 204
Bibb, Joseph, 98
Bilbo, Theodore G., 177
Birmingham, Ala., 14, 35, 181, 184,
    187, 222–23
Black, Hugo, 34, 218
Black Belt, 14
Black Cabinet, 31–32
black-Jewish coalition, 147, 157,
    160–66
black migration, 14, 16, 68, 182
Black Power, 197–98, 223
black vote, 14–15, 18, 25–26,
    39, 68, 81, 182–84, 188–89,
    222–23
Boston Globe, 81
Brooke, Edward, 207
Brotherhood of Sleeping Car
    Porters, 35, 100, 218
Browder, Earl, 108, 132
Brown, Edgar G., 95

Brown, Sterling, 117
Brown v. Board of Education, 11, 19–20, 219–20
Buber, Martin, 3
Buck, Pearl, 67
Bunche, Ralph, 32, 42, 59, 116, 207
Byrd, Harry F., 179
Byrnes, James F., 34, 73, 77

Cable, George Washington, 26
California Eagle, 96
Camus, Albert, 3
Carmichael, Stokely, 197, 209
Carr, E. H., 8
Chicago, Ill., 74, 114, 152, 204
Chicago Defender, 44, 70, 96–97, 110, 112–13, 163, 189
Civilian Conservation Corps (CCC), 24, 27, 30
civil liberties, 134–36, 142
Civil Rights Act (1964), 207, 215–16, 223
civil rights movement, 4–5, 7–8, 12–13, 16–17, 20, 209–10, 220–23
in World War II, 80–81, 115
Civil Rights Section (Justice Department), 17, 38, 185
Civil Works Administration (CWA), 24
Clifford, Clark M., 176, 178–80, 188
Cold War, 5, 15, 177, 218
Columbia University, 4–5, 131
Commission on Interracial Cooperation, 104
Committee on Civil Rights, 19, 177–79, 182–83, 188
Commonwealth College, 108
communists, 21, 26, 54, 96, 107–9, 118, 132–36
and blacks, 190

concentration camps, 150
Congress, 15, 17, 36–37, 181–82, 187, 207, 222–23
Congress of Industrial Organizations (CIO), 26, 54, 107–9, 118, 189
Congress of Racial Equality (CORE), 18, 44, 67, 94, 101, 104, 221
Connor, Eugene "Bull," 184, 222
consensus history, 5–6, 8
Costigan, Edward, 37
Coughlin, Father Charles, 53, 132
Cowan, Paul, 166
Crisis, The, 37, 154, 156–57, 159–60

Daily Worker, 109
Daniels, Jonathan, 77–79
Darrow, Clarence, 3
Daughters of the American Revolution, 35, 177
Davis, Benjamin, 108
Dawson, William L., 189
Democratic Party, 15, 26–27, 38–40, 131, 139, 142–43, 179–81
Department of Justice, 17, 38, 185, 188
Department of the Interior, 28
Detroit, Mich., 43, 54–58, 65, 75–76, 113, 140, 159
1943 race riot, 46–52
1967 race riot, 207
Paradise Valley, 46–48, 50–51
Dewey, Thomas E., 176, 180, 184, 186, 188
Dies, Martin, 54, 131
Dirksen, Everett, 216
"Double V," 44, 67, 99, 113, 137
Douglas, William O., 34, 218
Drew, Dr. Charles, 96

DuBois, W. E. B., 37, 96, 116–17, 151, 154, 164, 189
Durham, N.C., 104–5, 114

Early, Stephen T., 57, 77
Eastland, James, 219–20, 222
Eisenhower, Dwight D., 180, 185, 220
"Eleanor Clubs," 75, 109
Ethiopia, 149
Ethiopian Pacific Movement, 97
Ethridge, Mark, 78
Evers, Medgar, 94
Executive Order 8802, 18, 69, 80, 94, 218

Fair Employment Practices Committee (FEPC), 18, 28, 46, 69–70, 74, 78, 80–81, 94, 101, 106, 116, 175, 218–19
Farm Security Administration (FSA), 28
farm tenancy, 23–24, 28
fascism, 26, 97, 115, 141–43, 149, 218
Faubus, Orval, 220
Federal Bureau of Investigation (FBI), 53, 199, 208
Federal Emergency Relief Administration, 24
Federal Housing Administration, 25
Federal Works Agency, 28
Fifteenth Amendment, 17
Fifty Years Later: The New Deal Evaluated (Sitkoff), 22
Fisk University, 73, 109
Flynn, Edward J., 184
Fourteenth Amendment, 17, 190, 219
Frankfurter, Felix, 34, 218

Franklin, John Hope, 6, 9, 41
Frazier, E. Franklin, 116–17

Garfinkel, Herbert, 97
Garner, John Nance, 181, 215
Garvey, Marcus, 151
Garrison, William Lloyd, 3
Graham, Frank P., 78
Granger, Lester B., 78, 98–99
Graves, John Temple, 78
Great Depression, 6, 12, 22–23
Greensboro, N.C., 14, 114
Gunther, William, 50–52, 62

Hancock, Gordon B., 105, 118
Harlem, N.Y., 68, 70, 77, 101, 112, 151, 153, 188
Hastie, William, 32, 68
Herndon, Angelo, 108
Highlander Folk School, 108
Hitler, Adolf, 69, 114, 148–59, 164
Hollywood, Calif., 129, 133–34, 137–38, 154
Holocaust, 148–49, 161, 164–66
Hoover, J. Edgar, 58, 79
Hopkins, Harry, 24, 29, 78
Horton, Myles, 108
House Un-American Activities Committee (HUAC), 54, 131
Howard University, 67, 101, 117, 200
Hughes, Langston, 96, 112, 118–19, 160
Hull, Cordell, 155
Humphrey, Hubert H., 183

Ickes, Harold, 28, 31, 132
imperialism, 16, 129–30, 138–39, 201, 205
Indiana, 130, 143
International Labor Defense, 54

interracial violence, 45–49, 51, 57–
58, 65, 71–77, 110–14, 139

Jackson, Jesse, 199
Jackson, Miss., 14, 180
Japanese Americans, 136
Jeffries, Edward, 47–51, 53–55
Jewish organizations, 7, 114
Jewish Survey, 161–62
Jews, 2–3, 7, 116, 137, 142, 147–51,
160–61
  and blacks, 151–54, 156–58, 165
Johnson, Lyndon B., 11, 13, 15,
200–201, 203, 207, 215, 218–
19, 223–24
Jones, LeRoi, 116
Jordan, Leonard Robert, 68

Kelly, Harry F., 49–53, 58
Kemp, Jack, 22
Kennedy, John F., 11, 215–16,
221–23
Kennedy, Robert, 8
Kester, Howard, 108
King, Coretta Scott, 198, 202, 208,
211
King, Martin Luther, Jr., 166, 197–
213, 217, 221–23
Knox, Frank, 77
Kristallnacht, 150, 155
Ku Klux Klan, 53, 57, 106, 131,
154, 158

labor movement, 21, 26, 107, 181
LaGuardia, Fiorello, 155
Lawson, James, 202, 211
Left, the, 26, 79, 107–9
Leuchtenburg, William, vii, 147
Levison, Stanley, 199, 204, 207
liberalism, 6–7, 15, 79–80, 130,
199

and civil rights, 7, 17, 21, 80,
107–8, 116, 181–86, 190
Lincoln, Abraham, 22, 140–41,
179, 217
Little Rock Central High School,
3, 220
Logan, Rayford, 100, 117
"long" civil rights movement, 1, 7,
11
Lorraine Motel, 212–13
Los Angeles, Calif., 45–46, 74
Louis, Joe, 96, 184
lynching, 21, 38, 45
Lynn, Winfred W., 98

March-on-Washington Movement,
18, 44, 54, 67, 69–70, 78, 81,
100–101, 104, 108–9, 160
Marshall, Thurgood, 98, 102, 162,
219
Marx, Karl, 3, 7, 135, 208
Maslow, Will, 162–63
Mays, Benjamin, 105
McGrath, J. Howard, 180, 183, 187
McIntyre, Marvin, 73, 77
Memphis, Tenn., 211–13
Miller, Kelly, 153, 159
Mississippi, 54, 153, 186
Missouri, 18, 182, 187
Mobile, Ala., 46, 111
Montgomery, Ala., 14
  bus boycott, 3, 16, 221
Moon, Henry Lee, 32
Morehouse College, 105
Morgan, Irene, 101
Muhammad, Elijah, 68
multiculturalism, 5
Murphy, Frank, 34, 135
Mussolini, Benito, 149, 158
Myrdal, Gunnar, 16, 41, 67–68,
116–17, 119

National Advisory Committee on Education, 33
National Association for the Advancement of Colored People (NAACP), 3, 12, 18, 25, 32, 34–35, 39, 44, 47, 56, 67, 71, 77–78, 80–81, 98–99, 102–6, 108–10, 112, 115–16, 129, 137–38, 141, 143, 149, 153–55, 219–20
    and Franklin Roosevelt, 35, 39, 69, 77, 78
    and Harry Truman, 178, 186
    and the New Deal, 18, 32–33, 39
    and World War II, 149–50, 153–55, 158–60, 218
National Council of Negro Women, 163
National Labor Relations Act, 25
National Lawyers Guild, 54, 71
National Negro Congress, 25, 44, 95, 104, 108
National Recovery Administration (NRA), 24
National Student Association, 4
National Urban League, 12, 25, 29, 44, 69, 78, 95, 98, 102–3, 158, 160, 163, 204
National Youth Administration (NYA), 27, 29, 32
Nation of Islam, 97
Native American history, 5
Nazism, 16, 97, 44, 143, 148–50, 154–55, 159, 218
    See also fascism
Negro press, 44, 67, 96–98, 103–4, 110
Newark, N.J., 74, 207
New Deal, 6, 7, 21
    and African Americans, 7, 21, 23–31

and civil rights, 17, 21–42, 217–18
New Deal for Blacks, A (Sitkoff), 7, 21, 40
"new history," 5–6
New Left history, 5–7, 43, 65, 175
"New Negro," 16, 120
New York Age, 151
New York Times, 204, 206
Niles, David, 77
Nixon, Richard M., 6
Nobody Knows My Name (Baldwin), 166
nonviolent direct action, 20, 197
Norfolk Journal and Guide, 111, 164
Norris, J. Frank, 53
Norris, Tenn., 24

One World (Willkie), 139, 143
Ottley, Roi, 97
Overton, John H., 179
Owen, Chandler, 153

Parks, Paul, 166
Parks, Rosa, 221
People's Voice, 44
Philadelphia, Pa., 75
Philadelphia Tribune, 151
Pittsburgh Courier, 30, 99, 111–13, 133, 141, 153, 160, 206
Plessy v. Ferguson (1896), 34
Poor People's Campaign, 198–99, 211
Popular Front, 107, 183
Powell, Adam Clayton, Jr., 44, 59, 101, 109, 112, 152–53, 158, 160, 177
Progressive Party, 183–84, 189
Public Works Administration (PWA), 28–30

Queens College, 3

race relations committees, 79,
113–14
race riots
in 1960s, 6, 43, 207–8
in World War II, 6, 43–45, 65,
72–78, 94–140, 152
racial discrimination
in armed forces, 44, 69–71, 94–
95, 97, 137, 185, 187
in defense program, 35, 39, 69,
94–95
in employment, 18–19, 23, 28–
29, 39, 43, 69, 94, 114, 177–78,
185, 216, 218–19
in interstate travel, 18, 178
in jury service, 18–19, 218
in relief programs, 24–25, 29
racial restrictive covenants, 19, 188
Ramparts magazine, 199–200
Randolph, A. Philip, 18, 44, 67,
69–70, 81, 94, 96–97, 100, 104,
106, 116–17, 160, 163, 218
Rankin, John, 54, 106
Reagan, Ronald, 215
Red Cross, 69
Republican Party, 39, 55, 78, 132–33,
139–43, 184–85, 188–89, 198
Robeson, Paul, 3, 96, 160, 189
Robinson, Jackie, 3, 94, 207
Rogers, J. A., 99, 153
Roosevelt, Eleanor, 32, 34–36, 54,
67, 77, 139, 217
Roosevelt, Franklin D., 2, 7, 131,
137, 218
and African Americans, 7, 15,
17, 19, 21–23, 29–31, 45, 66,
77–78, 133, 181, 217
and civil rights, 22, 26–27, 32–33,
36–40, 68–69, 79, 133, 176

and World War II, 57–58, 69, 73,
153
Roosevelt, James, 183
"Roosevelt Court," 34
Russell, Richard B., 179, 216
Rustin, Bayard, 204
Rutledge, Wiley, 34

Schneiderman, William, 134–35
Schuyler, George, 153
"Second Reconstruction," 22, 27,
176, 188, 215–24, 224
segregation, 67, 77, 117–18
in armed forces, 19, 70–71, 97,
110, 187, 219
in housing, 19, 23–25, 43
in interstate commerce, 18–19, 101
in public education, 18–20, 23,
114–15
Selma, Ala., 14
Shepard, Dr. James, 78
"Silent South," 26
Sitkoff, Harvard, 1–9, 11, 21–22, 43,
65, 93, 129, 147, 175, 197, 215
Smith, Gerald L. K., 53
Smith, Lillian, 106
socialists, 21, 54, 99, 130
social scientists, 21, 26, 79
Social Security Act, 25
Sojourner Truth Housing Project,
46, 73
South, the, 12, 14, 19, 217, 222
and the New Deal, 23, 24–27,
37–38
and the Truman presidency, 178–
82, 218–19
and World War II, 78, 95, 101,
104, 120
Southern Christian Leadership
Conference, 12, 198–201, 204,
209–10, 221

Southern Conference for Human Welfare, 35, 106–7
Southern Negro Youth Congress, 25, 95, 108–9
Southern Regional Council, 106
Southern Tenant Farmers' Union, 7, 108
Soviet Union, 15, 19
Spock, Dr. Benjamin, 204
States' Rights Democratic Party, 187, 219
Steffens, Lincoln, 3
Stimson, Henry, 51–52, 77
Struggle for Black Equality, The (Sitkoff), 9
Student Nonviolent Coordinating Committee (SNCC), 202–3, 209, 221
Styron, William, 147
Supreme Court, 11, 15, 18–20, 33–34, 101, 116, 135–36, 177, 181, 188, 190, 218–20

Taylor, Glen H., 184
television, 13, 16, 222
Tennessee Valley Authority (TVA), 24, 131
Thomas, R. J., 54
Thurmond, J. Strom, 179–80, 187, 219
Time, 187, 206
Tindall, George B., 102
To Secure These Rights (Committee on Civil Rights report), 19, 178–79
Townsend, Willard, 189
Truman, Harry, 6, 15, 19, 175–81, 184–90, 218
Tuskegee Institute, 68, 72, 118

United Auto Workers, 54

United Nations, 67, 165, 177, 201
University of New Hampshire, 2
U.S. Housing Authority (USHA), 28–29

Vietnam War, 5, 198, 200–207
Voting Rights Act (1965), 13, 201, 204, 223

Wagner, Robert, 37
Wallace, George, 223
Wallace, Henry, 57, 67, 139, 176, 179–82, 184
War Department, 49–50, 71–72, 110
War on Poverty, 198, 205, 207
Warren, Earl, 184, 219
Washburn, Patrick, 97
Washington, Booker T., 106, 118
Washington, D.C., 179, 184
Washington Post, 206
Wechsler, James, 3
What the Negro Wants (Logan), 100, 117
Where Do We Go from Here (King), 199, 208
White, Josh, 96
White, Walter, 41, 137–38, 140–41
and World War II, 47, 60, 62–63, 77, 154–56, 160–62
white backlash, 198
white primary, 18, 177
Why We Can't Wait (King), 208
Wilkerson, Doxey A., 109, 117–18
Wilkins, Roy, 32, 117, 153–54
Williams, Aubrey, 27, 31
Williams, Hosea, 199
Willkie, Wendell, 7, 57, 67–68, 129–45, 176
Wise, Rabbi Stephen, 161–62
Witherspoon, J. H., 53–56, 63

Woodward, C. Vann, 6, 8
Works Progress Administration
    (WPA), 29–30
World War I, 44, 66, 97–98, 109,
    111
World War II, 6, 15–17, 93, 147–50
  African American support for,
    95–99
  and civil rights, 17–18, 66–69, 94,
    114–15, 119–20, 130, 140, 218

and interracial violence, 43–46,
    65, 71–77, 80, 110–11
and racial militancy, 44–45, 65–
    77, 80, 93–95, 110
Wright, Richard, 96, 109, 112, 117

Young, Andrew, 202, 211, 213
Young, Whitney, 203

"zoot-suit riot," 45–46, 74, 112